SOVIET FOREIGN POLICY TOWARDS EGYPT

SOVIET FOREIGN POLICY TOWARDS EGYPT

Karen Dawisha
Lecturer in Political Science
University of Southampton

St. Martin's Press   New York

Library of Congress Cataloging in Publication Data

Dawisha, Karen.
  Soviet foreign policy towards Egypt.

  Bibliography: p.
  Includes index.
  1. Russia—Foreign relations—Egypt. 2. Egypt—
Foreign relations—Russia. I. Title.
DK68.7.E3D38 1979   327.47'062   78-10539
ISBN 0-312-74837-X

For my mother, and my father

Contents

List of Figures and Tables

Preface

When the Soviet Union negotiated its first arms deal with Egypt in 1955, its influence in the Middle East and the Third World was practically non-existent. In the fifteen years following that deal, its involvement grew until, by the early 1970s, the Soviet role in the determination of Egypt's domestic and foreign policy was decisive. Now, in the eighth year of President Sadat's rule, the Soviet position in Egypt has been reduced to one of little more than an interested bystander. The rift with Egypt has had far-ranging repercussions on Soviet foreign policy. Thus, the exclusion from Egyptian Red Sea and Mediterranean ports has necessitated the reassessment of Soviet strategy in the Indian Ocean. Moreover, the failure of Egypt to continue its progress toward the establishment of a socialist system has led to the questioning of Soviet ideological assumptions, while the refusal of the Sadat regime to repay its economic and military debts to the USSR has given rise to debates amongst Soviet decision-makers over the diminishing returns of its aid programme to Egypt and other countries with similarly unpredictable leaders. The study of Soviet relations with Egypt, therefore, is important not only in itself, but also in so far as it highlights both the potential of Soviet influence and the impotence of Soviet power.

The objectives of this study are two-fold. In the first part of the book, the history of Soviet–Egyptian relations is analysed; and attention is focused in particular on the extent of Soviet influence, the impact of such external factors as inter-Arab rivalries, the Arab–Israeli conflict and East–West relations, and the decisive role of personality in affecting the outcome of Soviet policy. Part Two goes beyond the constraints imposed by a purely chronological account and sets Soviet–Egyptian relations within the broader context of Soviet foreign policy as a whole. In doing so, this section assesses the various external and internal influences operating on the formulation of policy towards Egypt and outlines the main features of the decision-making process, including the role of interest groups and competing elites. The objectives pursued by the Soviet Union are counterposed with the instruments used to achieve these aims, thus highlighting both the depth of the Soviet commitment to Egypt and the difficulties for the decision-makers in achieving the desired correlation between inputs and outcomes, or between aid and influence. The final chapter then considers the record of Soviet relations with Egypt and suggests the reasons for the various successes and failures of Soviet policy.

In acknowledging my debt to those individuals and institutions who, in both direct and indirect ways, contributed to the ideas expressed in the book and in the preparation of the manuscript itself, my first thanks must go to Geoffrey Stern of the London School of Economics, who painstakingly read the manuscript in all of its many phases and provided invaluable advice and encouragement at every juncture. I would also like to thank Professor Philip Reynolds of the University of Lancaster who made it possible for me to transfer my studies from the United States to his department and who subsequently, through his teaching, led me to appreciate the value of analytical thinking. Similar thanks go to Professor Joseph Frankel of Southampton University and Professor Geoffrey Goodwin of the London School of Economics who both made incisive comments on various parts of the manuscript and who helped to shape the framework used in the study. For the many discussions on strategy and Soviet capabilities, I also am indebted to my colleague at Southampton, Dr. John Simpson.

This book would not have been possible without the help of the following: Professors Peter Richards and Kenneth Hilton of the University of Southampton for promoting my application for study leave and financial assistance; to the University of Southampton and the British Council for supporting my research in the Soviet Union; and to Professor Fred Northedge and the Department of International Relations at the London School of Economics where I was fortunate to be an Academic Visitor during 1977–78. In Moscow, Barbara Hay and Jenny Diamond of the British Embassy and Dick Miles of the American Embassy were instrumental in making a success of my visit. My thanks also go to the staff of the Institute of Orientology in Moscow for the use of their facilities and especially to Dr B. M. Potskhveriya for all the time and effort he devoted to arranging interviews for me. Considerable insight into the Soviet policy process and Soviet objectives in Egypt was gained through the long and informative discussions I had with many research workers, including Dr G. K. Shirokov, the Director of the

Institute of Orientology, Professor G. I. Mirskiy of the Institute of World Economy and International Relations, Professor L. D. Freedman of the Institute of Asia and Africa, Dr A. Kislov of the Institute for the Study of the USA and Canada, Dr Ludmila Zvereva and Dr I. Usupov of the Institute of Africa, and with officials of the Soviet Ministry of Foreign Affairs and the Egyptian, Iraqi, Syrian, Lebanese and Tunisian embassies in Moscow. A special thanks must also go to the staff of the main and press libraries of the Royal Institute of International Affairs whose unrivalled expertise and diligence made my research both more productive and more enjoyable. Similarly, my gratitude goes to the secretaries of the Department of Politics at the University of Southampton, who have valiantly struggled against overwhelming odds to meet impossible deadlines in the past, and who no doubt will continue to do so in the future! A special mention must also be reserved for Macmillan's staff, for their helpfulness, efficiency, and their flexible and dynamic editorial policy. Finally, I would like to thank both my husband's family, for their continual support, and last, but never least, my husband, Adhid, whose relentless encouragement and vigorous sense of humour kept me working when the will was weak.

London
April 1978

Karen Dawisha

THE SOVIET UNION AND THE MIDDLE EAST

PART ONE
THE DYNAMICS OF
SOVIET–EGYPTIAN
RELATIONS

1 The Historical Foundations of the Policy

Prior to 1955, the establishment of full and cordial relations with Egypt and the other states of the developing East was not high on the list of Soviet objectives. Rather, priorities lay more with domestic economic growth and the establishment of a socialist order in the industrialised West. Nevertheless, both geographically and demographically Russia has always stood between East and West; and it was not unnatural, therefore, for the Bolsheviks to conclude that the October Revolution had 'built a bridge between the Socialist West and the enslaved East'.[1] In the years following the revolution, the Bolsheviks tried to strengthen this bridge by advocating that all communists and Eastern nationalists should join forces in a united front to bring about the collapse of imperialism and the victory of socialism. The decision to adopt united front tactics was taken at the Second Comintern Congress in 1920 against the bitter opposition of many Eastern communists who claimed, not without justification, that the national bourgeoisie in the East were unreliable allies and that they would turn against the Communists at the first opportunity.[2]

Egypt was granted independence from the British in 1922, and in the parliamentary elections held the following year, Sa'ad Zaghlul's Wafd Party, which had led the struggle for independence, attained an overwhelming majority. The Comintern, in line with the united front tactics, advised the newly established Communist Party and its leader, Joseph Rosenthal, to support Zaghlul. However, the communist–nationalist alliance in Egypt proved as shortlived as did similar alliances elsewhere. When communist-supported strikes broke out in Cairo in January 1924, the Communist Party was suppressed and its entire Central Committee imprisoned. It is instructive that, in commenting on this event, Stalin emphasised that 'the struggle of the Egyptian merchants and bourgeois intelligentsia for the independence of Egypt is . . . an objectively

3

revolutionary struggle in spite of the bourgeois origin and bourgeois status of the leaders of the Egyptian national movement, in spite of the fact that they are against socialism'.[3]

By the end of 1927, Soviet domestic and foreign policy had been subjected to a thoroughgoing revision. The failure of united front policies throughout the East, and particularly in China; the reappraisal of the value of 'peaceful coexistence' with the West; the ascendancy of Stalin within the Party apparat; and a shift in economic priorities toward forced collectivisation and industrialisation had contributed to this change in direction. Whereas the continued existence of Soviet Russia had previously been made dependent upon the success of world revolution, with the promulgation of 'socialism in one country', world revolution was now increasingly dependent upon the continued strength and survival of Soviet Russia. Moreover, from this time forward the Comintern gradually lost what little independence from Soviet directives it had previously enjoyed, and policies for foreign communist parties were formulated to correspond with the current situation in the Soviet Union. In this way, since cooperation between communists and private farmers and traders (or 'nepmen') had been ended inside the USSR, the communists abroad were now advised to stop cooperating with other parties and groups, including Social Democrats and the national bourgeoisie.

However relevant 'class against class' tactics may have been to the domestic Soviet situation, when applied to foreign communist parties, they proved both irrelevant and counterproductive. In Germany especially, the resultant struggle between the Communists and Social Democrats blinded both groups to the threat of nazism. In Egypt, too, the communists split with the nationalists, labelling the ruling Wafd party as 'bourgeois–landlord–counter-revolutionary–national-reformism'.[4] In Egypt and throughout the Arab world, however, where the communist parties were for the most part still politically insignificant, the promulgation of radical tactics only contributed to the isolation of the communist movement from the mainstream of Arab politics.

When the Seventh and final Comintern Congress convened in 1935, it was apparent that the 'class against class' tactics, by preventing an alliance between communists and Social Democrats, had aided Hitler's rise to power in Germany. Consequently, it was decided by the Congress that a return to the broadest united front policy was the only effective deterrent against the further spread of fascism. A common front of all 'democratic nations' against 'the authoritarian regimes' was established; and it was further resolved that this front was to be under the leadership and direction not of the Comintern, but of the USSR since 'the interests of the defence of the Soviet Union determine the attitude of the world proletariat to war'.[5]

This new policy was likewise extended to the colonial world where any activity which might weaken the anti-fascist front was discouraged. This effectively meant the postponement of any national liberation movement seeking independence from Britain and France who were also part of the new united front. In an address on this subject, Maurice Thorez, the French Communist Party leader, made an interesting distinction between the rights and duties of communists in the colonial world:

> Recalling a formula of Lenin, we have already told our Tunisian Comrades who approved of our attitude, that the *right to divorce* did not mean the *obligation to divorce*. If the decisive question of the movement is the victorious struggle against fascism, the interests of the colonial peoples lie *in their union* with the French people . . . .[6]

The Egyptian Communists also followed the line set down by Moscow and renewed their alliance with the Wafd Party.

After the war, the Soviet leadership was preoccupied almost exclusively with the consolidation of Soviet power in Eastern Europe and the reappraisal of relations with its former allies. With the beginning of the Cold War and the promulgation of the 'two-camp' thesis in 1947 which conceptualised the international system in rigidly bipolar terms, Eastern Communists were once again advised to pursue a policy of non-cooperation with the national bourgeoisie.[7] Communists were told that 'the ruthless exposure of reactionary bourgeois – nationalist ideology in its various forms— be it Kemalism or Gandhism, Zionism or Pan-Arabism—hastens the process of the national and social emancipation of the peoples of the colonial and dependent countries . . . .'[8] Soviet commentators were equally disparaging of any attempts to encourage cooperation between the two contending 'world systems' and in particular attributed little value to the growing body of neutralist and non-aligned sentiment amongst many leaders of the newly independent states of Asia and Africa. Until the early 1950s it was steadfastly held in the Soviet Union that there could be no middle ground between the two camps. In an article in *Voprosy ekonomiki*, Yevshei Zhukov made this assessment of neutralism and its adherents:

> National-reformists in the colonial and semi-colonial countries mendaciously insist upon their desire 'to remain outside' of the struggle between the two camps and their 'neutrality' in the so-called 'ideological conflict' between the USSR and the USA, whereas in reality they, with the reactionary bourgeoisie, slander the USSR and actively assist the imperialists . . . .[9]

The Soviet view of the new Egyptian regime continued to be hostile well into 1954 with numerous articles appearing in which it was stated, for example, that the Egyptian revolution 'did not bring about any essential changes in the situation. The reaction in Egypt has increased'.[10] It is, of course, true that the establishment of close Soviet–Egyptian relations was not exactly the first priority of the Naguib–Nasser regime either. Indeed, the suppression of the Egyptian Communist Party continued, and relations between Egypt and the West were initially very cordial.

Despite Soviet criticism of the new bourgeois nationalist regimes, there are indications that a new trend based on a growing appreciation of non-alignment and the benefits of closer economic and political cooperation with the developing countries was beginning to emerge as early as 1951. At the Singapore Trade Conference in October of that year, a Soviet delegate for the first time suggested that 'the USSR might replace the West as a market for Asian exports and as a source of industrial goods and machinery'.[11] Some months later at the 1952 International Economic Conference in Moscow, Soviet officials expressed an awareness of the economic and political problems facing the governments of the Third World, and stated that the Soviet Union was prepared to enter into full trading relationships with these countries based on the principle of complete equality.[12] Even at the 19th Party Congress in 1952, it is possible to detect the bare outlines of what might have become a major reorientation in foreign policy. In what was to be his last speech to the Party, Stalin spoke of the added strength of the socialist camp now that the USSR was surrounded by friendly 'shock brigades' in the form of Peoples' Democracies. Malenkov took up the theme of the effect of shifts in the global balance of power by saying that, because of the greater strength of the socialist camp, wars between socialism and capitalism could be averted. While wars amongst capitalist states were inevitable, Malenkov stressed that the coexistence of the two camps was now entirely possible.[13] However, Stalin's death and the subsequent succession struggle postponed the re-evaluation of foreign policy until 1955.

In many ways, the decision-making environment which has characterised the Soviet Union since 1955 bears little resemblance to the one which existed under Lenin and Stalin. The USSR has emerged as a recognised Great Power in international affairs and as a leader of a number of socialist states. It has also overcome many of the initial problems caused by economic underdevelopment and political instability. The CPSU also has undergone tremendous changes. Its leaders are no longer first generation revolutionaries, nor have they experienced the turmoils and challenges of the early Lenin period. Neither do they wish to be associated with the xenophobic and excessive policies of the Stalin period. For these reasons, it might be difficult to see how the policies pursued by Lenin and Stalin in any way served as an historical foundation for the policies pursued by Khrushchev and his successors.

In just as many ways, however, the decision-making environment of the last two decades has been tremendously influenced by the historical precedents established in the first quarter century of Soviet rule. Firstly, it could be said that the Soviet penchant for rewriting history is not out of disregard for it, but rather out of a too-zealous concern for consistency with past policies, particularly those of Lenin. An apparent, if not actual, uniformity with Leninist precepts and policies is certainly a major source of legitimacy for Soviet leaders. As such, concern over the accurate representation of history is not as important in this respect as the fact that history itself is regarded as an important foundation of Soviet policy. Moreover, events in history, if not history itself, have had an important impact on, and serve as a foundation for, Soviet policy. Thus, for example, while Soviet leaders have condemned Stalin's regime and attempted to dissociate themselves from its excesses, many of these leaders are the products of that regime, and it is difficult to conceive how they could have failed to be influenced and shaped by it. Similarly, although the course of history may be shaped by a nation's leaders, the decisions which are open to those leaders are very much influenced by a set of relatively constant factors such as a nation's geographicial situation, its economic resources, its demographic composition and so forth.[14] It is for these reasons that many historians of Soviet affairs have stressed the consistency of Russian and Soviet foreign policy and the importance of past precedents and policies in the determination and formulation of Soviet policy towards Egypt after 1955.

2 Soviet–Egyptian Relations under Khrushchev 1955–64

1955–58

Apart from lack of motivation to expand its relations with Egypt prior to 1955, Soviet inactivity must equally be attributed to lack of opportunity. Despite isolated outbursts of anti-Western sentiment, such as the 1948 demonstrations in Iraq against the Portsmouth Treaty and the 1952 'Black Saturday' riots in Cairo against British activities in the Canal Zone, the Arab governments and public remained generally pro-Western in outlook. Moreover, following the defeats suffered by the Arab armies in the Palestine war, the Arab–Israeli front remained fairly free from conflict in the period between 1949 and 1954, and relations between the Arab governments themselves were cordial. In Egypt, the new regime led by General Mohamed Naguib and Colonel Gamal Abd al-Nasser concentrated on domestic affairs in the two years following the 1952 overthrow of King Farouk. If the sum total of these events precluded the expansion of Soviet activity in the Arab East during the period 1949–54, a series of events in 1954–55 was to alter radically both the Soviet motivation and opportunity for a more active Middle Eastern policy.

The root of the change can be traced to the attempts by the Arab regimes to obtain arms from the West beyond the levels set down by the 1950 Tripartite Agreement. Britain and the United States, for their part, were engaged throughout the early 1950s in efforts to create an Arab-based regional defence system. Both countries let it be known that Arab requests for arms would be met upon accession to a Western-sponsored act, and indeed in April 1954 Iraq signed an arms agreement with the United States after agreeing in principle that Iraq would join a Western defence alliance in the near future.[1]

In Egypt, Nasser had told John Foster Dulles during his visit to Cairo in May 1953 that the only Communist threat to Egypt emanated not from the Soviet Union but from the local communist parties whose strength would only be reinforced if Egypt were to accede to Western requests.[2] Nasser preferred instead to elicit support for the existing Arab Collective Security Pact created in 1950 under the auspices of the Arab League. The success of such a pact depended both on acquiring those arms necessary to make it a viable organisation and on discouraging other Arab states, particularly Syria and Saudi Arabia, from joining Iraq in a Western-sponsored pact which would have isolated the Egyptian stand. To this end, the Egyptian government continued to negotiate with the West for arms throughout 1954 and 1955, and received assurances from the Iraqis that a final decision on Iraqi membership in a Western pact had not yet been reached.[3] When, soon after, Iraq precipitately announced the conclusion of a Turkish–Iraqi alliance, the first step in the formation of the Baghdad Pact, Nasser's prestige was clearly at stake and an Egypt–Iraqi break seemed unavoidable. Nasser called an immediate Arab summit conference in Cairo on 22 January 1955 to condemn the Iraqi action. While the conference inconclusively aired the opposing views on the admissibility of alliances with the West, it did mark the beginning of a more activist phase in Egypt's foreign policy.

Egypt's anti-Western stand was reinforced by the takeover in Syria on 13 February 1955 of a leftist coalition led by Sabri al-Asali, Akram Hourani and Khalid al-Azm, who immediately declared their support for Egypt and its regional policies. However, Nasser's position lacked credibility so long as Egypt was unable to obtain arms both for her own defences and for the strengthening of the Arab Collective Security Pact. Indeed, the vulnerability of Egyptian defences was highlighted by the Israeli attack on an Egyptian military camp in the Gaza strip on 28 February 1955 which increased domestic and external pressure on Nasser and strengthened his growing conviction that military hardware had to be obtained from any source. The final event which marked the emergence of Egypt on both the Arab and world scenes was the Bandung Conference of non-aligned states in April 1955. It was at this conference that Nasser enunciated 'positive neutralism' as an independent, if rather anti-Western, line in both domestic and external policy. Evidently influenced by his meetings with China's Premier Chou En-lai and Yugoslavia's President Tito, Nasser, in a speech following the conference, stated that 'a socialist society must be founded in this country so that the government may rule on behalf of the majority and not on behalf of a minority. . . . It will work for Egypt alone, not under the guidance of any foreign force, either Western or Eastern.'[4]

These events, which together created the opportunity for greater Soviet activity, coincided with a change in policy by the Soviet leaders. This reappraisal was signalled by a Foreign Ministry statement on the eve of Bandung in which the pressures being imposed on Syria and Egypt to join the Baghdad Pact were condemned, the threat to Soviet security presented by Western military alliances was enunciated, and the preparedness of the Soviet Government 'to support and develop cooperation with the countries of the Middle East' was made public. The statement went on to say that 'the Government of the Soviet Union would support any steps . . . towards strengthening the national independence of these countries and consolidating peace and friendly cooperation among the people'.[5] Thus, by the spring of 1955, the Soviet Union possessed both opportunity and motivation for increasing its relations with the Arab East.

When Nasser announced on 27 September 1955 that an agreement with Czechoslovakia for the purchase of arms had been negotiated, an immediate controversy broke out on the actual source, timing and quantity of the deal.[6] However, it has subsequently become clear that Czechoslovakia was used by the Soviet Union merely as an intermediary in order, as Mohamed Heikal relates, to prevent 'a deliberate breach of the spirit of Geneva'.[7] The Soviet decision to dissociate itself from the deal in order to safeguard the temporary relaxation in Cold War tensions marks the first of many instances in which Soviet behaviour in the Middle East was clearly influenced by, and subordinated to, the wider consideration of East–West relations.

Despite the varying accounts of the origins and size of the deal, its impact was enormous and irrefutable. Egypt's own centrality in the Arab and Afro-Asian world was reasserted and strengthened; Iraq's position was undermined; and in the months following the deal, the armed forces of Egypt, Syria, Saudi Arabia and the Yemen were placed under a joint Egyptian-dominated command. On the Soviet side, in so far as the Czech arms deal was designed primarily to alleviate pressure on Egypt to join a Western-sponsored pact, the agreement certainly did assist the Soviet decision-makers in achieving their primary objective of reducing the perceived threat to Soviet security by isolating, while not eradicating, the Western military presence in the Arab world. Moreover, the enthusiasm with which the deal was greeted in the Middle East served to undermine the position of those in the Politburo who had argued against it;[8] and as a result, articles in Soviet newspapers and journals began to adopt a more positive approach to non-alignment in general and to Egypt in particular.[9] Finally, the arms sale had the effect of generating intense Soviet diplomatic and economic activity not only in the Middle East, but throughout Africa and Asia. In the months following the deal, not only were similar, if less substantial, agreements signed with Syria and the Yemen, but Soviet missions were also established in Sudan, Libya, Liberia, and Ethiopia. Relations between the Arab and socialist countries generally were at a high level during this period, culminating in the establishment by both Syria and Egypt of diplomatic relations with the Chinese People's Republic in 1956.[10]

While the Czech arms deal served to strengthen the prestige of both Nasser and Khrushchev and to discourage the proliferation of Arab membership in the Baghdad Pact, it did not, and indeed was not meant to result in the total convergence of outlook between the Soviet and Egyptian decision-makers. Thus, the suppression by Nasser of the Egyptian Communist Party did not cease or even decrease. It was clear from Arab statements that 'Communism is one thing and cooperation with the Soviet state is another'.[11] That the Soviet leaders seemed to accept this state of affairs was indicated by an article entitled 'The New Spirit of Egypt' which condemned one faction of the Egyptian Communist Party as '*provocateurs* in Egypt who call themselves communists and who dare to come out against Nasser.'[12]

From the Arab point of view, the main point of divergence with the Soviet Union centred on the latter's policy toward the Arab–Israeli dispute. Not only was the dispute peripheral to Soviet objectives in the area, but an outbreak of war could have been directly counterproductive by highlighting the USSR's inability to intervene decisively on the Arab side, beyond the supply of weapons.[13] In a Soviet Government statement issued in April 1956, and during talks in Britain between Eden and both Khrushchev and Bulganin, the Soviet leaders made it clear that, while they were critical of Israel's policy, they recognised Israel as a legitimate state, and favoured a peaceful settlement of the dispute which could take into account 'the just national interests of the parties concerned'.[14] It emerged even more clearly at the London conference that the arms supplied to Egypt were not intended primarily for use against Israel, as witnessed by Khrushchev's proposal for a total Great Power arms embargo to the Middle East. However the proposal, which, if implemented, would have led almost certainly to the breakup of the Baghdad Pact, was rejected by Britain, and resulted in a temporary strain in relations between the Soviet Union and Egypt. Despite these problems, if one considers that the primary and overriding objective of the Soviet Union during the period 1955–58 was the protection of Soviet security through the isolation and ideally the dissolution of the Baghdad Pact, then the Czech arms deal certainly contributed to the achievement of this objective.

Although the popular enthusiasm created by the deal constrained Jordan and Lebanon from joining the Pact, it did not affect the relations these countries had with the West on the diplomatic and economic level. If anything, Nasser's own policy of 'positive neutralism' was based on the desire to maximise relations with both camps without commitment to either. This policy met with initial success when, in December 1955, the United States, Britain and the World Bank offered to assist Egypt in building the Aswan Dam. However, this offer allegedly was provisional upon Egypt's acceptance of conditions which Nasser felt were tantamount to foreign control of the Egyptian economy, and he threatened to seek Soviet financing unless the conditions were minimised.[15]

In the West, reaction to the scheme was equally mixed. In the House of Commons, those favouring the withdrawal of British finance from the project cited Nasser's disruptive influence on Arab politics, his alleged complicity in Hussein's dismissal of General Glubb, and his animosity toward Iraq, Britain's main ally in the region. In the American Congress, the cotton lobby could hardly have been expected to support a project designed to increase the cotton acreage of one of its main competitors. Both the Formosa lobby, angered by Egypt's recognition of the CPR, and the powerful Jewish lobby supported Secretary of State Dulles' own antineutralist sentiments which opposed giving aid to countries hostile or even ambivalent to American interests.[16] Moreover, the World Bank was hesitant about the ability of the Egyptian economy to sustain such a project, particularly in view of Egypt's increased foreign indebtedness following the Czech arms deal. All of these factors culminated in the American decision to withdraw from the project. Britain and the World Bank soon followed suit. Nasser was furious at Dulles' blunt and public announcement that the American withdrawal was necessary because 'the ability of Egypt to devote adequate resources to assure the project's success has become more uncertain than at the time the offer was made'.[17] Nasser responded, not by seeking Soviet backing, which in any case might not have been forthcoming, but by declaring that, since the West would not help to build the Dam, Egypt must depend upon its own material and human resources. To this end Nasser announced on 26 July 1956 the nationalisation of the Suez Canal Company.

The first official Soviet response to Nasser's nationalisation was contained in a speech by Khrushchev in which he upheld Egypt's right to take control of the Canal and maintained that 'the situation in the Suez Zone will not become tense unless it is artificially aggravated from outside'.[18] Thereafter, during the period preceding the Israeli invasion on 29 October, in notes to the Governments of Britain, France, Israel and the United States, in speeches by Soviet delegates at the United Nations, and in the international conferences on Suez from which Egypt was usually absent, the Soviet Government consistently upheld Egypt's legal right to nationalise the Company and repeatedly protested against French and British military preparations.[19]

From the moment of the tripartite invasion, the Soviet leaders made it clear to Nasser, through Syria's President Quwatly who was in Moscow at the time, that Egypt should not expect Soviet intervention to end the crisis and that the crisis must be resolved by political and diplomatic means.[20] The Soviet Union was in any case preoccupied with the situations in Poland and Hungary, and so the most Soviet diplomacy could offer was the mobilisation of world public opinion against the invasion. India and Indonesia, as the leading nations in the neutral 'bloc', were urged to convene a second Bandung conference on Suez—a proposal they rejected. At the United Nations, which had been rendered ineffective in previous months through a combination of Soviet vetoes and British and French preoccupation elsewhere, Soviet and American representatives successfully worked together to obtain a ceasefire. In addition, the Soviet Union, in an effort to take advantage of this unexpected convergence of views between the two super powers, proposed joint Soviet–American military action in Egypt. Not unexpectedly, the proposal was rejected by President Eisenhower, who affirmed that a joint Soviet–American alliance against Britain and France was unthinkable, particularly in the light of the current

Soviet invasion of Hungary. Following this rebuff, the Soviet Union rather belatedly threatened missile attacks against the capital cities of the aggressors in the now famous series of notes dispatched on 5 November, the day preceding the ceasefire.[21]

Mohamed Heikal was later to suggest diplomatically that 'Russia's support of Egypt's position both in the United Nations and outside played a vital part in the mobilisation of world opinion against the aggression'.[22] This statement aptly sums up the extent of Soviet activity during the crisis. Constrained by its actions in Hungary, the absence of a Soviet naval presence in the Mediterranean and its inability, unlike the United States, to impose effective economic pressure on the invading powers, the Soviet Government proved essentially unable either to prevent the invasion or to mediate to end it. France's Foreign Minister Pineau was later to assert that, while Soviet diplomatic intervention had certainly played a part in ending the crisis, its influence had not been as important as the pressures exerted by British public opinion, by the American Government or even by the United Nations.[23] Nevertheless Soviet diplomatic activity did secure additional prestige for the Soviet Union in the Arab world where the population seemed to be impressed with the style, if not the substance, of the Soviet stand. In the immediate postwar period supplies of food, medicines and arms replacements to both Egypt and Syria contributed to Soviet popularity.

For Britain and France, the Suez crisis resulted in a long period of poor economic and diplomatic relations with the Arab East. Trade with the Arab world reached an alltime low; cultural exchanges were negligible; and diplomatic relations were severed by Egypt, Syria and Saudi Arabia, with Iraq breaking relations with France and refusing to sit with the UK in Baghdad Pact meetings.

As with the Czech arms deal, although the Soviet Union was an indirect beneficiary of the increase in anti-Western sentiment, Nasser was the real beneficiary. The Suez crisis was presented to the Arab world as a victory for Arab nationalism and Arab unity. In October of 1956, the new government of Jordan headed by Suleiman Nabulsi promptly joined Syria and Egypt in a military alliance which placed Jordanian and Syrian forces under an Egyptian commander-in-chief. In January of 1957, a Treaty of Arab Solidarity was signed by Egypt, Saudi Arabia, Syria and Jordan, designed to run for a ten-year period. Nasser's prestige outside the Middle East was also enhanced with congratulatory messages flowing in from the leaders of the Afro-Asian and socialist states.

However, Nasser's belief that the Suez crisis had proved the Arab's capability to defend themselves from external pressures was not shared by the United States government, which in January 1957, outlined a new American initiative to fill the 'vacuum' created by the Anglo-French 'withdrawal'. In his State of the Union message on 5 January 1957, President Eisenhower asked Congress for authorisation to extend assistance, including the despatch of American forces, to any country requesting aid 'against overt armed aggression from any nation controlled by International Communism'.[24]

Thus, at the beginning of 1957, for the first time, the United States and the Soviet Union found themselves face to face in the Middle East. The achievement of the Soviet objective of strengthening her security by weakening Western influence in the area, an objective which had been brought closer to realisation by the Czech arms deal and Suez, was now retarded by the intrusion of the United States into the Middle Eastern regional system. The Soviet Union responded first by condemning the latest Western initiative as an attempt to 'implant the former colonial system in the Middle East countries under a new signboard',[25] and by setting out a series of counterproposals designed to regulate Great Power activities in the Middle East. The proposals, which included the liquidation of foreign bases and the embargo on Great Power arms deliveries to the area, were summarily rejected by the American Government, and were given only a lukewarm reception in the Arab press, which generally deleted the Soviet suggestions for an arms embargo.[26]

In the Arab world, the Eisenhower Doctrine had the effect of aggravating latent rivalries, undermining Nasser's bid for hegemony in the area, and putting Cold War labels on traditional inter-Arab disputes. As Patrick Seale observed, 'the Soviet–American confrontation did not long remain on a two-power basis, for it was soon enmeshed in a tangle of local issues which largely determined the terrain on which it was fought'.[27] By the summer of 1957, Nasser's brief period as undisputed leader and spokesman for the Arab world had ended, with Jordan, Saudi Arabia, Lebanon and Iraq relying more heavily than ever on Western aid in an effort to check Nasser's growing influence. Egypt had only one remaining ally, Syria; and she was in the midst of an international crisis.

In August 1957, Khalid al-Azm, the Syrian Defence Minister,

signed a major agreement in Moscow for military and economic
aid. Upon his return three American embassy officials were expelled
for allegedly plotting with the deposed President Adib Shishakli to
overthrow the Syrian regime. Soon after, Azm appointed Afif al-
Bizri, an officer of supposed communist sympathies, as commander-
in-chief. These events led many observers to conclude that a
communist takeover in Syria was imminent.[28] Reports emanating
primarily from Beirut, Baghdad and Amman exaggerated the
strength of communist and Soviet influence in the country, largely
in an effort to deflate the momentum of the forces calling for Arab
unity under Egyptian hegemony and to increase the flow of
American assistance to their own strife-ridden countries.[29] Despite
repeated assertions by Syrian and Egyptian leaders to the effect that
'this Moslem country cannot become a Communist country',[30] and
even from Moscow Radio that 'Syria will never go Communist',[31]
the American government seemed convinced of the likelihood of a
communist takeover. On 24 August, the State Department sent Loy
Henderson to the Middle East to confer with the leaders of Iraq,
Jordan, Turkey and Lebanon. In his memoirs, President Eisenhower was to confirm that at a joint meeting the consensus emerged
that 'the present regime in Syria had to go; otherwise the
takeover by the communists would soon be complete'.[32] To this end,
Turkish troops massed along the Syrian border; the US Sixth Fleet
moved into the eastern Mediterranean; and the United States
began an airlift of arms to Jordan, Iraq and Lebanon.

The Soviet Union started an intensive propaganda campaign
against Turkey, the United States, and the Baghdad Pact and sent a
number of diplomatic communiqués to Turkish leaders, asking how
they would feel 'if foreign troops were concentrated on their
border'[33] and warning that military action against Syria would not
remain 'localised'.[34] In September, a Soviet naval squadron called
at the Syrian port of Latakia in a show of solidarity. By the end of the
month, those Arab governments who had originally advocated
action against Syria were forced, through the pressure of public
opinion, to disengage. Only the Turkish troops remained; and in a
dramatic, if rather unnecessary, gesture designed to underline his
commitment to Arab unity, Nasser airlifted Egyptian forces to Syria
on 13 October. On 24 October, in an equally flamboyant way, the
Soviet leadership ordered combined army and navy exercises in the
Trans-Caucasian and Black Sea areas. Soon after, Khrushchev
unexpectedly appeared at a Turkish embassy reception in Moscow,

announcing that his decision to attend the reception should be interpreted as a 'gesture toward peace'.[35] Following these moves, the crisis gradually came to an end.

Although Soviet initiatives were little more than token gestures, they served to reinforce opinion in the Arab world that both Egypt and the Soviet Union could be relied upon for support when it was needed. Thus, at the end of the crisis, the forces within Syria favouring Arab unity were strengthened rather than weakened; many Arab leaders were isolated for supporting what Egyptian propagandists now referred to as the 'second Suez'; public opinion within these countries was even more divided; Western influence in Syria had declined even further; and people of communist or Soviet sympathies were reinforced in their conviction by the Soviet stand during the crisis and by the conclusion of major credit agreements between the Soviet Union and both Syria and Egypt in the months following. The latest 'defeat' of the forces of 'Western imperialism' prompted a renewed Arab propaganda campaign against the Baghdad Pact and the Eisenhower Doctrine, with John Foster Dulles being singled out for 'special' treatment, as the lyrics from the following Arabic song, popular at that time, illustrates:

Dulles, O Dulles, O Hatcher of plots,
Stop intimidating us, O Beloved of the Sixth Fleet.
Dance on your Fleet, rock and roll!
You accuse us of Communism, while your eye covets oil.
Do not accuse us, you will not move us.
Syria is free and honest, you'll never deceive us . . .[36]

All in all, the first 'trial run' of the Eisenhower Doctrine seemed to indicate that the policy was not without its defects.

Although the international crisis over Syria had subsided by the end of October, the crisis in Syrian domestic politics remained, with the Communists, Baathists and the various conservative forces in a precarious balance which only produced a political stalemate. As is often the case in Syrian politics, it was the army who intervened to break the deadlock. In January 1958, a group of army officers decided to seek some form of union with Egypt, and a delegation was sent to Egypt to confer with Nasser. The Egyptian President reluctantly agreed to their demands for unity but insisted that the union should be on his terms and should include the dissolution of all Syrian political parties, and the replacement of the Syrian

Parliament with an Egyptian-style National Union. It was the Syrian delegation who now reluctantly agreed; and on 1 February 1958, the United Arab Republic was formally established.

The new constitution was promulgated soon after, and Nasser was elected President of both Syria and Egypt. The process of purging the communists began almost immediately. Khalid Bagdash and other leaders of the Syrian Communist Party went into exile, and a number of pro-Soviet army officers including Afif al-Bizri were dismissed. The USSR established diplomatic relations with the UAR soon after its creation, but the coverage of the merger in the Soviet press was far from enthusiastic. A *Pravda* article by 'Observer,' a pseudonym generally recognised as expressing official Politburo opinion, welcomed the formation of the UAR, but stated that the direction which unity might take was purely the internal affair of Egypt and Syria alone.[37] A more outspoken article in the March issue of *International Affairs* (Moscow) stated that only those trends in the Arab world 'closely associated with the people' would triumph in the long run and that 'being Marxists, we are by no means inclined to make a fetish of Arab unity as such or to ignore the fact that the idea may, in certain circumstances, be used for some time also by reactionaries'.[38] Despite these reservations, Nasser received a tumultuous welcome on the occasion of his first visit to the USSR in April 1958, where he held high-level talks with Soviet leaders and made an extensive tour of the Soviet Central Asian republics. A joint communiqué issued at the conclusion of the visit reaffirmed the basic principles of anti-imperialism, non-interference in domestic affairs, and peaceful coexistence.[39] The fact that economic and diplomatic relations between the two countries continued unabated, despite the suppression of the Syrian Communist Party, illustrates the primacy which Soviet leaders continued to place on Nasser's anti-Western foreign policy.

While Nasser was still in the Soviet Union, latent sectarian tensions were erupting in the Lebanon into civil war, between 'Moslems who supported a pan-Arab, pro-Nasser line, with whatever collaboration with Communist powers that that entailed, and Christians who looked to their coreligionists of the Western world for protection against Moslem domination'.[40] While the UAR gave at least moral support (although the Christian community led by President Kamil Chamoun claimed that this support extended to the supply of arms) via the 'Voice of the Arabs' to the Moslem community, Iraq and Jordan sided with the pro-Western President

Chamoun and the Christians. On 13 July Nuri al-Said ordered Iraqi troops stationed outside Baghdad to join their Jordanian counterparts in what was allegedly to have been a joint operation against Syria in support of Lebanon. Instead, the brigade led by Brigadier Abd al-Karim Qassem entered Baghdad and carried out a coup in which the monarchy was overthrown. The Iraqi Republic was proclaimed on 14 July 1958.

The governments of Lebanon and Jordan were now clearly in a precarious position, and fears grew of a united UAR–Iraqi attack on the remaining bastions of 'anti-union and pro-Western' sentiment. The two governments responded by appealing to the West for help, upon which American and British troops landed in Lebanon and Jordan respectively. Nasser learned of the Iraqi revolution and the American and British landings while returning to Egypt from a visit to Yugoslavia's President Tito. Upon hearing the news, he decided to return to Moscow for the second time that year to assess Soviet reactions and intentions. In a meeting with Khrushchev, Nasser was able only to get Soviet leaders to declare general manoeuvres on the Turkish–Bulgarian borders.[41] As in the Suez and 1957 Syrian crises, the Soviet leaders utilised limited military displays of force to back up intensive propaganda and diplomatic activity.

By August, the Lebanese situation had stabilised with the appointment of the universally respected commander-in-chief, General Fuad Shihab, as president. Although the crisis had subsided and Western forces had been withdrawn, the situation would never return to the *status quo ante*. With the formation of the UAR, the emergence in Iraq of a regime initially favourable to Egypt, the weakening of King Saud's position (following allegations of complicity in a plot to assassinate Nasser), the fall of President Chamoun, and the adherence of the Yemen to an Egypt-led Arab confederation, Nasser's position as the foremost leader of the Arab world was once again reasserted.

With the Iraqi Revolution and the fall of Chamoun's government, Western hopes for an anti-communist military alliance with the Arab states finally disappeared. The Baghdad Pact and the Eisenhower Doctrine had thus proved insensitive to, and unsuited for, the complexities of inter-Arab politics, which at their root had little to do with the Cold War mould in which they were cast. The objective which had shaped Soviet policy during the period 1955–58 was largely achieved with Iraq's withdrawal from the Baghdad

Pact. In addition, the Iraqi revolution had brought to power a regime in which many Communists were soon installed in positions of considerable influence. With the threat to Soviet security minimised, the Soviet decision-makers upgraded their objectives in the Arab world, by turning their attention increasingly to Arab domestic affairs and shifting their allegiance from Nasser to Qassem, thus instituting a new phase in Soviet relations with Egypt.

1958–61

In the months immediately following the Iraqi revolution, both the Soviet and Egyptian governments looked favourably upon events in that country. The new government announced its intentions to withdraw from the Baghdad Pact and to establish close and cordial relations with both the UAR and the Soviet bloc. Domestically, there was a revival of political activism which coincided with the release of political prisoners. The new regime also announced its adherence to the ideals of Arab nationalism and Arab unity.

It was not long, however, before different conceptions of Arab unity led to the revival of sectarian and political divisions in Iraq itself, as well as to the reopening of the rivalry between Iraq and Egypt for hegemony in the Arab world. One view of Arab unity rested upon the belief that loose federation (*ittihad fedrali*) rather than organic unity was the best form of cooperation between Iraq and the UAR. The adherents of this view broadly included the Communists, the Kurds, the National Democratic party, and the majority of the Shi'i Moslems, all of whom stood to lose politically by any kind of organic unity with the UAR. Organic unity (*wahda*) under Egyptian hegemony was called for by the Baathists, the Nasserites and the Sunni Moslems who, while numerically weaker than the Shi'is, held the monopoly of political power in Iraq and thus looked to the Sunni-dominated UAR to bolster their tenuous position. This divergence of views became evident within the Iraqi leadership itself when a struggle between Qassem and Deputy Prime Minister Colonel Abd al-Salam Aref developed with Qassem favouring federation and Aref seeking unity. In this struggle Qassem encouraged and received the support of the communists; and the arrest of Aref in November 1958 resulted in the pre-dominance of those groups including the communists who opposed immediate union with Egypt.

Nasser viewed the events in Iraq with alarm. The arrest of Aref, the failure in December 1958 of a pro-UAR coup led by Rashid Ali Gaylani, and the communist ascendancy all helped to dampen his original hopes that Iraq would soon be incorporated into the UAR. However, Nasser's alarm over the Iraqi situation went beyond his concern for the future development of relations with that country. The creation in Iraq of a viable popular alternative to Egypt-centred Arab unity threatened to undermine both the unsteady foundations of the UAR as well as Nasser's own position in the Arab world. In particular, the growth of Communist influence in Iraq was generating a resurgence of Syrian communist activity. In November 1958, the Syrian Communist Party issued a thirteen-point programme which asserted that Arab unity would fail unless democratic freedoms were allowed and the differing historical circumstances existing in each Arab country were taken fully into account.[42]

The scene was thus set for the reactivation of the traditional inter-Arab rivalry between Iraq and Egypt. At its source this rivalry was concerned with contending conceptions of Arab nationalism, different programmes for domestic development and personality clashes between the various leaders. However, just as the animosity between Nasser and Nuri al-Said, the Prime Minister of pre-1958 Iraq, had become focused on divergent views of the role the West should play in the Arab world, the rivalry between Nasser and Qassem came to centre on the influence of the communists and the role of the Soviet Union in the area. Nasser's speech at Port Said on 23 December 1958, in which he accused the Syrian Communist Party of seeking to undermine the gains of Arab unity,[43] marked the beginning of this phase. In the months to come, Nasser was to become more outspoken, calling the Syrian and Iraqi Communists 'agents of a foreign power' and intimating that the Soviet leadership was intending to establish Soviet satellites in the Middle East.[44]

The USSR was thus thrust into the midst of an inter-Arab conflict. Although Khrushchev initially refrained from answering Nasser's charges, maintaining that 'differences in ideological views must not hinder the development of friendly relations',[45] after the failure of an anti-communist UAR-backed coup in Iraq in March 1959, the Soviet silence on the rift was broken. During a speech to a visiting Iraqi government delegation, Khrushchev stated that in Iraq 'a more advanced system is being established than in neighbouring countries of the Arab East'. Khrushchev went on to say that 'it is natural that our sympathies should be on the side of those governments . . . which take into consideration the interests of their people'. On the subject of Soviet–UAR relations, while expressing regret over Nasser's recent anti-communist speeches in which the Egyptian leader had armed himself with 'the tongue of the imperialists', Khrushchev reaffirmed the Soviet Union's intention to maintain friendly relations with the UAR.[46] This speech represented the first signs of a major shift in the objectives of Soviet policy in the Middle East and the developing world as a whole. It was a natural reappraisal in the light of changed circumstances, but one which was nevertheless to introduce an added dimension to the Soviet Union's evaluation of the progressive nature of any given regime, an evaluation previously based almost solely on the behaviour of that state in the international arena.

In the UAR, Khrushchev's remarks were seen as a full-scale attack on Arab nationalism. Nasser, in a series of speeches delivered in Damascus in late March, accused the USSR of violating the Bandung principles of non-interference in the domestic affairs of other states. He maintained that during the Suez crisis Egypt had not in fact received any assistance from the USSR and he warned that the Soviet Union's ultimate objective was the establishment of a 'Red Fertile Crescent'.[47] In response, a *Pravda* editorial made the following statement:

> Recent events have justified those Arabs who believe that the union of Iraq and the UAR under present conditions would not increase the strength of the Arab peoples in their struggle for independence, economic development and progress. . . . Union will benefit the peoples only if the necessary economic and political conditions become ripe for it.[48]

For many months thereafter, the Soviet Union's relations with Egypt were affected by the former's support of the Qassem regime. However, in July 1960, the failure of a communist uprising in the northern Iraqi town of Kirkuk marked the beginning of the decline in communist influence within Iraq. As a result, Soviet policy in the Middle East went through a period of uncertainty and duality, possibly reflecting the conflicting and competing influences operating on the decision-making process at that time. On the intergovernmental level, the Soviet leadership made efforts to stabilise

relations with both the UAR and Iraq. The public dispute between
Khrushchev and Nasser subsided, and work on the first stage of the
Aswan Dam began late in 1959. Optimistic, if more cautious,
reports on the situation in Iraq still appeared in the Soviet press,
with a series of protocols and exchanges taking place throughout the
latter half of 1959. However, it was quite clear that the Soviet
leadership was far from pleased with the situation in the Middle
East. Not only was Communist influence on the decline in Iraq, but
in the UAR, authorities had begun a new wave of suppression,
including the arrest in Damascus of the influencial Lebanese
Communist Party leader Farajallah al-Hilu.

Nevertheless, on this occasion, the Soviet leadership refrained
from direct and public intervention on the side of the Arab
Communists, a decision no doubt influenced by the lessons of
Kirkuk as well as by Soviet preoccupation elsewhere. It was at this
time that the Sino–Soviet dispute first became apparent, with the
unilateral Soviet cancellation of the 1957 military aid agreement,
Khrushchev's visit to Peking, the first open exchange of polemics at
the Rumanian Party Congress, and the recall of Soviet technicians
from China. Soviet relations with the West were equally dynamic.
While Khrushchev's visit to the United States and the United
Nations in September 1959, and the ensuing 'Camp David Spirit',
may have improved East–West relations for a time, the U2 incident
and the abortive Paris summit in May 1960 marked the beginning
of a period of renewed Great Power rivalry in the Congo, Cuba, and
Berlin. The Middle East, by the end of the decade, was not the same
arena for Cold War competition that it has been in the preceding
years.

Equally, by the beginning of the 1960s, inter-Arab politics had
become more concerned with purely regional issues. Because of the
complexity of the issues involved, the area could no longer be so
strictly divided between the pro-West and pro-Soviet states; and the
language of politics included fewer references to 'imperialism' and
'Communism' and more to 'feudalism' and 'conservatism' or to
'positive neutrality' and 'Arab socialism'. The euphoria created by
the events of 1958 had begun to wear off, and Arab leaders
increasingly began to concentrate more on domestic consolidation.
By the winter of 1960, Soviet relations with the UAR had improved
tremendously after the low point reached in the spring of 1959.
However, the diverse pressures operating on the Soviet leadership to
adopt a more militant posture were to infuse new dynamism into

Soviet foreign policy following the November 1960 meeting of 81 Communist and Workers' Parties in Moscow.

While the proceedings of the Moscow meeting were never published, it is clear from accounts by various delegates, as well as from the statement issued afterwards, that Moscow's attempt to reconstruct its leadership over a monolithic bloc had been far from successful. In the ideological and strategic fields, the Russians were faced with China's militant and 'high-risk' attitudes towards the nature of the present epoch, the inevitability of a violent and revolutionary transition to socialism, and the necessity of positive support for communist hegemony in movements for national liberation. While the final statement of the conference, with its vague and contradictory phrasing, illustrates the unwillingness of either side to make fundamental modifications in their views, there was evidence of a shift in the Soviet view of the national bourgeoisie. This shift was outlined in the construction of a new historical phase through which a state might pass 'on its way to socialism'. This state of 'national democracy', was to be midway between a 'bourgeois democracy' and a 'people's democracy' and was defined in the following manner:

It is a state which consistently upholds its political and economic independence, fights against imperialism and its military blocs, against military bases on its territory; a state which fights against the new forms of colonialism and the penetration of imperialist capital; a state which rejects dictatorial and despotic methods of government; a state in which the people are ensured broad democratic rights and freedoms . . . .[49]

While it was clear that a state's foreign policy was to be given continued primacy, this new formulation nevertheless represented an attempt to accomodate Chinese 'leftism' without sacrificing Soviet 'gradualism' or the continuation of the tactical and temporary reliance on the national bourgeois governments of the developing world. While the Moscow statement contained no explicit references to whether communist parties should now seek hegemony in national liberation movements, articles published in the following months began to advocate communist leadership.

This divergence of views between the Chinese and Soviet positions on the role of indigenous communist parties also led to a split within the Soviet leadership itself. Although Khrushchev, writing in *Kommunist* in January, spoke generally of the need for all groups to unite to oppose imperialism without mentioning the need for communist hegemony,[50] other leading members of the Soviet hierarchy clearly advocated a more militant line. The more outspoken among these was the newly appointed head of the International Department of the Central Committee, Boris Ponomaryov, who, writing on the 'State of National Democracy' in May 1961, openly advocated communist takeovers in these states:

> In those liberated countries where the people are still without democratic liberties, the struggle for the creation of a national democratic state gives the progressive forces the opportunity to remove the remnants of the colonial administration, to seize the power from the national traitors who serve imperialism and take the fate of the country in their hands.[51]

During the early months of 1961, Khrushchev's more conciliatory approach seemed to be overshadowed by hardline criticism of the national bourgeoisie in general and of the UAR in particular. It was made clear that the UAR was not 'a state of national democracy', and such adjectives as 'dictatorial', 'terroristic' and 'repressive' were coupled with references to measures taken by Nasser. Various front organisations, as well as the Soviet press and radio, stepped up their campaign to secure the release of imprisoned Arab communists.

However, Soviet economic and diplomatic relations with Egypt were not initially affected by this campaign, with both Khrushchev and Nasser refraining from the exchange of mutual recriminations in the verbal dispute. Then, at the beginning of May, just as the propaganda 'war' was subsiding, Khrushchev held a reception for a visiting Egyptian delegation headed by Anwar al-Sadat. In the course of his speech, Khrushchev turned to the subject of nationalism and communism and forecast that some members of the Egyptian delegation would themselves eventually become communists. He went on to say that while Egypt and all states would turn to Communism of their own free will, for 'people cannot be driven to paradise with a stick', it was inevitable that this should happen since 'Arab nationalism is not the zenith of happiness'.[52] Needless to say Sadat and the delegation were stunned; and the remarks sparked off a new round of polemics, in which *Pravda*'s 'Observer' reminded the Arabs of the adage 'Cut not the tree that provides the shade'.[53] In response, Radio Cairo vehemently declared:

> In its campaign against us, *Pravda* quoted an old Arab saying . . . that one should not cut the tree which shades us. This is fine, but Russia is not a tree which shades us . . . We treat Russia as a bank. The bank which grants me a loan has no right to interfere in my own affairs.[54]

Sadat, in a written reply to Khrushchev in June 1961, stated that 'we do not believe that the historical development of man runs along the blind alley of which capitalism is the beginning and communism is the imperative end. . . . We refuse capitalism . . . But this refusal does not mean that communism will succeed in our country'.[55] This type of assertion represented the continuing Egyptian efforts to develop an independent domestic and foreign policy based on Arab socialism and positive neutralism, efforts which found fruition in the summer of 1961 with a series of radical domestic measures and the preparations for the Belgrade conference of non-aligned states. Moscow's turn to the left and its continuing dispute with Nasser somewhat tempered its reaction to the new reforms nationalising banks, financial institutions and all industries above a certain size in both Egypt and Syria. A Soviet commentator writing in *Pravda* noted rather cynically:

> In Cairo we had occasion to read articles in which the author claimed that the decrees of President Nasser on the one hand mean the building of 'Arab national cooperative socialism' and on the other hand have nothing in common with communism. . . . We can indeed confirm that this is far removed from communism. But it is also far from building socialism. In speaking of this we are not intending to lesson the importance of the President's decrees in the UAR.[56]

The Soviet leadership was at this time actively involved in a number of events, including the Berlin crisis, the continuing conflict in the Congo, the 22nd CPSU Congress, and Khrushchev's forthcoming trip to the United Nations—all of which tended to divert attention away from the Belgrade Conference. When Nehru, Tito, Sukarno, and the other Third World leaders gathered in Belgrade it was clear that the hopes that had brought them together at

Bandung six years earlier had failed to materialise since then. They had all become more preoccupied with domestic and regional problems, and progress towards the consolidation of the Third World into a viable and united non-aligned camp had been scant and sporadic. Indeed, the disarray into which the Third World had fallen was exemplified by the vast division over the Congo crisis. Nevertheless, the Bandung powers were determined to meet in Belgrade to discuss their own problems and hopefully to exert some influence on a still polarised world. However, on 31 August, the day before the conference was to open, the Soviet Government announced its intention to resume nuclear testing. Whether or not this decision was taken, as Robert Slusser suggests, by Kozlov and other hardliners without Khrushchev's consent while he was vacationing in the Crimea,[57] the neutralist leaders greeted it with considerable consternation and dismay.

Much of the conference was taken up with discussions of colonialism, although there was also a major debate on Great Power politics and the role of non-alignment. The delegates condemned the arms race and the Berlin crisis without singling out the Soviet Union for particular comment, and drafted a letter to both Kennedy and Khrushchev urging them to enter into direct negotiations. While American public opinion was astonished at the failure of the Belgrade delegates to specifically condemn recent Soviet actions, nevertheless the balance of non-alignment at Belgrade shifted perceptibly away from the USSR. The conference censured the Soviet Union and the United States equally for their failure to make greater progress toward disarmament and the lessening of international tensions. Moreover, the reforms of the United Nations proposed by the delegates bore little resemblance to Khrushchev's 'troika' plan; and the conference failed to draw up any concrete resolution on the German question or on the admission of Communist China to the United Nations.

For the Soviet Union, the conference was a disappointment, as the following characteristic commentary illustrates:

The attempts to prove that neutralism is a middle-of-the-road position of passive observers have two purposes. Firstly, they are intended to whitewash the aggressive military policy of the leading Western countries. Secondly, they are intended to push the neutral countries off their true path.[58]

However, in view of Moscow's decision to resume nuclear testing, the non-aligned states might have been expected to come out more openly against the USSR. Thus, their decision to bypass the more sensitive international issues and remain 'passive observers' may actually have benefited the Soviet leadership. The 'Cairo Summit' between Tito, Nasser and Nehru, as well as the meetings between Khrushchev and Nasser at the United Nations in September were postscripts to the conference. The fact that these meetings, like the conference before them, accomplished little was due less to irreconcilable differences between the participants than to a fluid and dynamic situation in the international arena, Great Power preoccupation elsewhere, and the pressure of domestic upheaval in the UAR which tended to focus attention away from foreign affairs.

The secession of Syria from the UAR on 29 September 1961 marked the end of a period in which Syrians and Egyptians alike had become disillusioned with this first experiment in Arab unity. Nasser's speech announcing his decision not to oppose the secession, while full of regret for the failure of an ideal, showed his own realisation of the perennial problems which had beset the union throughout its three-and-a-half troubled years. The Soviet press refrained from commenting on the break-up of the union for over two months, contenting itself with short reports of both Nasser's and the new Syrian leader's speeches and declarations. Apart from the establishment of diplomatic relations with the new regime, the Soviet Government also refrained from comment. However Khalid Bagdash, the Syrian Communist leader, speaking at the 22nd CPSU Congress in October, expressed his view that 'the disintegration of the union of Egypt and Syria does not mean a collapse of Arab unity, but the bankruptcy of the policy of anti-communism.'[59] Bagdash's speech was the only occasion at the Congress in which the causes or the implications of the break-up of the UAR were dealt with at any length. The Soviet leadership was far more concerned with mustering support for its denunciation of Albania and its attempts to isolate the Chinese position. Events in the Middle East were as a result hardly the central focus of attention.

Nevertheless, the leftward shift in Soviet foreign policy which had become more apparent following the November 1960 Moscow Meeting, was reaffirmed at the 22nd Congress when the Party programme proclaimed that henceforth it would not be enough for states to pursue a progressive foreign policy. Rather, Third World leaders must increasingly concentrate on radical domestic reforms since their newly won independence 'will be shaky and become fictitious if the revolution does not lead to deep changes in social and economic life, if it does not solve the essential tasks of national rebirth'.[60]

The pronouncements of the Congress coincided with the more progressive domestic policy pursued by Nasser after the summer of 1961. Nasser's belief that the union with Syria had been sabotaged by the feudal and bourgeois classes in Syria and reactionary elements in the Arab world as a whole led him to adhere more closely to the ideals of Arab socialism, thus marking the beginning of a period of ideological confrontation and isolation for Egypt in inter-Arab affairs.[61] This isolation was perhaps one reason why Nasser now sought to repair relations with the USSR. The high tide of Arab unity and non-alignment was at an end, and Nasser turned his attention more to domestic reconstruction, the implementation of Egypt's five-year plan, the completion of the first stages of the Aswan Dam, and the promulgation of the quasi-socialist National Charter in 1962.

1962–64

The National Charter declared Egypt's rejection of the capitalist path, and announced the necessity of peacefully eliminating class differences in Egyptian society. It also established the Arab Socialist Union to replace the dissolved National Union as Egypt's sole political party and reserved 50 per cent of all parliamentary seats for workers and peasants. Compared with the political and economic programmes being enacted by other Afro-Asian countries, the Charter and the nationalisation measures enacted the previous summer stand out as bold and progressive reforms. Despite this, articles in Soviet newspapers and journals were divided in their appraisal of the new policies.[62] The debate begun at the 1960 Moscow meeting over the national liberation movement and the concept of 'national democracy' had clearly yet to be resolved within both the Soviet press and the leadership. Khrushchev's outbursts to the Egyptian delegation which visited Moscow in May 1961 showed his continued adherence to the view that while the Egyptian leaders were not themselves representatives of the working class, they were nevertheless capable of taking Egypt towards socialism and of becoming eventual converts to communism themselves. This 'gradualist' view was opposed by Ponomaryov and other adherents to the more radical line who refused to accept that Egypt could enact truly socialist measures while denying the necessity of proletarian hegemony. Articles in various Soviet publications and in the *World Marxist Review*, an international socialist journal controlled by Ponomaryov's department in the Central Committee, continued to publish demands for proletarian hegemony and appeals for the release of Communists being held in Egypt.[63]

Any explanation of Soviet indecisiveness on the evaluation of the new reforms must take into account the changing international environment and the internal political upheavals of the early 1960s. Whereas in the mid-1950s with its rigidly bipolar international system, Egypt had been able to demand and receive a 'blank cheque' in return for a non-aligned foreign policy, in the fluid and polycentric conditions which had begun to emerge by the early 1960s, the importance of Egypt as a factor in superpower relations had markedly declined. In particular, with the failure of British and American efforts to enlist Arab membership in an anti-Soviet regional security system, the immediate threat to Soviet security had somewhat faded. Equally, with increased Chinese activity in the area, culminating in Chou En-lai's highly publicised visit to Cairo and other African capitals in the latter part of 1963, Soviet commentators became aware that it was no longer true (if it had ever been) that anti-Western regimes were thus by definition pro-Soviet. Chinese efforts to secure adherents to their own model of socialism led to more cautious and tentative Soviet appraisals of Third World trends, which now had to be assessed for both their anti-Western and their anti-Chinese content.

Internal political splits also exerted a decisive influence on the direction of Soviet–Egyptian relations during this period. The early 1960s are now generally recognised as a period of heated and divisive debate in the Politburo on matters of both domestic and foreign policy. The Sino-Soviet dispute, and the crises in Berlin and Cuba are but a few of the many instances in which the Politburo was split between opposing factions. Given these splits and Soviet preoccupation with intra-bloc and Soviet–American relations, it is hardly surprising that Soviet leaders refrained from expressing their own diverse views in public.

It was, however, symptomatic of Khrushchev's own diminishing stature after the Cuban Missile Crisis that the First Secretary, whose name had always been personally associated with the promotion of Nasser's regime in the Politburo, made no statement welcoming the Egyptian reforms. Moreover, a visit by Khrushchev to Egypt announced for January 1963 was cancelled without explanation.[64] One can only surmise that the majority of Politburo personnel felt that the domestic situation in Egypt did not yet warrant the blessing that would be implied by such a high-level delegation.

Nevertheless, Khrushchev continued to attach tremendous importance to Soviet relations with Egypt. In June 1963 Khrushchev's son-in-law, Aleksei Adzhubei, the editor of *Izvestiya*, was dispatched for top-level negotiations with Nasser on the question of the continued imprisonment of Egyptian Communists. Nasser relented and announced the following month that all political prisoners were to be released, concentration camps were to be closed, and Communists were to be invited to join the Arab Socialist Union as individuals, where they would be able to actively participate in the construction of socialism. *Pravda* greeted the announcement as a major step forward[65] and the way was now open for Khrushchev to visit the UAR.

His visit was universally hailed in Egypt and abroad as a success for Soviet foreign policy and as a watershed in the personalised style of diplomacy between Khrushchev and Nasser that had characterised Soviet–Egyptian relations over the previous decade.[66] However, the trip was reported neither fully nor enthusiastically in the Soviet press, for Khrushchev in the course of the visit displayed all those qualities which only five months later were to lead to his ouster – 'harebrained scheming, half-baked conclusions, hasty decisions and actions divorced from reality, bragging and bluster, attraction to rule by fiat . . .'[67]

In the first place he apparently agreed to give Egypt a far larger loan than had previously been agreed to by the Politburo.[68] He then proceeded to confer the highest honour the Soviet Union can bestow, the Hero of the Soviet Union, on both Nasser and the Minister of Defence, Marshal Abd al-Hakim Amer—and the latter award was made despite the fact that Amer had rudely interrupted Khrushchev during a speech broadcast live over Cairo Radio to demand more arms.[69] Soviet leaders were outraged that Khrushchev had awarded the medals, not only because they felt Amer at least was not worthy of the title, but also because Khrushchev did not have the constitutional authority to award such honours.[70] In his speech to mark the completion of the initial stages of the Aswan

Dam, Khrushchev created a further uproar. Apparently angered by the remarks on Arab unity made by the previous speaker, the Iraqi President Abd al-Salam Aref (who had overthrown Qassem in 1963), Khrushchev departed from his prepared speech and launched into a vicious denunciation of Arab unity, admitting to a stunned audience at the end that the editors in Moscow would now 'tear him to bits' for departing from his set text.[71] The Soviet press remained ominously silent, making oblique reference to the incident. Finally, while Khrushchev, in a review of the UAR's domestic reforms, proclaimed that the country was indeed 'embarking on the path of socialist construction',[72] the joint communiqué issued at the end of the visit was much less fulsome in its praise. The Soviet Union refrained from supporting the declaration of 'the Egyptian side' that the UAR had 'taken the road of socialist development'. Rather 'the Soviet side' referred only to the 'broad social and economic transformations' taking place in Egypt.[73]

On 14 October 1964, Khrushchev was ousted from power. Certainly his behaviour in Cairo must have been added to the long list of indictments levelled against him. His penchant for brash and spontaneous outbursts and his repeated interventions in intergovernmental affairs had resulted in several setbacks for Soviet–Egyptian relations, as witnessed by the heated exchange with Nasser in 1959, his remarks to the Egyptian parliamentary delegation in 1961 and his behaviour during the Egyptian tour. Nevertheless, Khrushchev's style was in many ways an asset. His own personal interest in Soviet–Egyptian relations and his close friendship with Nasser were highly appreciated by the Egyptian leader, whose own personal style was equally flamboyant. Moreover, it was Khrushchev, more than any other Soviet leader, who had promoted the development of the relations with the Third World. Beginning with his visit to South Asia in 1955, Khrushchev had witnessed and encouraged a decade of rapidly expanding economic, military and political ties with developing countries, with Soviet–Egyptian relations serving as a model. And it was this expanded presence which was perhaps his greatest and most lasting legacy to his successors.

3 Soviet–Egyptian Relations under Brezhnev and Kosygin 1964–70

If one of Khrushchev's greatest legacies to his successors was the expansion of relations with Egypt and the Third World, the Egyptian leadership was anxious following his ouster to ensure that these relations continued unaffected. Egyptian newspapers were quick to assert that 'we must not consider our relations with the Soviet Union as relations with any particular personality . . . we have built these relations on a general and not on a personal basis'.[1] In his weekly column in *al-Ahram* Mohamed Heikal went even further by claiming that Khrushchev's fall was no great loss to Egypt, since he had been the only Soviet leader with whom Egypt had ever quarrelled and since he had never been able to eradicate completely the remnants of Stalinism.[2]

Despite Cairo's initial signs of anxiety, relations between the two countries were not significantly influenced by the change in leadership. In November, a high-level Egyptian delegation headed by Marshal Amer held talks in Moscow with the new Soviet leaders on the future direction of relations between the two countries. In December, Deputy Premier A. N. Shelepin headed a parliamentary delegation to the UAR, a trip which coincided with the arrival of Egyptian trade officials in Moscow. Throughout the spring and summer months in 1965, a variety of military, economic, and governmental delegations were exchanged, including in March the first in a series of high-level Soviet naval visits to the UAR, in this instance headed by the commander-in-chief of the navy, Admiral S. G. Gorshkov.

This series of exchanges was a prelude to a five-day visit by Nasser to the Soviet Union in August. Although a variety of subjects were discussed, including Vietnam, the forthcoming Afro-Asian summit, the Sino-Soviet conflict, and Soviet aid to Egypt, the primary purpose of the visit was to establish close personal relations between Nasser and the new Soviet leaders. The Minister of Defence, R. Ya. Malinovskiy, is reported to have asked Nasser why he did not wear the order of Hero of the Soviet Union bestowed on him by Khrushchev, with President Mikoyan making it clear that the Soviet Union still regarded Nasser as a 'real hero of heroes'.[3]

Nasser's visit set the tone for what was to be a period of strong and stable relations between the two countries, characterised by a much more pragmatic and far less flamboyant approach by the Soviet leadership. Although the new leaders remained cautious in their assessment of Egypt's own brand of socialism, nevertheless they welcomed and encouraged the dissolution of the Egyptian Communist Party in 1965 and the absorption of its members into the Arab Socialist Union. The Communists were given the task of cooperating with other ASU members in order to transform that organisation into a vanguard party. To this end the Russians organised study sessions both in Egypt and in the Soviet Union for ASU members and established several ideological institutes in the UAR. The distinction between Moscow's brand of 'scientific socialism' and Nasser's own variant became blurred as Soviet ideologues began to focus on the more positive features of the regime. Thus, despite the fact that the Egyptian revolution was being carried out almost totally from above, Soviet observers by now were willing to concede that although 'it is a particular feature of the situation that those who lead the Egyptian revolution are not Marxists, they are putting into practice measures which in many respects are similar to the measures taken by Communists at a certain stage of a social revolution'.[4]

This period of greater optimism and flexibility resulted not only from leadership changes and ideological reassessments but also from shifts in the international system during 1965 and 1966 which enhanced the importance for the Soviet Union of establishing closer ties with Egypt. In particular, China's continuing efforts to enlist allies amongst the Third World states underscored the necessity of carefully nourishing those regimes which remained friendly to Moscow. In January 1965, China extended an $80 million credit to Egypt for industrial projects in an effort to win Egyptian support for the Chinese move to exclude the Soviet Union from the forthcoming Afro-Asian conference in Algiers. However, Nasser upheld the Soviet presence there; and as a result, when it was convened in the summer of 1965, the Chinese succeeded in having it first postponed and then cancelled, thereby destroying any semblance of unity which the Afro-Asian movement had managed to maintain.

A further worrying trend from the Soviet point of view was the downfall of a number of leftist regimes in the Third World. In the last years of Khrushchev's rule, the Soviet leadership had been heartened by the emergence of pro-Soviet regimes in Algeria, Ghana, the Yemen, the UAR and Indonesia. However, the overthrow of the Ghanaian and Indonesian regimes, the continuing war in the Yemen and the temporary flirtation of Algeria's new government with China upset Moscow's views on the 'irreversibility' of the pro-Soviet and non-capitalist paths and further motivated the Soviet leaders to protect their gains.

The new and more hostile phase of Soviet–American relations ushered in by the American bombing of North Vietnam also affected Soviet policy towards Egypt and the Middle East as a whole. With the escalation of the war, Soviet and East European supplies to North Vietnam of weaponry, oil and other materials increased dramatically. As such, the Suez Canal assumed a major importance as a vital link in the maritime route from the Black Sea ports to Hanoi. This was especially true both after the Chinese began to interfere with Soviet shipments through China's territory and during the winter months when the Trans-Siberian railway was often unusable and the seas off Vladivostok were frozen. As major users of the Canal in the years prior to the June 1967 Middle East war, one can understand why the Soviet and East European leaders worked so hard to have it reopened after the war. In this way the Middle East assumed a vital strategic role for the Soviet involvement in Southeast Asia.

However, the war in Vietnam had a further and less tangible, yet probably more important, impact on the formulation and conduct of Soviet policy in the Middle East and elsewhere. The American decision to escalate the war by the massive involvement of her own personnel and by the use of all military means short of nuclear weapons had a singular effect on Soviet decision-makers. The cautious optimism which had intermittently characterised Soviet–American relations in the early 1960s was at an end, with the Soviet Union now convinced that the Americans would meet any Soviet response with further escalation. As such, in a situation of uncertainty about the upper limit to which the American government was willing to go to protect its interests, the Soviet leaders adopted a much more reactive and defensive posture. Their decision not to match every American escalation with a Soviet counterescalation was taken not only because of their perception that the Americans were willing to continue escalating, but also because the Americans at that time possessed a far greater capability than the Soviet Union for the use of conventional weapons in limited wars. In particular, the Soviet Union had not yet developed the capability to transport, land, supply, and protect large numbers of her troops in marine-type operations on foreign soil. The Soviet perception of American bellicosity and the Soviet realisation of the greater ability of the Americans to conduct foreign military operations were to have a decisive impact on the Soviet Union's reaction to the crisis which developed in the Middle East from mid-1966 onwards.

THE 1967 CRISIS

If the early and mid-1960s was a period of relative tranquillity in inter-Arab and Arab–Israeli relations, by 1966 there was every indication that this phase was rapidly coming to an end. Egypt's intervention on the side of the republicans in the indecisive Yemeni civil war was having a debilitating effect on her economy and was straining relations with Jordan and Saudi Arabia, who supported the royalist faction in the Yemen. Furthermore, beginning in December 1965, Saudi Arabia's King Faisal started to enlist support from the Shah of Iran and King Hussein of Jordan for an Islamic summit to fight against all those forces alien to Islam, a pointed reference to Nasser's brand of 'Arab Socialism'. The fact that Faisal's initiatives coincided with the announcement of a $350 million arms deal between Saudi Arabia and the United States was enough to convince both Egypt and the Soviet Union that this was the beginning of a new drive by the Americans to weaken the 'anti-imperialist' and 'progressive' forces in the area. In an important interview with *Izvestiya* in February 1966, Nasser expressed both Egyptian and Soviet fears.

> The forces of colonialism and reaction inside and outside the Arab world are launching a new offensive and, therefore, all progressive forces inside and outside the Arab world should close their ranks, solidify their unity, and redouble their vigilance and thus become effective.[5]

This call for unity coincided with a coup in Syria which brought to power an extremely left-wing and neo-Marxist section of the Baath Party, headed by Dr Nureddin al-Atassi, who became head of state, and by Colonels Salah Jadid and Hafiz al-Assad. Quick to support the new regime, the Soviet leaders called for the creation of a united front of revolutionary forces—including Algeria, Iraq, Yemen, and Syria, and with Egypt at its head.

It soon become apparent that the Syrian leaders were radical and activist not only in their approach to inter-Arab relations but also in their attitude towards Israel. They called for a Chinese-style revolutionary war of liberation and gave the al-Fatah Palestinian guerrillas increased support for their raids into Israel. Hoping to stabilise the still shaky regime, the Soviet Union promised Syria $133 million of aid for a number of projects, including a commit-ment to build the Euphrates Dam. Soviet leaders also denounced what seemed to them to be a series of Israeli and American provocations designed to topple the new government. In May, Kosygin visited the UAR to promise continued military, economic and political support for Nasser's more radical policy in the Arab world. Attempts were made by the Russians, the Syrians, and the Palestinians to bring Egypt into a firm anti-Western and anti-Israeli pact with the exposed and isolated Syrians. However, Nasser resisted these efforts for many months, no doubt cognisant of his already burdensome commitment in the Yemen and of the Syrian ability to involve Egypt in a conflict which it could not control. Finally, on 4 November 1966, Nasser relented and signed a mutual defence agreement with Syria. All the ingredients for a Middle East war were now present: Arab–Israeli enmity, Great Power rivalry, a radical Arab front, a series of binding agreements, and a fluid and volatile situation in the Fertile Crescent area. All that the participants required were ammunition and a spark.

Ammunition was hardly in short supply, because a fullscale arms race had been going on since the end of 1965, with the Soviet Union supplying the UAR, Syria and Iraq, and the United States supplying Israel, Jordan and Saudi Arabia.[6] The sparks, in the form of numerous clashes along Israel's borders with Jordan and Syria, were also abundant.

On 7 April 1967 a practically routine exchange between Israeli and Syrian artillery over Israeli cultivation of the demilitarised zone escalated into a fullscale air battle in which six Syrian jetfighters were shot down. Some Israeli jets then flew on to Damascus, making victory swoops over the city. Almost immediately there were calls from the Arab world for Nasser to come to Syria's defence, but for the time being he did nothing. The Soviet leaders were equally slow to react, and it was not until two full weeks after the clash that the Israeli ambassador to the Soviet Union was summoned to the Ministry of Foreign Affairs. There he was told that the incident was a 'dangerous playing with fire on the part of Israel in an area near the borders of the Soviet Union'; and he was warned that Israel's continued verbal and physical threats against Syria would 'result in serious consequences'.[7] At the same time, right-wing colonels carried out a successful coup in Athens, toppling the Greek monarchy and smashing left-wing hopes for victory in the forthcoming elections. This event was viewed in Moscow as further evidence of renewed American efforts to establish anti-Soviet systems in the area. As such, Israel's hostile posture towards Syria was seen by the Soviet leaders as part of a much larger 'plot' by America and her supporters to destabilise and overthrow progressive Arab regimes.

On 25 April, the Israeli ambassador was again called to the Soviet Foreign Ministry where he received a written note stating that 'the Soviet Government is in possession of information about Israeli troop concentrations on the Israeli–Arab borders at the present time. These concentrations are assuming a dangerous character, coinciding as they do with the hostile campaign in Israel against Syria'.[8] Four days later an Egyptian parliamentary delegation headed by Anwar al-Sadat arrived in Moscow, and according to Mohamed Heikal, Premier A. N. Kosygin told Sadat that Israel had massed two brigades on the Syrian border. By now, Soviet, Syrian and Egyptian leaders were all convinced that these troop movements were a build-up for a military intervention designed to topple the Damascus regime. Although it may never be known exactly what Israeli intentions actually were at the time, Nasser in a speech after the war stated that Soviet leaders had told Sadat of their conviction 'that the invasion of Syria was imminent'.[9]

This conviction was reinforced by a series of bellicose statements made by high-ranking Israeli leaders during the weekend of 12 May. In addition to the public speeches made by Levi Eshkol and General Rabin, there was also a United Press despatch from Jerusalem quoting a 'highly placed Israeli source' as saying that 'if Syria continued the campaign of sabotage in Israel, it would immediately provoke military action aimed at overthrowing the

Syrian regime'.[10] In a speech by UN Secretary-General U Thant to
the Security Council on factors aggravating the present crisis, he
dealt specifically with the effects on the Arab world of these
statements by Israeli leaders. He warned that 'reports emanating
from Israel have attributed to some high officials in that State
statements so threatening as to be particularly inflammatory in the
sense that they could only heighten emotions and thereby increase
tensions on the other side of the lines'.[11] This was precisely their
effect.

Nasser's reaction to the Israeli statements was to begin moving
Egyptian troops into Sinai. On 16 May, he asked the United
Nations Emergency Force to withdraw from those positions which it
had occupied since the Suez crisis. It was widely believed outside
Israel that this was a political demonstration by the Egyptians,
designed both to appease those Arabs who had accused Nasser of
hiding behind UNEF and to relieve some of the pressure on Syria.
Without referring directly to Egyptian troop movements, the Soviet
press stepped up its condemnation of efforts by the United States,
Britain and Israel to overthrow the Syrian government, making it
clear that 'Syria has reliable friends who will not leave her in
need'.[12] It is interesting however that the UAR, Iraq, and
Lebanon—but not the Soviet Union—were listed as states which
would come to Syria's defence.

On 22 May, Nasser announced that Egyptian forces had
reoccupied Sharm al-Sheikh and closed the Straits of Tiran to
Israeli shipping, thereby initiating the final stage in the prelude to
war. From this time onward, the Soviet leaders cautioned restraint
on all the parties concerned. Egyptian actions, which they had
initially encouraged as a show of force to bolster the Syrian regime
against American and Israeli provocations, had now developed a
momentum of their own. At any moment, either the Arab or the
Israeli side, convinced that the other was preparing an invasion,
might take pre-emptive military action to gain the upper hand. The
Soviet Government did not openly support Egypt's decision to close
the Straits (perhaps fearing that were they to do so the Turks might
reply by closing the Dardenelles); and they made it clear through
unofficial channels that Nasser had not consulted the Soviet Union
prior to his decisions to withdraw UNEF and reoccupy Sharm al-
Sheikh.[13] An official Soviet Government statement issued on 24
May emphasised that the Soviet support for the Arabs was neither
unlimited nor unconditional and that the Soviet Union could not

condone a military solution to the crisis. A crucial portion of the statement read as follows:

> But let no one have any doubts about the fact that should anyone try to unleash aggression in the Near East, he would be met not only by the united strength of Arab countries but also by strong opposition to aggression from the Soviet Union and all peace-loving states. It is the firm belief of the Soviet Government that the people have no interest in a military conflict in the Middle East.[14]

In case the Egyptians did not appreciate the full meaning of the statement, Kosygin told Shams al-Din Badran, the Egyptian Defence Minister, who was in Moscow between 25 and 28 May that 'we are going to back you. But you have achieved your point of view. You have won a political victory. So it is time now to compromise, to work politically'.[15] Evidently however, Badran misunderstood Kosygin; and Nasser got the impression from Badran that the Russians were willing to give him unlimited support, an impression he conveyed in a speech on 29 May. Hearing the speech the Egyptian Under-Secretary of State, who was also at the Moscow meeting, reportedly sent Nasser accurate minutes of Kosygin's statement.

From this time until the beginning of the war, both the Soviet Union and the United States made every effort to restrain their respective clients from firing the first shot. Robert Stephens was told by French diplomatic sources that the Russians had emphasised to both the Egyptians and the Syrians that 'not only would they not support them if they attacked Israel and so risked confronting the United States as well, but also that they would not give the two Arab states military support in the event of an attack by Israel alone'.[16] This message was repeated by the Soviet ambassador to Cairo, who at 3.00 am on 27 May awakened Nasser with a message from the Kremlin that on the basis of Israeli intelligence, the Russians had been told by the Americans that Egypt was going to attack in the morning. Despite Nasser's reassurance that there was no truth in the allegations, the ambassador cautioned Nasser not to fire the first shot because whoever did so would be in an untenable political position.[17]

The buildup continued on both sides with Jordan's accession to the Syrian–Egyptian unified defence command and the establishment in Israel of a new government of national unity with Moshe Dayan as Minister of Defence. After Iraq's announcement on 4 June that she would join the unified Arab command, Israel became convinced that war was now inevitable.

Israel opened its offensive early on Monday 5 June 1967; and although the war lasted for six days, victory was assured for Israel after three hours. The Israeli air force launched an all-out attack first on Egypt's airfields and then on bases in Syria and Jordan. Egypt was caught totally by surprise. Her airforce was destroyed; her airfields were made unusable; and as a result the Egyptian army in Sinai was left without any air cover for the ensuing battles. The result was a devastating defeat in which Egypt lost not only her entire airforce but also 11,500 men killed and 5,500 captured, and 700 tanks and thousands of guns and trucks.[18] A similar fate befell Syria and Jordan, and by the afternoon of 10 June when the ceasefire came into effect, Israel had occupied Sinai, east Jerusalem, the territory west of the Jordan river, and the Golan Heights.

The Soviet reaction to the Israeli attack was immediate yet restrained. In a statement issued on 6 June, the Soviet Government condemned the Israeli action, declaring its resolute support for the Arab side; and ambiguously reserving 'the right to take all steps that may be necessitated by the situation'.[19] It was obvious from the moment hostilities broke out that the Soviet leadership's prime concern was to prevent a direct confrontation between the USA and the USSR. One of Kosygin's first actions was to open the hotline with Washington in order to express concern over the Israeli attack and to urge President Johnson to exert pressure on the Israelis for an early ceasefire. Despite the total destruction of the Arab airforce, the Soviet leadership was evidently remaining true to its prewar stand that it would not provide military support in the event of an attack by Israel alone. It was apparently to invoke Soviet military intervention that the Arabs made misleading accusations about the participation of American aircraft in the Israeli attack. Kosygin received American reassurances that their planes had not been involved; and when justifying Soviet non-intervention, he reportedly informed the various Arab envoys that their leaders' accusations had been false.[20]

Up until 9 June, Soviet activity was centred around efforts to obtain an unconditional ceasefire. When on 9 June the Syrians announced that they too would accept the ceasefire, and the Israelis nevertheless continued to advance, the Soviet Union's involvement in the crisis escalated. Obviously afraid that the Israelis and their 'supporters' were about to achieve their initial objective—the overthrow of the progressive regime in Damascus—the Soviet Union broke off diplomatic relations with Tel Aviv, stating that unless Israel ceased hostilities, the Soviet Union would adopt other sanctions against it.[21] On the same day, a statement was issued by the Communist Party leaders of the USSR and all the East European states with the exception of Rumania. The signatories to the statement threatened that if Israel did not stop its offence, they would do 'everything necessary to help the peoples of the Arab Countries administer a resolute rebuff to the aggressor . . .'.[22]

On 10 June, when the fighting on the Syrian front continued, the Soviet government finally threatened unilateral military intervention. The Soviet statement emphasised that unless the Israelis adhered to the ceasefire immediately, the Soviet Union would be forced to take all 'necessary action, including military'.[23] Although the Soviet High Command had placed some of their paratroop divisions on alert, their naval build-up in the Mediterranean did not contain sufficient amphibious landing or non-nuclear capabilities for an immediate low-level intervention.[24] What is more, the Soviet leaders' failure to airlift any replacements to the Arab armies during the fighting (replacements did not start to arrive until 23 June) supports the view that the Soviets' overriding objective was to obtain a speedy ceasefire, both because of the apparent inability of the Arabs to defend themselves and because of the unpreparedness and the unwillingness of the Russians either to resupply the demoralised Arabs forces or to intervene on their behalf. The Americans reacted to the Russian threat by moving the Sixth Fleet closer to the Syrian coast and by putting greater pressure on the Israelis to accept the ceasefire. In the afternoon of 10 June, the Israelis finally acquiesced and halted hostilities. The war had ended.

THE GROWTH OF SOVIET INFLUENCE

Officially the Soviet leaders attributed the Arab defeat to Israel's surprise attack and the support she received from the West.[25] Unofficially, however, it soon became abundantly clear that incompetance, miscalculations, and even disloyalty on the part of the Egyptian command were also considered to have contributed to the 'setback'. Articles began to appear in the Soviet press which dealt explicitly with the question of why the UAR's armed forces, with their 'first class, up-to-date weapons', had lost. While there were many variations on the theme, Soviet analysts were in general agreement that the Egyptians had been defeated, as one journalist stated, 'mainly because some generals and senior officers, who in their hearts had never accepted the revolution, were in the event not prepared to do their military and patriotic duty. They were biased against the Government's basic policy of effecting social changes in the country'.[26] However, these criticisms were limited to the military command and were not intended to signal a lack of confidence in Nasser's own commitment to a socialist transformation. The Soviet press cited the popular demonstrations which followed Nasser's resignation speech as proof of the Egyptian people's continued loyalty to him and to the progressive aims of his government. Nor did press reports indicate that Soviet leaders no longer regarded the UAR as the head of progressive forces in the Arab world. Rather it soon became evident that what was being called for was a purge from both the military and the government of all those leaders who were concerned about their own privileges and lifestyle and who had resisted any profound social change.[27] Mohamed Udah, of the Egyptian newspaper *al-Jumhuriya*, wrote an article in *Pravda* which indicated the coincidence of views between leading Soviet and Egyptian circles.

> One urgent task now facing the UAR at home is the creation of a truly new army, able to defend the revolutionary regime which has declared socialism to be its choice. Parallel with this, the creation of a political party is of tremendous importance, a party which will become the main pivot of political life in the country and not a complex bureaucratic organisation.[28]

In the three years between the end of the June war and Nasser's death, Soviet influence in the domestic affairs of the UAR reached a level which has not been equalled since either in the UAR or elsewhere in the Middle East. It was in the army that Soviet influence was most profound. Immediately following the war, Soviet President Podgornyy came to Cairo to make a first-hand assessment of the situation, accompanied by the Armed Forces Chief of Staff, Marshal M. V. Zakharov. As a result of this and subsequent meetings, the decision was taken to completely reorganise the Egyptian army. One of Nasser's first acts after the war had been to sack Marshal Amer and 50 other top army and airforce commanders. This process was continued until practically the entire upper echelon of the military had been replaced, with 1500 Soviet training advisers attached to all Egyptian military units above brigade level, under the overall supervision of Marshal Zakharov, who had remained in Egypt. Soviet military supplies began to arrive in vast quantities. In the week following Podgornyy's visit, an estimated 130 combat aircraft arrived in Cairo; and throughout July, Heikal reported that Soviet aircraft carrying equipment and military supplies 'arrived in Cairo at the rate of one every ten minutes'.[29] The efforts to retrain and resupply the Egyptian forces proceeded at such a rate that by the beginning of November 1967 Zakharov was able to tell Nasser: 'Mr. President, I think that Egypt can now stand up to anything Israel can deliver. I have no fears for the Egyptian front. The defences are perfectly all right'.[30]

The Russians also played a more direct part in Egyptian defences in the post-1967 period. In the days following the war a number of Soviet warships arrived in Alexandria and Port Said, with Rear-Admiral Moloshov declaring 'We are ready to cooperate with your armed forces to repel any aggression'.[31] The Soviet naval presence in Egyptian ports increased, with the Egyptian authorities granting them extensive autonomous facilities. In October 1967 a fresh outbreak of hostilities seemed possible after Israel bombed Egyptian refineries in Suez, in retaliation for the sinking of the *Eilat*. Soviet ships that had departed from Egypt in previous days steamed back to Egyptian ports, in an obvious display of military support. Nasser welcomed this increase in Soviet naval strength in the Mediterranean, hoping that it would balance the omnipresence of the American Sixth Fleet. This certainly corresponded with Soviet strategic objectives, for it was under Brezhnev and Kosygin that the Soviet navy witnessed a massive buildup—a buildup which required a concomitant expansion of maritime routes and ports of call. A statement made by Vice-Admiral Smirnov in 1968 clearly indicated that the Soviet navy now considered the Mediterranean to be a legitimate and permanent sphere for Soviet activity:

Our state, which is, as is known, a Black Sea and consequently also a Mediterranean power, could not remain indifferent to the intrigues organised directly adjacent to the borders of the USSR and other socialist countries. No one can be allowed to turn the

Mediterranean into a breeding ground for a war that could plunge mankind into the abyss of a world-wide nuclear missile catastrophe. The presence of Soviet vessels in the Mediterranean serves this lofty noble aim.[32]

The size of the Soviet Union's naval presence was also eventually matched by an equally massive commitment to the UAR's air defence. With Egypt's airforce in ruins and Israeli troops sitting on the east bank of the Canal, Nasser was rightly anxious to come to an agreement with the Russians over air defence. Both Heikal and Sadat concur that during Podgornyy's visit to Egypt, Nasser asked that the USSR enter into a mutual defence agreement with the UAR, in which the Soviet Union would assume immediate but temporary responsibility for Egyptian air defence. On this occasion, the Soviet leaders declined what they must have thought would be an entangling alliance.[33]

However at the height of the 'war of attrition' in 1970, the Soviets did take responsibility for a large part of Egypt's air defence. Soviet pilots began to fly operationally against Israeli Phantoms, and Soviet techncians manned SAM-3 missile sites on the Canal. This was the first time that Soviet military personnel had been engaged in active operations on such a scale outside the socialist bloc, and Heikal's account of Nasser's January 1970 meeting in Moscow indicates clearly that this was not a decision that the Soviet leaders took lightly. After Nasser had threatened to resign because of his inability to defend Egyptian territory without greater Soviet involvement, the entire Politburo and a group of Soviet marshals were called into a joint session. Following a meeting which lasted well over six hours, Brezhnev told Nasser that they had reluctantly agreed to the Egyptian request, adding that it was a decision 'fraught with grave consequences', and one that would require considerable restraint on the part of the Egyptians.[34] The Soviet leaders were quite clearly prepared only to stop the Israeli penetration of Egyptian air space west of the Canal, and were most concerned not to become involved either in any Egyptian effort to liberate occupied territory or in any direct confrontation with the United States.

The desire to prevent an American escalation led to the Soviet decision to signal their new involvement in several muted ways. On their arrival in Egypt, the SAM-3 missiles were driven openly through the city streets with their Russian crews waving to the crowds on route; and Soviet pilots sent to intercept Israeli jets communicated openly on their intercoms in Russian. The Israelis and the Americans clearly got the message; and Israel's deep penetration bombing ceased after 18 April, although the continuing war over the Canal was to lead to the subsequent downing of at least four Soviet-piloted aircraft.[35]

By Nasser's death, therefore, Soviet military involvement in Egypt had been extended to all levels. Soviet military advisers were in Egypt, and their Egyptian counterparts were receiving training in the Soviet Union. Arms supplies increased quantitatively and qualitatively to include the latest and most sophisticated weaponry. The buildup of the Soviet naval presence in the East Mediterranean and the introduction of Soviet military personnel into operational positions on the Egyptian–Israeli front were both precedents in the expansion of the Soviet Union's military role in Egypt. It was, nevertheless, an important feature of this buildup that however massive it may have appeared to the Western observer, it was first of all the product of Nasser's own demands and secondly it always fell short of these demands. One can in no way say that the Soviet military presence was imposed on Egypt any more that one can deny that this increased presence gave the Soviet Union considerable strategic advantage in the Mediterranean, enhanced prestige in the Middle East, and added influence over the formulation of Egypt's domestic and external policy.

Soviet analysts looked on Egypt's domestic policy in a very favourable light in the post-1967 period. Following Nasser's purges of right-wing military and governmental officials and his reaffirmation of the necessity to pursue a socialist course, R. A. Ul'yanovskiy, Ponomaryov's assistant in the International Department of the Central Committee, was able to report optimistically that in those national democracies such as the UAR,

> the state sector . . . is developing at a more or less accelerated rate. Foreign capital is being nationalised. . . . Political structures are being established in the nature of one-party regimes exercising a revolutionary anti-imperialist dictatorship. . . . A progressive foreign policy is being carried out.

Turning to discuss the UAR specifically, Ul'yanovskiy noted that the UAR Charter which was now being implemented had 'felt the

effects of scientific socialism, the international communist movement and the world socialist system'.[36]

It had been in the Charter, introduced in 1962, that the
formation of the Arab Socialist Union was first announced. In 1968,
following riots demanding greater political and press freedom,
Nasser put forward his '30 March programme'. While promising
greater personal freedom, the programme did not allow for the all-
party elections which some had demanded. Rather the ASU was to
be given greater day-to-day responsibility for decision-making; and
in order to fulfil this new role the ASU Central Committee was to
remain in permanent session. Nasser did not sanction the creation of
an inner political vanguard within the ASU which the Soviet Union
and the Egyptian left-wing had been pressing for, but he did
announce that the ASU was to be rebuilt 'by free elections from top
to bottom'. Despite the fact that the programme's pledges fell far
short of the Soviet objective of transforming the ASU into an
effective political vanguard styled on the CPSU, the Soviet press
was generally enthusiastic about the reforms, saying that they
represented 'a victory for the progressive forces in the Egyptian
revolution'.[37] One *Pravda* article, however, attributed the ASU's
failure to be transformed into a vanguard party to 'traditional fears
that, if a party is established, persons outside it would start
struggling against it, which might increase class "collision" in the
country and many other things. Nevertheless there is a growing
tendency to establish parties within the ASU'.[38]

This last statement was certainly true, with a pro-Soviet circle led
by the ASU's General Secretary Ali Sabri becoming particularly
influential within the ASU Central Committee after 1968. When
Ali Sabri and some of his protégés were demoted by Nasser in
September 1969, the official explanation was that Sabri's entourage
had tried to smuggle in excess goods on their return from a visit to
Russia. Unsubstantiated rumours abounded, however, that Sabri
had been involved in an unsuccessful left-wing coup against Nasser.
One can only agree with Robert Stephens's speculation that the
series of demotions 'may have been intended as a warning to the left-
wing of the Arab Socialist Union and perhaps also to the Russians
about the limits of their influence'.[39] Time would show that
President Sadat was not prepared to be as patient as Nasser had
been with Ali Sabri's pro-Russian sympathies.

If the Soviet Union's role in shaping the reform of Egyptian
political structures was rather limited, her influence on Egypt's

economic development and financial solvency was decisive. The June war had been a tremendous drain on Egyptian resources, and one which could have been devastating had the Soviet leaders not decided to re-equip the Egyptian armed forces free of charge.[40] Nasser later revealed that the Soviet Union had also agreed to cancel half of Egypt's debt to the Soviet Union and to reschedule the remainder.[41] These three factors, combined with an inflow of Arab aid and investment and favourable commodity prices for increased Egyptian exports, surprisingly produced what in the short term was a relatively healthy economy. Indeed in 1968–69, Egypt had its first trade surplus since the 1930s. The rescheduling of the Soviet debt was of course a false economy designed to gain a breathing spell. Nasser hoped that with the expansion in arable land which would accompany the completion of the Aswan Dam and with the recovery of the oil fields in Sinai and the reopening of the Suez Canal, which could only be achieved by an Israeli withdrawal from occupied territory, the Egyptian economy could free itself of dependence on any overseas aid. Yet when Nasser died in September 1970, although the Aswan Dam was all but finished, there was still no hope in sight of a settlement to the Arab–Israeli problem.

THE ARAB–ISRAELI FRONT: ACTIVITY WITHOUT PROGRESS

Efforts by the UN, the Great Powers and the participants themselves to bring about a resolution of the conflict began almost immediately after the cessation of hostilities in 1967 and continued unsuccessfully until Nasser's death. While in the United States for the UN General Assembly's special session on the Middle East, Premier Kosygin and President Johnson held an informal summit in Glassboro, New Jersey at the end of June. Although a communiqué was never released, it was admitted that the Middle East had been discussed. President Johnson later confirmed in a televised report on the meeting that while Soviet and American views on the Middle East had diverged, they were 'a long way from total difference' since both sides had at least agreed that all states had a right to exist.[42]

The Arab Heads of State meeting in Khartoum at the end of August 1967 decided to lift the oil embargo imposed since June on the West; to provide economic aid to Egypt and Jordan in recompense for war damages; and to enforce 'the principles of non-recognition and non-negotiation, and to make no peace with Israel for the sake of the rights of the Palestinian people in their homeland'.[43] While Israel interpreted this resolution as being militant and uncompromising, it was in many ways a victory for the 'moderates' headed by Nasser. Because the conference had agreed to seek a settlement by political rather than military means, Nasser and Hussein were able to interpret the resolution to mean that the Arab states would not extend *de jure* recognition to Israel, they would not negotiate *directly* with Israeli officials, and they would not conclude an *official* peace treaty with the Government of Israel. The loopholes in the resolution therefore offered Arab leaders room for manoeuvre.

Following Khartoum, and the threat which the *Eilat* incident in October presented for the renewal of hostilities, the efforts to find a solution shifted to the UN. On 22 November 1967, the Security Council unanimously adopted Resolution 242 which outlined the components of a peaceful settlement and requested the appointment of a special UN representative to seek agreement on the resolution's implementation. However, the wording of the resolution was sufficiently ambiguous to allow varying interpretations. As a result, the arduous efforts of Gunnar Jarring, the UN envoy, to secure an agreement were doomed to failure, despite his practically non-stop shuttle diplomacy between New York and the Middle East during the year and a half after the November meeting. By the end of 1968, it had become apparent that the resolution would not be implemented until a common understanding of its meaning had been agreed by the Great Powers, who could then hopefully bring their respective clients into line.

The Soviet Union was particularly anxious to seek a settlement. Palestinian commando raids were on the increase; the Egyptian people were pressing for a military offensive; and the Soviet Union, diplomatically in quasi-isolation after the invasion of Czechoslovakia in August 1968, was more than ever dependent on Egypt (as one of the few Third World countries which did not condemn the invasion) as an opinion-leader in the non-aligned camp. When Nasser visited Moscow in July 1968, he found that while the Soviet leaders were willing to support the Egyptian demands for a complete Israeli withdrawal from all occupied territories, they were reportedly still reluctant to do anything which would risk 'a hot confrontation with the United States'.[44] Articles in *Pravda* also indicated that it was only the anti-progressive sections of Egyptian society which were pressing for a renewal of hostilities, hoping that such a renewal would lead either to the downfall of the present government or to the abandonment of socialist programmes.[45] When the Jarring mission proved unproductive, therefore, Foreign Minister Gromyko flew to Cairo in December 1968 to seek Egyptian approval for a memorandum to be sent to the United States, Britain and France setting out Soviet proposals for a settlement.

Talks between the Big Four began in March 1969 and continued inconclusively for several months, with Israel expressing repeated concern about the possibility of an imposed solution. Meanwhile, hostilities increased until, by July, Egypt was waging a fully-fledged 'war of attrition' against Israeli positions along the Canal. In December, the US Secretary of State put forward an American peace plan which was rejected first by Nasser and then by the Soviet Union. By the beginning of 1970, Egypt was inflicting heavy losses on the Israelis. Utilising its complete air superiority, the Israelis retaliated first by neutralising Egypt's radar and anti-aircraft system and then by carrying out deep penetration raids on civilian and military targets around Cairo. It was at this time that Nasser flew to Moscow and demanded an escalation of Soviet involvement. By the end of 1970, an estimated 12,000 to 15,000 Soviet military personnel were stationed in Egypt, including many pilots and missile crews who were participating actively in Egypt's air defence.[46] The increased Soviet military presence promoted a renewed effort by the United States to bring about a settlement.

On 25 June 1970, Secretary Rogers announced that the US was seeking the reactivation of the Jarring mission to obtain a 90-day ceasefire and a reaffirmation by both sides of adherence to the main elements of Resolution 242—Israeli withdrawal from occupied territories and Jordanian and Egyptian recognition of Israeli sovereignty. Nasser went to Moscow on 29 June for talks lasting three weeks. In the final communiqué issued on 17 July both sides condemned Israeli aggression, called for the implementation of Resolution 242, and reaffirmed their mutual desire for 'the speediest possible settlement of the Middle East conflict'.[47] On 24 July, Nasser announced his decision to accept the ceasefire proposals; and Jordan and Israel soon followed suit. *Pravda* supported Nasser's decision and acknowledged that to take such a stand criticising Arab militarism required 'great political courage'.[48] Brezhnev also upheld 'the constructive position taken in this matter by the UAR government' and praised Nasser as an 'outstanding statesman'.[49]

However, while the ceasefire allowed the Egyptians a breathing spell along the Canal, it reactivated inter-Arab rivalries between those who accepted the ceasefire—including the UAR and Jordan—and those who rejected it—including the Syrians, Iraqis and Palestinians. Jordan's acceptance of the US proposals led to an escalation of domestic tensions between the Jordanian government and the Palestinians. The country dissolved into civil war, and once again as Syrian and Israeli forces prepared and threatened to intervene, the Middle East seemed poised on the edge of another war. The Soviet Government statement issued on 23 September stated that 'firm confidence has been expressed from the Soviet side that everything should be done to end as soon as possible the fratricidal fighting in Jordan. Permanent contact is being maintained with President Nasser of the United Arab Republic on all questions linked with the developments in Jordan'.[50]

Once again, Soviet leaders were depending on Nasser to exercise his influence as leader of the Arab world to bring about a settlement of the dispute. Indeed a conference convened by Nasser in Cairo between Hussein and Arafat succeeded in bringing about the cessation of hostilities. It ended on 27 September and was to be Nasser's last meeting. After nearly two years of diabetic and coronary ailments, the strain of this last summit proved to be too much for him: he died on 28 September.

The official Soviet statement on Nasser's death was very similar to the statement which Egypt had released following Khrushchev's ouster, emphasising that the friendly relations between the two countries were 'a constant factor, independent from any changes in the international situation'.[51] However, the Soviet leaders were just as worried about the effect of Nasser's death on Soviet–Egyptian relations as Egyptian leaders had been following Khrushchev's fall. And indeed, the Soviet leaders had good reason for concern. While it would have been difficult in 1964 for Brezhnev and Kosygin to enact an immediate and extensive change in the Soviet Union's carefully formulated policy towards Egypt, in the new and volatile states of the Middle East, the impact of personality is far more decisive. Soviet leaders had spent years building up their relationship not just with Egypt, but with Nasser himself. Nasser, and not just Egypt, had become the linchpin of their policy throughout the Middle East and the Third World. In a review of the unsteady state of Soviet–Egyptian relations during the year following Nasser's death, Heikal himself admitted that 'the Soviet Union used to base its relations with the Arab nationalist revolutionary movement on . . . Nasser, who was not just a leader, but the symbol of a huge historical upsurge'.[52] One need only repeat a portion of Nasser's speech in Khartoum, delivered several months before his death, to realise how much Nasser had come to share the Soviet vision of Egypt's future.

> We fought the battles to build socialism, in the sense of achieving political leadership by the people's working forces, in the sense . . . of the people's working forces' control over the means of production . . . in the sense of equal opportunities, and in the sense of rights to medical, educational, employment and insurance services.[53]

Because of her centrality in the Middle East, Egypt would remain the linchpin of Soviet policy, but Egypt's new leaders would no longer so readily adhere to the Soviet vision of Egypt's future.

4 Soviet-Egyptian Relations under Sadat, 1970-78

If Nasser pursued a policy in his last years of 'leaning to one side' in favour of firmly cementing his ties with the Soviet Union, one of Sadat's major objectives after becoming President was to redress what he considered to be a basic imbalance in Egypt's foreign policy. As a result, Egypt's relations with the West witnessed a marked improvement and her relations with the Soviet Union a corresponding deterioration. Egypt accepted America's pre-eminent role in the settlement of the Arab-Israeli dispute and also re-established both diplomatic and economic relations with the West.

The explanation for this shift in policy lay in Sadat's own personality, the nature of his leadership, and the changing Egyptian perception of Soviet objectives and capabilities. In the first place, Sadat was a much more devout Muslim than Nasser had been. Prior to the 1952 revolution, Sadat was in charge of liaison work between the Free Officers and the Muslim Brotherhood, and his zealous attachment to Islam continued after the coup when he was appointed secretary of the Islamic Congress and Nasser's chief adviser on Saudi Arabia and the Gulf. Sadat tended to share the views of many devout Muslims that communism and Islam were irreconcilable, a view undoubtedly reinforced by Sadat's own personal experience during his 1961 trip to Moscow, when Khrushchev unwisely forecast that many members of the Egyptian delegation would eventually become converts to communism.[1]

Secondly, while Nasser's influence had extended well beyond the boundaries of Egypt, Sadat could not hope to fill Nasser's legacy in this sphere. He possessed neither Nasser's charismatic authority nor his preoccupation with Egypt's Arab and world role. Whereas Nasser had been able to exercise considerable influence over Soviet decision-makers as a result of his stature as a Third World leader, Sadat was not able to use this as a bargaining ploy. Heikal appreciated this important difference between the nature of Sadat's and Nasser's leadership, as well as the effect which this difference would have on Egypt's relations with the Great Powers. 'By his influence, Nasser extended the frontiers of Egypt. If you deal with either of the super powers from the context merely of your own frontiers, well, you are a country much like another; but if you deal with them as the head of a movement, that confers much greater power. It was a power that President Sadat could not hope to possess'.[2] However, if Sadat was not a leader with the same international stature as Nasser, he was still the president of one of the most important countries of the Third World. As a result, Sadat's overtures towards the United States justifiably caused serious concern in the Soviet Union; and it is possible that in the beginning Sadat could have used these overtures as bargaining counters with the Russians.

However, the decline in Soviet influence can be attributed not just to Sadat's own personal dispositions and leadership style, but also to popular resentment of the Soviet Union's growing influence. Just as Britain and the United States had been blamed, rightly or wrongly, for Egypt's military and economic setbacks in the 1950s, the Soviet Union was being held responsible for Egypt's problems in the 1970s. To a certain extent, therefore, Sadat was able to bolster his own prestige by criticising the Soviet Union and turning to the United States. Whereas the Soviet Union could prepare the Arabs for war, it had been recognised by the Egyptians since 1970, when Nasser accepted the Rogers Plan, that it was only the United States who could bring pressure to bear on Israel and thereby achieve peace. For all of these reasons—Sadat's natural suspicions as a Muslim of communism, his desire to bolster his domestic prestige and bargaining position with the Soviets by turning to the West, the antipathy which any party feels when it is in an unequal relationship with a stronger party, and Egypt's realisation of America's unique role in the settlement of the Arab–Israeli dispute—Sadat's first eight years as president were characterised by a growing enmity towards the Soviet Union.

One can not help but feel that this antipathy to some extent was reciprocated by the Soviet decision-makers. After Egypt's defeat in the 1967 war, Nasser decided that Egypt's interest lay in 'internationalising' the Arab–Israeli dispute. By encouraging the Soviet Union's active participation in Egypt's military defence and economic reconstruction, he hoped to increase the Soviet Union's commitment to the Arab cause against Israel. His policy succeeded, and the Soviet Union did upgrade its commitment by allowing its pilots to fly missions against Israeli Phantoms.

However, Soviet support for the Arab cause was secondary to the Soviet Union's primary objectives—the encouragement of an anti-Western stance in Egyptian foreign relations and the strengthening of 'progressive' tendencies in Egyptian domestic policy. Under Nasser, the Soviet decision-makers used their support for Egypt's stand against Israel as a means of obtaining greater influence over Egypt's domestic and external policies. And as long as Nasser lived, Soviet–Egyptian relations remained amicable; for although their priorities may have differed slightly, there was a basic coincidence of views between both sides. When Nasser died, however, Soviet decision-makers were faced with a dilemma. Although Sadat continued to expect Soviet support for his stand against Israel, he certainly did not see this support as a means toward an end—he saw it as an end in itself. As a result, Soviet leaders were placed in a situation where they were expected to continue supplying aid for the client's own ends (the defeat of Israel), and not for their own (the promotion of a progressive domestic and foreign policy in Egypt). The dilemma was magnified by the fact that Soviet military supplies substantially increased the likelihood of a war which might escalate to global proportions, thereby threatening the Soviet Union's major foreign policy priority—the continuation of Soviet–American *détente*. Thus after Sadat came to power, there was constant tension between the two countries over the Soviet role in Egyptian foreign and domestic affairs and the 'price' which Egypt should expect to pay for Soviet military and economic aid, with the Soviets trying to prevent the improvement of Egypt's relations with the United States, while also making every attempt to protect their own relations with Washington. It was these themes which shaped the development of Soviet–Egyptian relations after 1970.

THE ARAB–ISRAELI CONFLICT: THE FAILURE TO FIND A SOLUTION

The period from Nasser's death in September 1970 until the signing of the Soviet–Egyptian Treaty of Friendship and Cooperation in May 1971 was marked both by continuing, yet unsuccessful, efforts to find a solution to the Arab–Israeli conflict and by a persisting power struggle within the Egyptian leadership between President Sadat and the group led by Ali Sabri, the pro-Soviet vice-president who was also a leading member of the ASU. The Rogers Plan for a partial Israeli withdrawal along the Suez Canal was revived in December 1970. Soviet, American and Egyptian exchanges continued throughout January, with Sadat announcing on 4 February 1971 that he was prepared to extend the ceasefire for a month and begin clearing the Suez Canal, provided that Israel was willing to make a partial withdrawal in Sinai as the first stage in a complete withdrawal to pre-1967 borders. Then on 8 February, the UN envoy Gunnar Jarring asked the Egyptian and Israeli governments to declare in writing their commitment to the implementation of Resolution 242. While Egypt responded with an equivocal acceptance of Jarring's proposal, Israel flatly declared its unwillingness to withdraw to pre-1967 borders. Soon after, on 4 March, Sadat received a message from President Nixon stating that while the United States also favoured a political settlement of the dispute, Sadat should be more patient and give both the Americans and the Israelis more time.[3]

Soviet decision-makers, who had reluctantly supported Egypt's acceptance of the American initiative, were convinced even before Nixon's letter arrived that the Israelis were pursuing a policy of deliberately sabotaging any peace initiatives. In a Soviet government statement at the end of February, the Soviet leaders reminded Israel that the dispute could be settled by either political or military means. Although the Soviet Union favoured a political settlement, if Israeli leaders were hoping that the sabotage of these efforts would lead to

> the overthrow of the progressive regimes that have asserted themselves in the UAR and other Arab countries, they should remember that such plans are doomed to failure. The Soviet Union is a friend of the Arab peoples and gives them all the necessary assistance . . . in the struggle for the liberation of the land captured by the Israeli aggressors, and this aid will continue.[4]

Soviet leaders asked Sadat to come to Moscow at the beginning of March for urgent consultations on ways to clear the impasse caused by the breakdown of the Rogers–Jarring mission. It was in Moscow that Sadat made the first of a series of demands for more advanced weaponry, including MIG-25s and missle-launching Ilyushins, in order to fulfil his promise that 1971 would be the 'year of decision' in the Arab–Israeli dispute. The Soviet leaders are reported to have promised Sadat a wider range of armaments, although they requested that the more advanced weaponry be kept under Soviet control until Egyptian crews could be properly trained in their use.[5]

However, the Soviet leaders remained cautious about advocating a military solution to the Arab–Israeli dispute. In May 1971, a Syrian communist party delegation led by Khalid Bagdash went to Moscow to seek the resolution of a dispute within the Syrian party over the proper tactics relating to the liberation of Palestine. They had talks with Mikhail Suslov, Boris Ponomaryov and other theoreticians and politicians; and upon returning to Damascus, the dissident wing of the Syrian party leaked the transcript of the meeting, thus providing a unique opportunity to examine the Soviet position on the Arab–Israeli question. During the course of discussions, the Soviet side made it clear that it did not support the renewal of war against the Israelis, both because it feared that the war might escalate to global proportions and because 'in the estimate of our experts, the two armies [Egypt and Syria] are incapable of defeating the Israeli army'.[6] The Soviet leaders also revealed a basic divergence of opinion with elements of the Syrian party over the existence of the state of Israel and the overall objectives which should be pursued in the area. The Soviets repeatedly stated that 'the existence of Israel is a fact. The idea of annihilating it as a way of achieving self-determination for the Palestinian Arab people is self-contradictory'. Rather, the Syrian communists were told to strive for establishment of a socialist government in Israel which would reject Zionism as the ideological foundation for Israeli policy. Further, it was made clear that communists could not separate the Palestine problem from the problems facing the entire Arab national liberation movement, or treat the solution to the Palestine problem as the factor which would determine the success or failure of all other objectives. The Soviet side was adamant in insisting that the Palestine problem was not the pivotal issue. 'The pivot is the formation, strengthening and expansion of Arab progressive democratic movements in all the Arab countries and the victory of socialism in these countries'.[7] As for direct Soviet involvement in another Arab–Israeli war, the Soviet leaders told a Lebanese government delegation in September

1971 that although the USSR would continue to supply the Arabs with arms, it would not agree to fight in their place.[8]

THE DOWNFALL OF THE ALI SABRI GROUP

However, it was abundantly clear by this time that a substantial section of Arab and Egyptian opinion did not agree with the Soviet formula, as expressed in the Syrian document, that the victory of socialism 'will solve everything'.[9] The power struggle which broke out in Egypt almost immediately after Nasser's death was concerned with this issue, as well as questions of the relationship between the presidency and the Arab Socialist Union, and the role of the Great Powers in the Middle East. In December 1970 and January 1971, the Soviet Union and Egypt exchanged three high-level delegations. In December, Ponomaryov headed a Soviet delegation to Egypt for talks on ways to strengthen the links between the CPSU and the ASU. At the same time Ali Sabri was in the Soviet Union working out agreements on economic cooperation; and in January, Podgornyy came to Egypt to open the Aswan Dam and assess Egyptian views on future relations between the two countries. On all these occasions, Sadat's statements on cooperation with the Soviet Union were guarded, while the most vociferous pledges of friendship emanated from members of the group who were beginning to coalesce around Ali Sabri—including Abdel Mohsen Abu al-Nur, Secretary General of the ASU; Diaddin Daoud, member of the Higher Executive Committee of the ASU; Sharawy Gomaa, Minister of Interior and Secretary in charge of political organisation within the ASU; and Sami Sharaf, Minister for Presidential Affairs. On the occasion of Ponomaryov's visit to the new Socialist Studies Institute established to train ASU cadres, Diaddin Daoud noted that the 'CPSU's experience in the selection, ideological education, and training of personnel is of tremendous importance for the cause of our revolution'.[10] Commenting on the agreement reached during the visit to strengthen relations between the ASU and the CPSU, Moscow Radio made the following optimistic assessment:

No longer are relations being developed and strengthened only between the two states: they are also being developed and strengthened in the party sphere. This is a logical development.

The UAR, which has been following the progressive path in all fields of national life, is increasingly turning to the experience of the Soviet Communist Party, that rich experience acquired in building and developing the first socialist society in the world.[11]

In an article on the 24th Party Congress convened in March 1971, Ponomaryov himself emphasised the significance of relations with the ASU and other ruling parties in the Third World. He stated that 'ties of this kind . . . actually represent a fundamentally new form of solidarity between the world communist movement and the forces of national liberation'.[12]

One can readily assess from these quotes both the pro-Soviet sympathies of leading members of the ASU and the importance which Soviet leaders were attaching to the strengthening of inter-Party links. Both groups hoped that the ASU's role as the fulcrum of decision-making in Egypt would continue to be enhanced, particularly now that the Presidency was in the hands of a man whose sympathies did not rest so wholeheartedly with socialism.

The crisis over whether the President would yield his powers to the Higher Executive Committee of the ASU came to a head in mid-April. Without consulting the ASU, Sadat announced the formation of a federation between Syria, Egypt and Libya, with Sudan having the option of joining later. Ali Sabri rallied his supporters in the ASU to oppose the federation, and Sadat was heckled in a Central Committee meeting when he tried to speak. On 1 May, despite a hostile popular demonstration organised by the Sabri group against the President, Sadat made a speech in Helwan in which he openly expressed his intention to liquidate all 'centres of power'. On the following day, Sadat dismissed Ali Sabri; and two weeks later, Sabri's followers, who now included most of the Executive Committee of the ASU and the ministers responsible for information, intelligence and the armed forces, resigned *en masse*. However, their strategy failed: the government did not collapse. Relying on troops and officials loyal to him, Sadat accepted their resignations, appointed a new government, and eventually brought them all to trial on charges of conspiring against the state.

Soviet leaders were naturally very concerned about the effects which these changes would have on relations between the two countries. Prior to the attempted coup, Sami Sharaf had been sent to Moscow to discuss the possibility of signing a treaty with the

USSR which would put relations between the two countries on a formal basis.[13] It was agreed that discussions on the matter would continue in Cairo at the end of May. Although the Soviet leadership apparently had refused earlier requests by Nasser to enter into a more binding agreement,[14] they obviously felt that with the downfall of the Sabri group, it was time to protect the gains they had made in Egypt. A treaty would also have the effect of answering Western press reports that the downfall of the Sabri group was intended as a rebuff to the Russians. It has also been suggested by East European sources that 'the Russian leadership had asked for the treaty as a piece of window-dressing to help silence criticism at home of continued aid to Egypt'.[15] When Podgornyy, Ponomaryov and Gromyko flew to Cairo, they brought a draft treaty with them; and after some negotiations, it was signed on 27 May 1971.

THE SOVIET – EGYPTIAN TREATY

The Soviet–Egyptian Treaty of Friendship and Cooperation was the first such treaty signed by the USSR with a non-communist developing country, and it contained clauses which were of benefit to each side. While the statement in Article 1 that both sides adhered to the principle of non-interference in domestic affairs was of more benefit to Egypt, in Article 2 the Soviet side was successful in gaining Egypt's contractual adherence to socialism. Both sides undertook to enter into immediate consultation in the event of any threat to peace (Article 7), and to continue cooperation in the development of Egypt's military potential (Article 8). In an interesting passage, Article 9 proclaimed that neither party would enter into any alliances or take part in any grouping of states or in any actions or measures directed against the other party.[16] The Soviet side was apparently hoping that such a clause would end any movement in Egypt toward closer relations with the United States.

It was clear that for Sadat the Treaty was a means of guaranteeing the continuation of Soviet economic and military support for Egypt's stand against Israel. In his speech before the UAR People's Assembly, he declared:

> I tell you that . . . I shall not sleep a wink until I have a complete army fully trained in electronic equipment. Only this can protect our homeland against any new Zionist attack. It was because of

this that I insisted on concluding a treaty of friendship and cooperation with the USSR.[17]

The Soviet press for their part emphasised the extent to which the treaty, and especially Article 2, would both consolidate the advances Egypt had already made along the socialist path and serve as a model for future relations between the Soviet Union and the other Third World countries.[18]

The different conceptions held by the two sides of the advantages and obligations of the treaty soon became apparent. In July 1971, a pro-communist coup in the Sudan against the Numeiri government was foiled with the active assistance of President Sadat, who airlifted a Sudanese paratroop brigade which had been stationed in Egypt back to Khartoum. Ponomaryov, who happened to be in Egypt at the time, unsuccessfully sought Sadat's intervention to prevent the failure of the coup and the execution of its Communist organisers. The communiqué issued at the end of his visit contained a pointed reference to Egypt's part in the Sudanese affiar: 'The two sides expressed their conviction that anti-Communism is harmful to the liberation . . . of the peoples'.[19]

Apparently as a result of Soviet displeasure over Egypt's part in reinstating Numeiri, Soviet arms deliveries were slowed down. Sadat's impatience for the weapons grew with every passing month in his indecisive 'year of decision'. The promises made by the Soviet leaders to meet Egyptian requirements, agreed during Sadat's trip to Moscow in October 1971, were left unfulfilled when the outbreak of the Indo–Pakistani war necessitated the redirection of Soviet weapons to India and Bangladesh. In February and again in April 1972, Sadat travelled to Moscow for negotiations on military aid and on the nature and extent of Soviet support for the Arab cause.

By this time, however, Soviet leaders were preoccupied with President Nixon's forthcoming trip to Moscow, and they did not want to do anything which might endanger the success of the summit. Sadat became worried that they might negotiate a Middle-Eastern settlement prejudicial to Egyptian interests. As a result, during his April visit to Moscow, Sadat stressed that in the course of negotiations with Nixon on the Middle East, Soviet leaders should not accept any agreements relating either to arms limitations or the continuation of the state of 'no peace, no war', since both of these would benefit only Israel. Moreover, Soviet leaders should not enter into any negotiations with the Americans designed to fix the borders between Israel and her Arab neighbours. Although Brezhnev reportedly agreed that the Arabs were justified in using military means to achieve their objectives, he nevertheless warned Sadat, on this occasion and three other times prior to the October War, not to attack Israel within her pre-1967 boundaries.[20]

Despite Soviet reassurances that they had argued Egypt's case in the negotiations with Nixon, Sadat became convinced that Soviet leaders were giving top priority to strengthening *détente* with the United States and that there was a risk of the Soviet Union and the United States forming a condominium to prevent the outbreak of war in the region. The view from Cairo, as expressed by Heikal, was that Nixon and Brezhnev had agreed to 'exclude all local disputes from their bilateral relations. . . . This meant that the Soviet military presence no longer had any practical effect so far as the US and Israel were concerned, as if this presence on Egyptian soil had become an artillery piece for which no serviceable ammunition existed'.[21] When Brezhnev failed to supply Sadat with a comprehensive statement of Soviet intentions relating especially to the supply of long-awaited offensive weapons, Sadat took the decision to expel Soviet personnel from Egypt.

THE EXPULSION OF SOVIET PERSONNEL

On 7 July, Sadat told the Soviet ambassador, Vladimir Vinogradov, that the services of all those technicians who came in the wake of the June war would not be required after 17 July. He added that Soviet arms in Egypt should either be placed under Egyptian control or be withdrawn, and that those experts who were in Egypt for training purposes and who had arrived before the main body of experts would be allowed to stay, but would also have to be placed under Egyptian command. Under the terms of the Soviet–Egyptian treaty, Egypt also called for immediate high-level negotiations. The Soviet leaders had little choice but to comply with Sadat's demands, and although it subsequently became clear that Soviet naval facilities in Egypt's Mediterranean ports would not be affected, nevertheless, the Soviet military presence within Egypt was drastically reduced. Although estimates vary, it is generally agreed that by 17 July the number of Soviet personnel had been reduced from around 15,000 to under 1,000; and most of the advanced weaponry (including MiG-21s, MiG-25s, Su-11 interceptors and TU-16 reconnaissance aircraft, as well as the advanced SAM missile batteries) was also withdrawn.[22]

The Soviet reaction was restrained, with *Pravda* merely stating that in view of the fact that the Soviet advisers had fulfilled their mission, 'it has now been deemed expedient to bring back to the Soviet Union those military personnel who were assigned to Egypt for a limited period of time'.[23] However, Soviet leaders were unwilling to comply with Sadat's request for high-level negotiations. In August, both countries recalled their ambassadors, and relations ground to a halt for several months. Meanwhile, Sadat was declaring the Arabs' capability for self-reliance, while making initial enquiries in Western Europe and the United States about the possibility of purchasing arms. It was not long before the Soviet press and leadership began to openly criticise the new trends in Egypt. A *Pravda* editorial made the following assessment: 'The reactionary elements and certain nationalist elements seek to compromise the very idea of Arab–Soviet friendship and to counterpose appeals for "reliance on Arab forces alone" to the slogan of strengthening the united Arab front and militant solidarity with all the forces of progress on an anti-imperialist basis'.[24] Heikal reports that Brezhnev sent a similarly worded message to Sadat in August which contained some constructive proposals as well as the following paragraph to which Sadat, not surprisingly, took great exception:

> You may remember, Mr President, that the leaders of our two countries were agreed on the need to strengthen and consolidate your own forward march . . . .You yourself have several times spoken to us about . . . the efforts being made by rightist elements directly or indirectly allied with imperialism to halt Egypt's march along the progressive road. . . . Where is Egypt going? Where is it being driven by forces inside and outside its borders?[25]

The Russians were not the only ones who wanted to know where Egypt was going. The military were pressing for war, and demonstrating students carried placards asking 'What next?'. The Palestinian massacre of Israeli athletes at the Munich Olympics in August ended any possibility of obtaining arms from West European sources, while the preparations for the November 1972 American elections precluded the possibility of a breakthrough on that front. Sadat decided it was time to renew ties with the USSR; and early in October, the ambassadors for the two countries returned to their posts. In the same month, Premier Aziz Sidqi went to Moscow for talks on the improvement of relations. In a speech during the meetings, Prime Minister Kosygin strongly criticised the opponents of Soviet–Arab friendship, whose attempts to undermine that friendship had failed for a number of reasons:

> They failed because the ideas of socialism are a sure and powerful means to helping the people to rise up from the depths of exploitation and poverty so as to become architects of their own destiny. Now [these opponents] are circulating the invention that the Soviet Union had allegedly reached some 'collusion' with the imperialists concerning a Middle East settlement to the detriment of the interests of the Arab countries. We emphatically reject such inventions. The Soviet Union has one foreign policy, one political line in Middle East affairs. This is a line of all-out support for the Arab peoples and progressive regimes in the Arab countries in their struggle against Israel's aggression.[26]

The talks ended successfully; Soviet arms and technicians began to arrive again in Cairo; and by April 1973 Sadat was able to declare: 'The Russians are providing us now with everything that's possible for them to supply. And I am now quite satisfied'.[27] Preparations for a war against Israel could finally begin in earnest.

THE SOVIET UNION AND THE OCTOBER WAR

In June 1973, Brezhnev held talks with President Nixon in San Clemente and signed the 'Agreement on the Prevention of Nuclear War'. He also warned Nixon that the situation in the Middle East was explosive, and that any further delay in reaching a settlement would result in a further round of hostilities. (Following the October war, the Soviets answered American charges that the USSR had broken Article Four of the new Agreement, calling for 'urgent consultations' in the event of a risk of nuclear war, by reminding the American government that Brezhnev had warned Nixon of this possibility at their June meeting.[28]) Shortly after, Soviet leaders invited Hafez Ismail, Sadat's national security adviser, to Moscow for a first-hand account of the San Clemente talks. Ismail was evidently told that the Soviet leaders expected *détente* to last for 20 to 30 years,[29] leading Sadat to warn that Soviet adherence to the improvement of relations with the West could 'isolate' Moscow from the national liberation movement.[30] Despite the fact that Sadat was now claiming, in contrast to his statement the previous April, that 'our cooperation with the Soviet Union has really been facing problems' and that 'we are not fully satisfied' with Soviet arms supplies,[31] shipments of arms continued to arrive in Egypt throughout the summer and autumn months.

After Ismail's visit, both the Soviet leaders and the Soviet press became much more restrained in their protestations of full support for the Arab cause against Israel: and as one analyst notes, in the five major speeches made by Brezhnev between the Ismail visit and the October War, no mention was made of the Middle East problem at all.[32] Although the Soviet leaders must have been expecting an outbreak of hostilities, according to Sadat, they were not informed of the Arab plan until 3 October and were not told the exact date on which hostilities would commence until the following day. (Heikal maintains that the Soviets were informed on 1 October to expect an imminent attack.[33]) On 4 October, Brezhnev sent a note to Sadat saying that the decision to fight must be the Arabs' alone, although they could rely on Soviet support. He asked only that Soviet civilians be evacuated. This was done on Friday 5 October; and despite all the signs of an impending invasion, Israel was caught unprepared.

The joint Syrian–Egyptian offensive began on Saturday 6 October, with the Syrians pushing well into Israeli-held territory on the Golan Heights and the Egyptians overrunning Israeli positions at the Bar-Lev line on the east bank of the Suez Canal. The first Soviet response was a nervous one, with Ambassador Vinogradov pressing Sadat to accept a Syrian-proposed ceasefire only six hours after fighting had broken out. Following the war, Sadat's claim that the Soviet leaders had fabricated this ceasefire request was to cause a lot of ill-feeling between the two sides. Sadat complained that he had received no such communication from Syria, and that he, therefore, could only interpret the message as expressing Soviet lack of confidence in Egypt's military ability and Soviet fear about the effect of the war on *détente*. Heikal relates, however, that this episode was a misunderstanding based on the gradual distortion of the message which the Soviet ambassador to Syria, Nuradin Mukhitdinov, transmitted to Moscow. When Mukhitdinov asked Assad before the battle started whether the Syrians wanted the Soviet government to take any action in the Security Council, Assad apparently replied that they could put forward a proposal for a ceasefire. If the Arabs were doing well, it could be ignored; if not, it might be very useful. However, by the time the account of this conversation reached Sadat via Moscow, the war had started; and what was meant to be a tactical suggestion was interpreted as an urgent request and one which Sadat knew Assad would not make.[34]

After the initial reports of Arab successes, Soviet hesitancy began to fade. A Soviet government statement on 7 October said that 'the responsibility for the present developments in the Middle East and their consequences rests fairly and squarely on Israel and those external reactionary circles which have constantly encouraged Israel in its aggressive ambitions'.[35] On the same day, Brezhnev and Nixon exchanged messages through normal diplomatic channels indicating their total agreement that the war should not be allowed to damage Soviet–American *détente*.[36] Having established that the conflict should not escalate beyond the regional level, first the Soviets and then the Americans proceeded to mount massive airlifts of weaponry and ammunition to their client states.[37] During the first week of fighting, the Soviet Union also refused to support a UN resolution calling for a ceasefire and encouraged other Arab states to go to Syria and Egypt's aid.

However, the Arabs were unable to sustain their initial successes. By 10 October, the Syrian offensive on the Golan Heights had been repulsed, while on the Sinai front, the Egyptians were unable to break through to the Mitla and Gidi passes despite a major tank battle which occurred on 14–15 October. On the following day, just as the Israelis were beginning to cross onto the west bank of the Canal, Kosygin arrived in Cairo to assess the situation. He stayed in Cairo for four days, and while there the Israeli salient on the west bank began seriously to undermine previous Egyptian gains. On the 19 October Sadat agreed to allow the Russians to press for a ceasefire. Kosygin returned to Moscow and immediately requested that Kissinger come to the Soviet Union for 'urgent consultations'. The time had come for the superpowers to test the durability of *détente* and to exert more control over their client states.

By this time the Arab oil-producing states were announcing their decisions to cut off supplies to the West. This served as a strong incentive for the Americans to reach a ceasefire, and Kissinger duly arrived in Moscow on 20 October, despite Israeli objections.[38] The outcome of the negotiations was an agreement for a 'ceasefire in place', which the combatants were pressured into accepting. However, while the Israelis could do nothing to prevent a Soviet–American ceasefire resolution from being passed through the Security Council, they were determined to improve their position on the west bank, and fighting continued. By 24 October, Egypt's third army was completely cut off, and Sadat appealed for joint Soviet–American intervention. At this point the crisis escalated to global proportions.

The Soviet Union was faced with the prospect of an unacceptable level of defeat for her Arab client. Her representative at the UN, Yaakov Malik, announced that Egypt's proposal 'to send contingents of USSR and US forces to the area of conflict is fully justified and in accordance with the UN Charter'.[39] At the same time, Brezhnev sent a note to Nixon making it clear that if the US did not agree to a joint force to stop Israeli violations of the ceasefire, 'we should be faced with the necessity urgently to consider the question of taking appropriate steps unilaterally. Israel cannot be permitted to get away with the violations'.[40]

Certain unexplained Soviet actions led the Americans to fear that the Soviets might actually be preparing for unilateral action. Seven Soviet airborne divisions were placed on alert (three of these divisions had been on alert since 12 October).[41] Soviet transport planes made fewer resupply flights to the Middle East after 22 October, and American officials may have feared that the Soviets were recalling their planes to prepare for the transport of troops. American satellites monitored the takeoff of a massive convoy of Soviet planes on 24–25 October, but the Americans did not know until they arrived in Cairo on 25 October that they carried arms and not troops. The Soviet naval presence also increased in the Mediterranean; and although it never matched the firepower of the American fleet, in the fast-moving crisis conditions of these few days, it was certainly a cause for alarm.

The key members of the National Security Council met late on 24 October and took the decision to put all American forces (including those in charge of strategic nuclear weapons) on a 'Defence Condition Three' alert. Kissinger also increased his pressure on Israel to adhere to the ceasefire. Three further Soviet actions caused concern in the last days of the crisis, but were not thought to have contributed to the American decision for a Stage 3 alert. On 22 October, neutron emissions, indicating the presence of nuclear weapons, were monitored from a Soviet freighter passing through the Bosphorus. In itself this was not necessarily worrying, since the Soviet Mediterranean squadron was known to have been equipped for some time with nuclear weapons. It was not known, however, whether the freighter was to join the Soviet fleet or whether it was destined for an Arab port. Not until the day *after* the alert had been announced did the ship in fact dock in Alexandria: It is generally agreed that the Egyptians never took possession of nuclear warheads for their Scud missiles; and it has been reported that the Soviets decided against delivering them as a result of the American alert.[42] Furthermore, on 25 October, a small contingent of 70 Soviet personnel was despatched to Cairo to form part of the proposed UN joint force. However, Washington evidently was informed by Moscow on that day that they were being sent as observers only.[43] Finally, although the behaviour of the Soviet navy had been characterised by US Admiral Bagley as 'constrained and considerate' (in contrast to the Sixth Fleet which he described as being 'targeted for instant attack from multiple points')[44], on 25 October, between six and nine surface combat ships, including two amphibious landing craft, detached themselves from the Soviet squadron centred off Crete and started moving towards Egypt. When the crisis subsided later that day, however, they evidently changed course.[45] By then, the Israelis had acquiesced to supplying the Third Army with food and water, although it was still effectively encircled. The Russians dropped their proposal for a joint Soviet–American force and instead supported the establishment of a UN emergency force which would not include troops from any of the five permanent members of the Security Council. On 26 October the United States lifted its alert, and the most explosive state of the crisis came to an end. While the Soviet attempt to arrange a condominium had failed, her primary objective had been achieved— the saving of the Egyptian army.

On 26 October, Brezhnev made his first major statement on the war during a speech to the World Peace Congress. In a reference to the alert, in which the US government diplomatically was not mentioned, Brezhnev maintained that cooperation between the two superpowers would not be promoted by 'such moves of the last few days, [instigated] by certain elements in NATO countries, as the artificial drumming up of emotions with all kinds of fantastic rumours about the intentions of the Soviet Union in the Middle East'.[46] A *Tass* statement of the following day was even more outspoken about the effects on *détente* of the American action. The Soviet government felt that the alert, 'far from contributing to international *détente* . . . was obviously taken in an attempt to intimidate the Soviet Union. However, those behind it must be told that they have chosen the wrong address'.[47]

At the end of the war, the Soviet leaders, while condemning what they felt was American overreaction, had good reason for optimism about the outcome of the conflict. The Arab oil embargo was having a serious effect on Western economies and was causing a rift in the NATO alliance—a rift which had been aggravated by America's non-consultation with her European allies over the Stage 3 alert. The Egyptians, although still partially surrounded at Suez, were on the east bank of the canal and thus in a good bargaining position. The Syrians, on the other hand, lost substantial ground after their initial successes; and the Israelis were now in possession of Mount Hermon and the strategically important area around the town of Kuneitra. However, the Soviet leadership was less concerned with the loss of territory, which they felt could be regained by political means, than with the Arabs' overall performance. In an important article following the war, one of the foremost Soviet analysts of Middle Eastern affairs, Professor Georgi Mirskiy, outlined the major myths that had been dispelled by the war. The first two were the myths of the invincibility of the Israeli armed forces and the inferiority of Arab weaponry. Mirskiy observed that this second myth, 'which regrettably was voiced at times in Arab countries as well', had been disproved particularly by the anti-aircraft missiles and anti-tank rockets provided by the USSR. A third was the inability of the Arabs to form a strong and durable united front. In fact, Mirskiy claimed that Arab solidarity both in the battle and in the decision to use the oil weapon had had a decisive impact on the outcome of the War. The fourth myth that allegedly had been dispelled was the inadequacy of *détente*, which some people claimed should have been able to prevent the war or at least bring about an early ceasefire. Mirskiy, however, was optimistic about the positive effects which *détente* had had in preventing the escalation of the conflict. 'Who knows what might have happened', Mirskiy asked, 'were the cold war still at its height, had there been no relaxation of world tensions in the past year and a half or two?'[48]

Moreover, Soviet prestige in the Arab world was at its zenith after the war, and the Soviet Union had high hopes of working with the United States and the combatants in bringing about a political settlement to the dispute. By representing Arab interests at the international level, the Soviet Union hoped to gain recognition for itself as a Great Power, with legitimate interests in the Middle East and the right to influence events there. However, if this was a primary Soviet objective, it was equally the preoccupation of the American government to prevent the achievement of this objective. It was due in particular to the efforts of one man, American Secretary of State Henry Kissinger, that the Soviet Union's influence in Egypt fell from an all-time high at the end of the October war to an all-time low by the end of March 1976, when President Sadat unilaterally abrogated the Soviet–Egyptian Treaty of Friendship.

THE EXCLUSION OF SOVIET INFLUENCE

Immediately following the war, the Soviet Union was faced with two dilemmas: how to salvage and strengthen Soviet–American *détente* while still supporting the Arab oil embargo, and how to prevent the disintegration of the united front against Israel and the West which the Arabs had constructed during the war. As long as the Soviet leaders encouraged the continuance of the oil embargo, they could also expect American Congressional and public opinion to oppose the passage of any legislation which would aid the Soviet economy. Indeed in November, Nixon postponed the passage of a bill which would have given the Soviet Union most-favoured nation status in its trade relations with the United States. On the Arab front, any semblance of unity vanished almost immediately following the war when the Iraqi regime rejected the call for a ceasefire. A split between the Egyptians and the Syrians was also soon apparent. The Syrians refused to exchange prisoners of war with Israel and boycotted the December meeting of the Geneva conference. At the same time, Kissinger successfully completed the negotiations with Egypt for an exchange of prisoners (7 November) and for the disengagement of Israeli and Egyptian forces (18 January).

The Soviet leaders were deeply worried by these developments, and in particular they were concerned over their own exclusion from the American and Egyptian efforts to reach a settlement with Israel. They worked hard for the convening of the first Arab–Israeli peace conference which met in Geneva on 22 December and were bitterly disappointed when it failed, as a combined result of Syria's non-participation and of the forthcoming Israeli elections. In January 1974, Kissinger flew to the Middle East to arrange for the resumption of the Geneva talks and according to some accounts it was Sadat who suggested that instead of returning to Geneva, he would prefer Kissinger to seek an immediate disengagement agreement between the Israelis and Egyptians.[49] To the dismay of the Russians and Syrians, the agreement was reached on 18 January. The Egyptian Foreign Minister, Ismail Fahmy, was hurriedly despatched to Moscow to explain Sadat's decision. An article on the talks in *Pravda* contained the telling statement:

> It was stressed that an important factor in the struggle for a just settlement in the Near East is the close coordination of the actions of the Soviet Union and Egypt at all stages of this struggle including the work of the Near East Peace Conference and all the working groups which come out of it.[50]

Although Soviet commentators were willing to concede that the disengagement agreement had defused the immediate situation, nevertheless they maintained that the step-by-step approach would not result in, and even obstructed, an overall settlement of the two root causes of the conflict—Israeli occupation of Arab territory and the Palestinian problem. A solution to these two issues could not be found without the active participation of all the parties to the conflict, including both the Palestinians and the Soviet Union.[51]

By the spring of 1974, Sadat's policy of finding an opening (or *infitah*) to the West for the solution both of the Arab–Israeli conflict and of Egypt's economic problems was beginning to take shape. Diplomatic relations between the United States and Egypt were re-established; David Rockefeller, the director of Chase Manhattan Bank, announced in Cairo his intention to open a number of banks there; American businessmen were being invited to invest in Egypt; and property sequestration orders passed under Nasser were being reversed. And on 19 March, the Egyptians and Saudis succeeded in getting the other Arab oil-producers to lift the oil boycott.

By April, the Soviet leaders' patience with Egypt was wearing thin, and not surprisingly Sadat began complaining that the Soviet attitude towards arms supplies was drastically affecting Egyptian military efficiency. At the same time, Syria's President Assad was in Moscow for talks 'on increasing Syria's defence potential'.[52] Shortly afterwards, Sadat announced that Egypt considered itself free to buy arms from any source; and indeed during Nixon's tour of the Middle East in June, the Egyptians were promised American help in the development of atomic energy for peaceful purposes. Despite Kissinger's protestations prior to Nixon's tour that 'we have no intention of trying to eliminate Soviet influence in the Middle East',[53] *Pravda* was in no doubt that the real purpose of the visit was indeed 'to minimise the role of the Soviet Union in the Near Eastern settlement' and 'to undermine Soviet–Arab friendship'.[54] Following his Middle Eastern tour, Nixon flew to Moscow, amid mounting criticism at home that the Soviets had recently gained all the benefits from *détente* in the form of grain, trade, and advantageous terms in the SALT I agreement. In the final communiqué, while the Soviet leaders were successful in gaining a US commitment to reconvene the Geneva talks and to consider the question of Palestinian representation at those talks, they were not able to extract a precise date from the Americans for the conference, with the communiqué stating only that the conference would reconvene 'as soon as possible'.[55]

After Nixon's visit to Cairo, Sadat received a $200 million loan from West Germany and passed measures designed to safeguard and encourage American investments in Egypt. On 25 July, in the most outspoken attack on Sadat's pro-American policy to date, L. Tolkunov of *Izvestiya* insisted that 'the establishment of relations between the USA and a number of Arab states has in no way affected the provocative, aggressive nature of Israel's course'. On Sadat's policy of *infitah*, Tolkunov maintained that it had no long-term advantages and that it 'may in time, as the experience of history teaches, turn into a bitter hangover for Egypt, and especially for its people'.[56]

The sudden resignation of Richard Nixon in August 1974 had no immediate impact on Soviet–Egyptian relations. However, by October, Sadat, displeased with the American failure to produce any movement toward a settlement on the Arab–Israeli dispute and unhappy about remarks made by Israel's Premier Yitzhak Rabin in Washington, announced that Ismail Fahmy would be travelling to the Soviet Union to discuss the strengthening of Soviet–Egyptian relations and the renewal of Soviet arms supplies. During the talks, Egypt affirmed her support for a resumption of the Geneva peace conference and for the full and equal participation of the PLO in them. It was also agreed that Brezhnev would be making a visit to Cairo in January 1975.[57] For the time being, it looked as though Soviet–Egyptian relations had been patched up.

Late in November, Brezhnev and Ford met at Vladivostok to discuss, among many other things, the Middle East. The situation in the area was far from stable, with Soviet–American rivalry over Egypt stronger than ever and with Syria refusing to extend the mandate of UNEF on the Golan Heights. The communiqué's references to the Middle East were bland and non-commital; but perhaps as a result of Soviet pressure, Syria did extent the mandate shortly after the conclusion of the summit talks.

In Egypt, Sadat was emphasising the importance of Brezhnev's forthcoming visit, which he said in a speech on 17 December would 'undoubtedly be a turning-point in the friendship between our countries'.[58] However at the end of the month, two Egyptian ministers were unexpectedly called to Moscow where they were told that for reasons of health Brezhnev would not be making his tour of the Middle East. While no firm evidence has come to light suggesting that Brezhnev was cancelling his trip for political reasons, it is interesting that on the day the two ministers arrived in Moscow, *Pravda* carried an article critical of Egypt's economic policy which stated that 'the strengthening of private enterprise trends which one notes in the country, given the fairly complex class structure of Egyptian society, can complicate the struggle for the continuance of progressive transformation'.[59]

Despite a criticism by Sadat of Soviet arms supplies in January 1975,[60] relations did improve somewhat in February when the Soviet Union decided to resume these supplies following Gromyko's visits to Egypt and Syria. However, a comparison of the communiqués issued at the end of Gromyko's talks with Assad and Sadat shows how far the Soviets had gone in switching their support from Egypt to Syria. While the Syrian talks took place in an atmosphere of 'complete mutual understanding', the Egyptian talks took place in a 'friendly and businesslike atmosphere'. The Syrians called for an immediate resumption of the Geneva talks by February or March at the latest, while the Egyptians just called for a resumption without mentioning any date.[61] Sadat obviously preferred to go to Geneva only after Kissinger had attempted to bring about a second stage disengagement between Egypt and Israel. It was when this round of shuttle diplomacy failed in March that the Soviet Union was able to take the diplomatic initiative. Soviet leaders called for the immediate convening of the Geneva conference and invited the leaders of Iraq, Egypt, Syria and the PLO to Moscow, with Kosygin also making a visit to Libya. Foreign Minister Fahmy represented Egypt; and Gromyko, in a speech at a dinner honouring him, emphasised that the Soviet leadership, 'and Leonid Brezhnev personally', had more than once stated the Soviet Union's readiness to further deepen and enrich Soviet–Egyptian relations. Gromyko stressed, however, that 'it is, of course, possible to accomplish these tasks successfully only if Egypt and the Egyptian leadership pursue the same kind of policy with regard to the Soviet Union'.[62]

Yet Soviet efforts to reactivate the Geneva Conference were fruitless. The Arabs were by then too divided amongst themselves to pursue a united policy; the Soviet leadership was itself preoccupied both with internal disputes following the dismissal of Shelepin in April and with preparations for the long-awaited summit concluding the Conference on Security and Cooperation in Europe, which convened in Helsinki in August 1975. Sadat's policy of placing his trust in America bore further fruits in the summer of 1975 when the Suez Canal was reopened and when Egypt and Israel signed a three-year disengagement agreement in which the Rabin government agreed to withdraw from the Sinai passes, provided Israeli troops were replaced by radar stations manned by US civilian intelligence personnel.

After August, neither the Soviet Union nor Egypt made any major effort to improve relations; and it is interesting to note that it was in that month that the decision to revive the Egyptian Communist Party was taken.[63] The Soviet boycott of the Geneva signing of the Egyptian–Israeli disengagement agreement on 4 September had led Sadat to condemn the Soviet act as a 'flagrant incitement and an attempt at splitting the ranks of the Arab nations'.[64] On the same day, Sadat announced that he would be visiting the United States in October.

Following his visit, *Pravda* carried a major article on the Middle East situation signed by 'Observer' – a pseudonym generally recognised as representing Politburo opinion. On the question of Sadat's claim that the Soviet boycott at Geneva was aimed at splitting Arab ranks, 'Observer' maintained that it was not the Soviet action but rather Egypt's adherence to a 'step-by-step' policy that was leading to inter-Arab conflicts. 'The signing of this kind of agreement could not fail to deal a blow against the unity of the Arab peoples. This explains why some people are now trying to lay the blame at someone else's door, hurling reproaches at the Soviet Union for "undermining" Arab unity'. But the most vehement criticism was saved for denouncing Sadat's claim that the Soviet Union had been withholding arms supplies to Egypt:

> Only after having lost all sense of shame can some people now say that [following the October War] Egypt received 'only a few cases of spare parts' from the Soviet Union. Words bearing no relation to reality basically carry no more conviction for being scathing. Since the October war of 1973, the Soviet Union has been consistently continuing the policy of furthering friendly cooperation with Egypt in the military field in accordance with the existing agreements. *But cooperation, of course, is a two-sided matter. It cannot develop if one of the sides is pursuing a policy of undermining it.*[65]

Sadat, by this time, was not limiting his criticism of the Soviet Union to the question of Soviet arms supplies. He was equally critical of the Soviet refusal to refinance the Egyptian debt. Egypt was in a very bad economic situation. While Sadat's open-door policy had succeeded in attracting some foreign investment, it had also fuelled inflation, which by the end of 1975 was running at over 30 per cent per annum. As a result of the declining value of her currency, Egypt found it increasingly difficult to repay her foreign debts. Even before the October War, Egypt had begun to feel the burden of her external debt repayments; and in 1972, the service payments on the Egyptian non-military external public debt, which stood at over $2,000 million, was equal to 31.5 per cent of Egypt's exports of goods and non-factor services (compared with 15.3 per cent in 1965).[66] Following the war, the situation became even worse; and on 29 December 1975, Dr Zaki Shafei stated that Egypt's non-military debts now amounted to over $7,000 million. Egypt's non-military debt to the Soviet Union alone was given at $4,000 million and military debts to the Soviet Union a month later were stated to be about $7,000 million.[67] Given the severe economic difficulties faced by the Egyptians, it is not surprising that the Soviet refusal to cancel or even reschedule Egypt's debt proved to be a major breaking point in relations between the two countries. It was announced in Cairo on 14 December 1975 that Egypt had declined to sign a trade protocol with the Soviet Union for 1976 because of the Soviet refusal to reschedule the debt.[68] In February 1976, Cairo's *al-Jumhuriya* reported that the Soviet Union had this time postponed the conclusion of the trade protocol for 1976, despite the fact that the Egyptians were now prepared to sign.[69]

The stage was set for the final break in relations; and in a speech before the Egyptian Parliament on 14 March 1976, Sadat unilaterally abrogated the Soviet–Egyptian Treaty of Friendship. In explaining his decision, Sadat declared that Soviet–Egyptian relations had reached a 'complete deadlock' since the Soviet Union had neither supplied Egypt with arms nor accepted a moratorium on Egypt's debts. They had even demanded interest on debts for military supplies, although he claimed it was 'common for war debts to be cancelled'. Sadat went on to complain that 'after one and a half years, the weapons in my possession will be . . . scrap, [unless] I submit and bow'.[70] Three weeks later, Sadat also announced the immediate cancellation of Soviet naval facilities in Egyptian ports.[71] A *Tass* statement issued on 15 March simply announced that Sadat's abrogation was 'a new manifestation of the unfriendly policy with regard to the Soviet Union which he has been pursuing in practice for a long time. This puts a juridical seal on a situation in which, as a result of this policy, the operation of the Treaty . . . had been, in fact, paralysed'.[72] Other articles in the Soviet press stated that such a decision harmed the Arab cause, which was apparently why, according to the Soviets, the abrogation had been greeted with such jubilation in Tel Aviv, Washington and Peking.[73]

Because Egypt was the first Third World state (shortly followed by India and Iraq in 1971 and 1972) to sign a Treaty of Friendship with the Soviet Union, the abrogation of that treaty was naturally a major setback for Soviet foreign policy. Soviet prestige was undermined further by the fact that in his speech to the 25th Party Congress only three weeks before the abrogation, Brezhnev had praised the treaty as 'a long-term basis for relations conforming with the interests not only of our two countries but also of the Arab world'.[74] Throughout April, the Soviet press concentrated on refuting Sadat's charges that the Soviet Union had been an unreliable ally and that it had left Egypt unarmed to face the Israelis—an allegation that *Krasnaya zvezda*, for example, denounced as a 'blatant lie'.[75] Although the 1976 Soviet–Egyptian trade protocol was finally signed on 28 April (allowing for $640 million in trade for 1976—a drop of $160 million from the original figure negotiated the previous December[76]), nevertheless, political relations between the two countries remained acrimonious.

Following the abrogation, Soviet leaders increased their efforts to improve relations with the other states in the Middle East, and in particular with Iraq, Libya, Algeria, South Yemen, and Syria. The strengthening of ties with Damascus, however, was made more difficult by the Syrian intervention in the Lebanon on the side of the Christian and right-wing forces, an intervention which began on the same day (1 June) that Kosygin arrived in Damascus for a state visit. The Soviet Prime Minister reportedly told Assad that while the USSR approved of Syrian actions in the Lebanon, the Syrians should not expect any public declaration of support because of the Soviet commitment to the Palestinians.[77] The Soviet stand, and its continued supply of arms to the Syrians, was thought to be based on strategic considerations arising out of Kosygin's attempts to form a united front between Syria, Algeria, Libya and Iraq and requests for port facilities in Latakia for the Soviet squadron. When both of these efforts failed, Brezhnev sent two letters to Assad in July, appealing to the Syrian leader 'to end military operations against the resistance and the Lebanese national movements', since not to do so would allow 'the imperialists and their collaborators to bring the Arab people, the area's progressive movements and the Arab states with progressive regimes under their control'.[78] Although arms supplies were curtailed to Syria after July, they were never entirely cut off.

Endeavours to obtain a Syrian withdrawal from the Lebanon and to find a solution to that problem characterised Soviet activities in the Middle East throughout the summer and early autumn of 1976. By September, the Palestinians and leftist forces, under attack from the Syrians, were also being criticised by the Soviets. An article by 'Observer' in *Pravda*, which appeared on 8 September, maintained that only further bloodshed would be caused by the 'attempts to reject out of hand any peaceful proposals—as has been done by some leftist elements within the Palestinian resistance and the patriotic forces front'. Still cognisant of Egypt's central role in the Arab world, the Soviets also reportedly sent two messages to Foreign Minister Fahmy seeking Egyptian intervention to bring about a solution.[79] The renewal of contacts between Moscow and Cairo was prevented, however, by Soviet support for Libya in its dispute with Egypt during August.[80]

It was not until 15 October that a Lebanese ceasefire agreement was worked out between the leaders of Egypt, Syria, Lebanon, Saudi Arabia, Kuwait, and the Palestinians in Riyadh. The summit sanctioned the Syrian intervention, reconciled Syria and Egypt, and resolved to request the member states of the Arab League, which was to meet in Cairo soon after, to form and finance an Arab

Peacekeeping Force (which would in fact consist predominantly of Syrians) for the Lebanon. While Brezhnev welcomed the Riyadh agreement in his speech to the October Central Committee plenum,[81] its side-effects, as one Soviet observer noted, were less welcome—the emergence of Saudi Arabia as the broker and paymaster in the Arab world and the collapse of any attempts to form a united front of progressive regimes to isolate Egypt.[82]

Put on the defensive once again, the Soviets invited Foreign Minister Fahmy to meet Gromyko in Sofia following the US Presidential elections early in November. Perhaps because of Sadat's uncertainty over the line which the new American administration might take towards the Middle East, the Egyptians accepted. The talks were not a success, however; and although Gromyko did agree to return 50 MiG-21 engines to Egypt, out of a total of 173 previously sent to the Soviet Union for repair,[83] little progress was made on bilateral relations. The only positive outcome of the meeting was the renewed commitment which both sides gave to the reconvening of the Geneva conference—a commitment which was reaffirmed by both Syria and Egypt the following month, when the leaders of the two countries agreed in Cairo that the Geneva conference should reopen before March 1977, with the full participation of all parties, including the PLO.[84]

Much of 1977 was taken up with efforts to find a solution to the Arab–Israeli conflict—efforts which proved to be futile due both to disagreement amongst the original participants over the role of the Palestinians in any negotiations and to continued disputes amongst the Arabs themselves and between the Egyptians and the Soviets over a variety of issues. In January, the extensive riots in Cairo over attempts by the government to lift food subsidies were blamed on Egyptian communists and their Soviet and Libyan supporters, an allegation rejected by the Soviets, who subsequently postponed, for the third time, the signature of the 1977 trade protocol.[85] Progress was made towards Geneva as a result of the tour of the Middle East undertaken in early February by the head of the Middle East department of the Soviet Foreign Ministry, Sytenko. Although no communiqués were issued after any of his visits, a Foreign Ministry official described the tour as 'useful' and stated that 'near and common approaches to Geneva' had emerged.[86] Once again, any semblance of unity was broken by the publication in Cairo of Sadat's memoirs denigrating past Soviet behaviour in Egypt. *Pravda*, on 19 February, claimed that the memoirs were based on 'lies, slander and falsification' and that they went 'far beyond the limits of elementary propriety and generally accepted norms in relations between states'.

In March, Brezhnev's speech to the Soviet Trade Union Congress put forward new proposals for the settlement of the Arab–Israeli conflict which would include the gradual Israeli withdrawal from all territories occupied since 1967, the establishment of internationally recognised and inviolable borders, the creation of demilitarised zones on both sides of the frontiers between Israel and her Arab neighbours, freedom of navigation through international waterways, and the provision of 'guarantees' (unspecified) by the Great Powers.[87] The speech set the stage for American Secretary of State Vance's trip a week later to Moscow, where the two sides agreed that mutual cooperation was 'essential to bringing about a just and lasting peace in the area'.[88] Vance and Gromyko met again in Geneva from 18–21 May, where they established the machinery for regular bilateral consultation on the Middle East and expressed their commitment to a timetable for an overall settlement. On 1 October, the two Superpowers issued a joint declaration on the Middle East, calling for the opening of the Geneva conference by the end of the year. They also reaffirmed their commitment to Israeli withdrawal from territory occupied in 1967, and called for the acknowledgement of the 'legitimate rights' of the Palestinians, the ending of the state of war in the area, and mutual recognition of all the parties to the conflict.[89]

If the views of the Soviet Union and the United States broadly coincided during this period, there was no such agreement amongst their respective client states. Israel had adopted a much more hardline approach to the withdrawal from occupied territories and the recognition of the Palestinians ever since the Likud victory on 17 May. Soviet relations with both the Syrians and the Palestinians had improved following the separate visits to Moscow of Assad and Arafat in April (with Arafat making a second trip in August). The Soviets were beset with continuing problems, however, in their relations with Egypt. In April, the Soviet government sent a series of letters to Arab leaders accusing Egypt of 'trying to stir up an armed clash' with Libya.[90] Despite the furore which this created in Cairo, Egypt accepted a Soviet invitation for talks between Fahmy and Gromyko. The meeting eventually took place in Moscow between 8 and 11 June; and the final communiqué acknowledged the existence of 'difficulties' in Soviet–Egyptian relations, but stated that 'constructive talks' had considered 'possible ways of strengthening the appropriate political foundation of relations between the two countries'.[91] The clashes on the Egyptian–Libyan border between 21 and 24 July once again prevented the improvement of Soviet relations with Egypt. The Egyptian bombing raid on a Libyan radar station, which reportedly led to the death of three Soviet technicians, brought immediate condemnation from Moscow as well as Egyptian countercharges of active Soviet involvement on Libya's side.[92] Sadat responded by suspending the export of cotton to the USSR in August[93] and withdrawing all the remaining students and military personnel being trained in the Soviet Union and Eastern Europe the following month.[94] As a result, Moscow cancelled the return visit which Gromyko was to have made to Cairo in September. Following Sadat's announcement on 26 October that debt repayments to the Soviet Union would be suspended for a ten-year period beginning in January 1978, Soviet–Egyptian relations came to a standstill.

It was under these circumstances that Sadat took the decision to go to Jerusalem between 19 and 21 November. His trip met with the immediate condemnation of most other Arab states, as well as the Soviet Union, who urged all progressive forces to form a united front both against 'the aggressor and against those who are willing to bargain with him'.[95] On 5 December, Egypt broke off diplomatic relations with Libya, Syria, Algeria, South Yemen and Iraq; and two days later closed the Soviet cultural centre in Cairo, as well as the Soviet consulates in Alexandria, Port Said and Aswan.

Following the Sadat initiative, Soviet–Egyptian relations were characterised by mutual recriminations and Soviet efforts to isolate the Egyptian stand. A string of visitors to Moscow attested to Soviet activities: Syrian Foreign Minister Khaddam in December, Algerian President Boumédienne in January, Libyan leader Major Abd al-Salam Jalloud and Syrian President Assad in February, and PLO chairman Yasser Arafat in March 1978. Sadat's own efforts to break the deadlock in the Arab–Israeli conflict met with only limited successes, with the establishment of bilateral military and political committees between Egypt and Israel and the promise of increased American arms supplies, following Sadat's US trip in February. The initiative virtually collapsed, however, as a result of Israel's invasion of southern Lebanon in March. Although Sadat's policy had suffered a serious setback, there seemed no prospect of an immediate improvement in relations with Moscow.

If the impact on the Soviet Union's foreign policy of its break with Egypt was decreased to some extent by Soviet successes in shifting its influence to other states in the region, it was equally diminished by Great Power preoccupation with other issues and areas after 1976—in particular with the Strategic Arms Limitation Talks and Soviet activities in Africa. Unlike the first decade of Soviet–Egyptian relations, when Egypt represented the foundation and linchpin of Soviet policy in the Middle East and the Third World, by the end of the second decade of these relations, the Soviet Union had diversified its influence throughout the area and had shown a greater flexibility in its policy. But if there was one 'constant' factor in Soviet–Egyptian relations, it was their dynamic and volatile nature. Relations between the two states often have been punctuated by disputes and disagreements; and thus while the latest break has been particularly serious, one cannot definitively say it is permanent. Soviet commentators continue to maintain that despite Sadat's efforts to reach a separate settlement, 'the Soviet Union still considers Egypt the foremost Arab country'.[96] However, the Soviet Union is unlikely to allow any settlement in the area which excludes its active participation. Soviet efforts to gain recognition of its legitimate role in the region have dominated Moscow's policy for the last two decades, and as maintained by the Soviet press 'nobody can undermine this role, whether in the Middle East or anywhere else in the world'.[97] It is ironic indeed that although Sadat now seeks to expel the Soviet presence from the area, it was primarily through Egypt that the Soviet Union established that presence in the first place.

PART TWO
THE MAKING
OF SOVIET POLICY
TOWARDS EGYPT

5 The Research Design

In the preceding chapters, the development of Soviet–Egyptian relations was outlined, with particular emphasis placed on the importance of Egypt in Soviet global calculations and the efforts made by the Soviet leadership to establish and maintain influence in that country. However, a chronological account of the type presented above raises almost as many questions as it answers. It does not in itself provide insights into the Soviet decision-making process which would allow a more complete explanation of not only the reasons for the successes and failures of Soviet policy toward Egypt, but also the more general features of Soviet foreign policy formulation as a whole.

The foreign policy of a state can only be understood if individual consideration is given to every component part of that policy and to the process by which the policy is formulated. Thus while Part One dealt with Soviet–Egyptian *relations*, it is only in Part Two that the Soviet Union's *policies* are examined. The two parts complement, and are mutually dependent upon, one another. The analysis of Soviet policy formulation contained in Part Two tends to be rather static in so far as it concentrates on isolating the various components and scrutinising them in some depth. It is only when wider consideration is given to Soviet–Egyptian relations that the dynamic aspects of the policy can be seen. In particular, the analyst can observe the Egyptian response to Soviet policy and the extent to which these responses are 'fed back' into the Soviet decision-making process to produce a reformulation of Soviet policy. Equally, it is difficult to understand the development of Soviet–Egyptian relations without a clear and detailed conception of all the factors which have combined to act as motive forces behind these relations. Thus if one examines Figure 5.1, it is clear that Part One elucidated the spiralling effect produced by the implementation of Soviet policies, the formulation and application of appropriate Egyptian responses and their subsequent feedback into the Soviet decision-making process. However, only in Part Two is consideration given

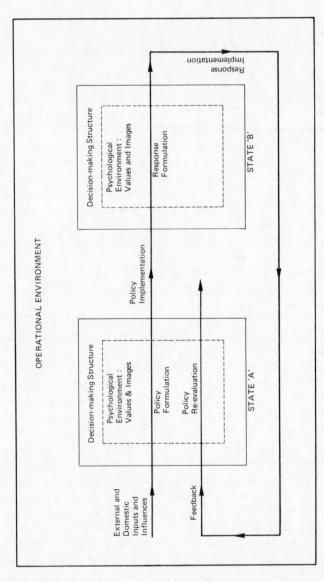

Figure 5.1 Model of Policy Formulation and Bilateral Interaction

to such important factors as the nature of the external and domestic inputs and influences, the disparity between the operational and psychological environments, the structure of the decision-making process and the utility of one instrument over another. For these reasons, the two parts must be seen as explanations of different sections of the same process.

In the past, the systematic analysis of Soviet foreign policy has been hampered by the paucity of reliable data and by resistance among Soviet specialists to the building of models applicable to socialist-type states. Thus, despite the fact that David Easton's pioneering study of political systems appeared in 1957,[1] the first rigorous efforts to extend his and other models to the Soviet Union did not appear until the late 1960s, with works by such authors as Hoffmann and Fleron, Triska and Finley, and Frederic Barghoorn.[2]

Instead, Soviet specialists on the whole continued to insist that the Soviet foreign policy process was unique, and that as such it was not subject to the same influences and processes as Western pluralist systems. Yet while they were generally unified in their belief that the Soviet policy process was unique, they were far from agreed on why this was so. Some analysts, notably George Kennan, W. W. Kulski, Adam Ulam, and Richard Pipes, saw Soviet foreign policy as the outcome of the interplay between traditional Tsarist expansionism and Soviet ideology.[3] Others, such as Robert Tucker, attributed Soviet behaviour to such specific features of the Soviet system as idiosyncratic personality factors.[4] The study by Bauer, Inkeles and Kluckhohn explained Soviet foreign policy by reference to a number of elite characteristics, such as a conspiratorial mentality, puritanical discipline, xenophobia, national chauvinism, and devotion to certain features of Marxism–Leninism.[5] However, these perspectives pale into insignificance when compared with the influence which the totalitarian approach has exercised on Western analyses of the Soviet Union since the Second World War. First developed by Hannah Arendt,[6] and Carl Friedrich and Zbigniew Brzezinski[7], this approach explained Soviet foreign policy as the products of the expansionism inherent in Bolshevik ideology and of a system whose survival depended upon the use of terror. While different in their points of emphasis, all of these perspectives contended that Soviet policy was the outcome of decisions made by a centralised and unified elite acting to maximise Soviet capabilities according to a clearly defined and purposive set of values, principles and objectives. As such, most of these studies of Soviet foreign policy would fall within what Graham Allison termed the 'classical' or 'rational actor' model, in which behaviour is explained as the more or less purposive acts of unified national governments.[8] In addition, most of the approaches tended to ignore the decision-making process, seeking an explanation for foreign policy behaviour in a variety of externally determined variables.

However, there now exists a growing corpus of literature which seeks to explain Soviet foreign policy in terms of its domestic sources and decision-making processes. The majority of the earlier works in this area concentrated primarily on treating policy outcomes as the direct and exclusive result of power struggles within the ruling elite. The influence of other institutional or socioeconomic sources of foreign policy were minimised in favour of the analysis of struggles within the Politburo. Many of these so-called 'Kremlinologists' assumed that conflicts between top leaders, with unstable positions, were the primary determinants of policy outcomes. As a result, policies were seen as emerging not so much from a process involving the rational calculation of capabilities, means, objectives and possible external responses, but more from *ad hoc* changes in internal power clusters. Kremlinology, with its emphasis on bargaining and conflict within the elite, was in many respects the antecedent of the bureaucratic politics model associated with Graham Allison and Morton Halperin.[9] It was Allison himself who stated that 'the *dominant* feature of bureaucratic politics in the Soviet Union is the continuous "struggle for power" '.[10] The utility of this model, and the problems involved in applying it to the Soviet Union will be discussed in greater detail in Chapter 6 below.

A recent example of efforts made to extend and clarify the analyst's understanding of the foreign policy process has been the work done by Michael Brecher to combine the concepts of the psychological and operational environments with an analysis of those factors which in any given 'issue-area' are likely to affect decision-making.[11] According to Brecher, the totality of all those variables which potentially may influence a state's foreign policy may be termed 'the operational environment'. However, these variables, such as a state's military and economic capability, its political structure, and its 'standing' in the international system, are transformed from potential into actual influences on the formulation of decisions only when the decision-makers consciously take them into account. In so doing, decision-makers may over-estimate or underestimate the importance of some of these factors, either because of gaps in their information or because of the countervailing influence of such subjective considerations as the individual personality traits and values of those taking the decisions. These subjective considerations form 'the psychological environment' of the decision-makers. Decisions taken are, therefore, the product of the interaction between objective factors in the operational environment and subjective and idiosyncratic factors in the psychological environment. While the two environments do not coincide, the closer the decision-makers' psychological environment corresponds to the operational environment, the greater is the likelihood of the policy's success.[12] Brecher views the relationship between the operational and psychological environments as 'the master key to a valuable framework of foreign policy analysis'. He goes on to state that 'the operational environment affects the results or outcome of decisions directly but influences the choice among policy options, that is, the decisions themselves, only as it is filtered through the images of decision-makers'.[13] Thus it is argued that in seeking to explain why one policy alternative was chosen over another, the analyst must consider not just the objective capabilities and constraints within which the decision-makers operated but also the way in which these influences were perceived by those decision-makers. Brecher's research design is set out in Figure 5.2, and forms the basis for the analysis of Soviet foreign policy formulation presented in the next four chapters.

However, in applying such models to the Soviet policy process, the analyst is faced with rather acute methodological problems. While it is accepted that policy outcomes are the result of the interaction between the decision-makers' images and the various external and internal influences, the difficulties involved in operationalising this statement are enormous. Without access to Politburo minutes, political memoirs, or records of open debates, it is almost impossible to draw any conclusions about the values, images and motivations of Soviet leaders. It is equally difficult to assess the relative importance of various factors or to isolate and measure the specific impact of any single variable.

Nevertheless, since the 20th Party Congress, more material has become available. This is largely the result of an increase in Soviet research on international relations and the Middle East,[14] as well as a reaffirmation of the importance of such public bodies as the Central Committee, the Party Congress and the Supreme Soviet, and a tendency for wider public discussions to take place during

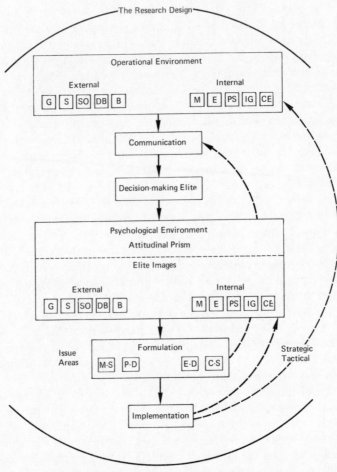

Figure 5.2 Brecher's Research Design

G = Global System; S = Subordinate System; SO = Subordinate Other; DB = Dominant Bilateral; B = Bilateral; M = Military Capability; E = Economic Capability; PS = Political Structure; IG = Interest Groups; CE = Competing Elites. M–S = Military Security; P–D = Political–Diplomatic; E–D = Economic–Developmental; C–S = Cultural–Status *Source*: M. Brecher, *The Foreign Policy System of Israel: Setting, Images, Process* (London: Oxford University Press, 1972), p. 4.

periods of leadership struggles, as occurred throughout the decade following Stalin's death. Thus, while a wealth of primary material still does not exist, nevertheless, the study of the influences on, and the outcomes of, the Soviet foreign policy process has been facilitated by these developments.

6 The Influences on Soviet Policy

In Brecher's research design, presented in the preceding chapter, he isolates ten variables which serve as inputs into the decision-making process, including five external and five internal variables. The military capability, including geostrategic considerations, and the economic capability, including the demographic input, are dealt with in this chapter, as is ideology and the various influences from the external system. The inputs emanating from the Soviet Union's political structure, and the role within it of competing elites and interests groups, are analysed in Chapter 7.

MILITARY CAPABILITY

A major determinant of Soviet policy towards Egypt has been the status of its military capability at any given time. Throughout the 1950s and early 1960s, the Soviet ability decisively to influence events in the Middle East was constrained by her relative maritime weakness and by her limited logistical capability. This weakness was the result not only of the regime's preference for conventional ground forces and coastal defence, but also of the decision to shift maritime appropriations away from the destroyer fleets toward the merchant and fishing fleets. As a result, in the 1956 Suez crisis, the 1957 Syrian crisis, the 1958 Lebanese civil war, and the 1967 Arab–Israeli war, the nature of the Soviet response was largely restricted to diplomatic protests and military manoeuvres along its own borders. However, by the 1970s, the Soviet military capability *vis-à-vis* the West had been much improved. With innovations in communications systems and weapons technology, including the development of satellites, missiles and nuclear submarines, traditional military considerations had lost much of their previous importance to both the USA and the USSR. In particular, the perceived threat to Soviet security posed by Western bases in the Middle East was substantially decreased as a result of this development. Moreover, the Soviet Union set out in the mid-1960s to rethink completely its strategic doctrine, with the result that by the 1970s, the USSR had developed both a limited capability to airlift troops and supplies beyond its own borders and a Mediterranean fleet to rival the American presence. These developments played an important part in giving the Soviet decision-makers the capability for a more flexible response to the October 1973 war, as has been shown in Chapter 4. Additionally, the strengthening of the Soviet navy and its deployment in the Mediterranean and Indian Ocean has significantly increased the importance to the Soviet Union of finding ports in that area capable of undertaking the repair and resupply of Soviet vessels. Moreover, because the Soviet fleet does not include any aircraft carriers (the *Kiev* being the only exception at present), it is dependent upon aircraft based in Baltic ports or friendly states in the Middle East and the Horn of Africa for the air cover and reconnaissance necessary for the protection of its fleet. The provision of port and base facilities by Egypt from 1968 to 1976 considerably enhanced both the Soviet Union's military capability in the area and Egypt's status as a major Soviet ally.

The Soviet Union's geographical location is also a factor which has affected not only its military capability, but also the way in which events in the Middle East have been viewed by Soviet decision-makers. Because of its position straddling both Europe and Asia, Soviet leaders have tended to regard the USSR not only as a European power, but also as an Asian and Mediterranean power. Indeed, a point often overlooked in the West, but never forgotton in the Soviet Union, is that the Soviet Union is much closer to the Middle East than any of the other Great Powers who claim to have legitimate interests in the area. As one observer has noted: 'The oilfields of Baku are closer to Iraq's, the Persian Gulf's and far closer to Iran's oilfields than Cairo is; and Cairo is closer to Soviet territory than it is to the capitals of Sudan, Saudi Arabia, either Yemen, Oman and the Union of Arab Emirates, Qatar, Bahrain, or Iran, not to mention Libya or the rest of the Maghreb'.[1] The Soviet Union's geographical proximity to the Middle East is shown in the map. Contrary to the prevalent Western view that the USSR is somehow 'external' to the area, geographically at least, the Soviet Union could be considered, and certainly considers itself, to be an important and integral part of the area.

There are a number of specific geographical factors which have influenced the formulation of Soviet policy towards Egypt in particular and the Near and Middle East in general (including Greece, Turkey, Iran, Afghanistan, the Levant, and North Africa). First of all, the Soviet Union shares common borders with Turkey, Iran and Afghanistan. Following the establishment of communist regimes in Eastern Europe and China, these three states were the only countries bordering the Soviet Union which had good relations with the West and which could be used to launch a direct land invasion of the Soviet Union (the border with Norway is too short and too far north to present a real military threat). The states on the Soviet southern perimeter have thus assumed great importance in the geostrategic calculations of both Soviet and Western decision-makers. Indeed, it was the Soviet Union's desire to 'jump over' and thereby encircle and isolate these states which provided a major motivation for the initial establishment of relations between Moscow and Cairo. Secondly, the Soviet Union has always been dependent upon the Black Sea, with its outlet to the Mediterranean through the Turkish Straits for its only year-round warm-water ports. The Soviet Union is predominantly a land power, but she has always had to defend widely dispersed fleet areas which cannot be easily reinforced unless the Black Sea fleet is able to navigate freely through the Straits and then sail either east through the Suez Canal or west through the Straits of Gibraltar. Russia's perennial maritime predicament was illustrated by her defeat in the 1905 Russo-Japanese war when Britain, then allied with Japan, closed the Suez Canal to Russian warships, necessitating an arduous and lengthy trip around the Cape, with the resultant delay contributing to the Russian defeat. The Soviet navy experienced similar difficulties in supplying North Vietnam following the 1967 closure of the Canal (see Chapter 3). All of these factors—including the increase in the Soviet military capability and the resultant strain on the Soviet economy (discussed below in the section on economic capabilities), the proximity of the Soviet Union to the Middle East, the vulnerability of the Soviet southern perimeter, the importance of the Suez Canal, and the increasing need for ports in the Eastern Mediterranean to maintain and protect the growing Soviet fleet—have contributed to the formulation of Soviet policy towards Egypt. In particular, they have served as a crucial determinant of Soviet strategic objectives (discussed in Chapter 8), and have also influenced the use and effectiveness of the military instrument (analysed in Chapter 9).

DEMOGRAPHIC INFLUENCES

The demographic factor includes the size, skills, distribution and compostion of a state's population and is one component in the decision-makers' assessment of their capacity to pursue a given course of action. Demographic statistics become significant only when they are related to other variables in a state's situation, such as the ability of that state to support its population, the government's willingness to tolerate ethnic and religious diversity, and its political objectives. Thus the population of the Soviet Union could be considered a source of strength due to its wide range of technical skills and its high level of education. Unlike India or Egypt, for example, the Soviet Union possesses the resources necessary to support her population, although rising expectations have strained the economy in recent years. Nevertheless, the demographic capabilities of the Soviet Union contribute both to the Soviet status as a Great Power and to her capacity to provide economic and military aid to the Arab states.

Beyond this general statement, however, three demographic factors have exerted a more specific influence on Soviet–Egyptian relations. The first is the national composition of the Caucasian and Central Asian Republics in which the ethnic boundaries of Arabs, Greeks, Kurds, Persians, Turks, and other nationalities extend beyond the frontiers of the Soviet Union into the Near and Middle East, as indicated in Table 6.1. This ethnic overlap has influenced greatly the formulation of Soviet policy in particular towards Turkey, Iran and Iraq. On the one hand, Soviet authorities have tried to prevent Soviet Arabs, Turks and Persians from identifying with their mother countries outside the Soviet Union while on the other hand lending occasional support to the more pro-Soviet Kurdish and Armenian movements for self-determination. However, these calculations have had only a secondary influence on Soviet–Egyptian relations. The Soviet Union's open support for fissiparous elements in the Arab world was often an issue in exchanges between Soviet and Egyptian leaders, but Egypt has not herself been directly affected by this aspect of Soviet policy.

This applies equally to the second demographic influence which

TABLE 6.1 Middle Eastern Nationalities in the USSR 1959 and 1970

Nationality	1959	1970
Abyssinians	21,803	24,294
Afghans	1,855	4,184
Arabs	7,042	–
Armenians	2,787,000	3,559,000
Greeks	309,308	336,869
Kurds	58,799	88,930
Persians	20,766	27,501
Turkomans	1,001,585	1,525,284

Source: *Itogi vsesoyuznoy perepisi naseleniya 1959 goda SSSR*, svodnyy tom (Moscow: Gosstatiz-dat, 1962), p. 201; *Itogi vsesoyuznoy perepisi naseleniya, 1970 goda*, tom IV (Moscow: Statistika Publishers, 1973), p. 9.

Note: All figures are taken from the 1970 census, except for the 7042 Arabs in the 1959 column. The 1970 census did not give figures for Arabs.

shapes the formulation of Soviet policy towards the Middle East—namely the influence of the links between the Jewish populations in the Soviet Union and Israel. While the presence of a cohesive, educated and influential core of Jews in the key urban centres has not apparently dissuaded the Soviet leaders from supporting the Arab cause against Israel, nevertheless the Jews' increasingly successful efforts to emigrate to Israel have been a point of contention between the Soviet Union and Egypt. After the 1967 war in particular, the Egyptian leaders often voiced their concern that while the Soviet Union was supplying the Arabs with arms, Israel was receiving a far more precious commodity—highly trained scientists, engineers and technicians.

Of all the demographic factors the one that has had the most direct impact on Soviet–Egyptian relations has been the religious variable, involving the strong religious bond between the Muslim population of the Soviet Central Asian republics and the other non-Soviet Islamic countries. Prior to the reformulation of Soviet policy toward the Middle East around 1955, Islam was denounced as a fraud deliberately invented by a class society and exploited by the imperialist powers for 'the enslavement of the peoples of the East'.[2] Despite Soviet attempts to eradicate Islam in Central Asia, in 1970 it was estimated that there were 30 million Muslims in the Soviet Union, 20 million of whom resided in Kazakhstan.[3] Further, although the number of registered mosques has declined, largely as a result of government policy, from 8,000 following the Second World War to only 400 in 1965,[4] nevertheless a large number of unofficial mosques and religious schools still operate, and the authorative *Voprosy filosophii* declared in 1966 that 'the presence of believers in the republics of the Soviet East is considerably higher than in the other Union Republics'.[5] In the case of these Muslim believers, their link with the religious capitals of the Middle East is reinforced by the Islamic strictures demanding that the Koran be read in Arabic only, thus forging a linguistic as well as a religious tie with the Arab world.

Following the improvement in Soviet relations with the Middle East, Soviet leaders increasingly came under attack from the Arab regimes for their suppression of national and religious freedoms in the Central Asian republics, with the result that these demographic factors began to constitute a constraint on the success of Soviet foreign policy in the area. Perhaps in the interests of expediency, the official Soviet view of Islam was partially revised. Since November 1954, after a break of over 25 years, small groups of Soviet Muslims have been allowed to make the annual pilgrimage to Mecca.[6] Moreover the 1972 edition of the *Great Soviet Encyclopaedia*, while hardly praising Islam, presents a far more realistic account of its history and development than the 1953 edition, and limits itself to the arid observation that Islam 'is incompatible with the principles underlying a scientific world outlook'.[7] Nevertheless, the Soviet record in the treatment of its Muslim population is still open to criticism from the Arab capitals, and Soviet publications on Islam in Central Asia remain basically defensive.[8] Yet the Soviet desire to prove to the Arab world that religious beliefs are protected in the Soviet Union has placed Muslims in a comparatively advantageous position *vis-à-vis* other religious groups. In 1969 the Mufti of Tashkent convened an Islamic conference in which he urged all Soviet Mulims to take a more active part *as Muslims* in the political and social life of the country, in order to extend the influence of Islam and protect the rights of believers. This movement has evidently spread and is presenting serious problems for the regime, who are constrained from suppressing it not only because of the numbers involved but also due to the possible ramifications such suppression would have on Soviet influence in the Middle East.[9]

If the Soviet treatment of its Muslim population constitutes a constraint on the Soviet leaders in the formulation of their policy toward the Middle East, the economic progress of the Soviet

Central Asian Republics is certainly perceived as a source of strength. The high level of education and the economic and technological advances of the Republics are often compared to the poorer record of the Middle Eastern states and are used as an example of the potential of the communist model of development. Soviet economists are eager to point out that the average annual rate of growth in Central Asia has far surpassed that achieved either in the Middle East or elsewhere in the USSR. Indeed an article in *Voprosy ekonomiki* in 1970 estimated that while the gross output of Armenia, Kirgizia and Kazakhstan had all increased by over 10,000 per cent between 1913 and 1966, the Russian Republic's output had increased by only 700 per cent.[10] It is a common theme for Soviet analysts to use the economic development of Central Asia to illustrate the possibilities open to those developing countries who adopt a similar path of development. For example, I. Potekhin, in arguing that the underdeveloped countries were capable of making the transition from feudalism to Socialism without having to pass through the bourgeois capitalist stage, asserted that

> the correctness of this theory has been proved in practice in the Soviet Union. . . . The peoples of Central Asia were in various stages of pre-capitalist, feudal society. . . . Today, all the peoples of the Soviet Union live in the conditions of socialism. This means that the people of Central Asia have passed from feudalism to socialism, bypassing capitalism, thanks to Soviet brotherly aid.[11]

While the Central Asian Republics may have grown at a faster rate than the Slavic and Baltic Republics, and while they may be at a higher stage of economic development than the Middle Eastern states, nevertheless if one compares the current levels of economic and sociocultural development of the various republics within the Soviet Union, one finds that on a wide range of indicators the Muslim nationalities (Uzbeks, Kazakhs, Azerbaidzhanis, Tadzhiks, Turkomans and Kirgizi) consistently come out on the bottom.[12] These demographic factors can thus be variously seen as both a constraint on and a capability for the Soviet decision-makers in the formulation of their Middle Eastern policy. The existence of Muslim nationalities who have obtained a relatively high standard of living *vis-à-vis* their coreligionists in the Arab world obviously provide the Soviet leaders with certain advantages in terms of facilitating low-level cultural links between the Soviet Union and the Middle East. However, there is a danger that such links might have undesirable effects both in terms of promoting Islam in Central Asia and in terms of leaving the Soviet Union open to criticism about the treatment of its religious and national minorities. As is true with all the domestic and external sources of foreign policy, the influence of the demographic factor has varied considerably over time.

ECONOMIC CAPABILITY

The economic strength or weakness of a country is a major consideration in the decision-makers' assessments of their capability to pursue a given policy. The level of economic growth, the performance of agriculture, the quantity and availability of natural resources, and the level and diversification of industry are all factors which determine the economic capability of a country. In the formulation of foreign policy, decision-makers must also take into account the extent to which their state is dependent upon foreign trade, the costs and benefits of pursuing economic relations with other states, and the degree to which economic constraints might necessitate the sacrifice of domestic economic growth if priority is given to defence spending.

The Egyptian leaders' desire to establish relations with Moscow grew out of the belief that the USSR possessed the ability to provide economic aid, armaments and advanced technology, as well as political and military support concomitant with the Soviet status as a Great Power—a status based on its level of economic development. Equally, however, the Egyptian leaders were to discover on numerous occasions that there were limits to the Soviet Union's capabilities—that because of strains within the Soviet economy and debates over the allocation of scarce resources, the USSR did not always have the economic ability (and also sometimes the political will) to meet all of Egypt's demands. The Soviet Union's economic objectives in Egypt will be discussed in another chapter, as will the use of economic and military aid and trade to support the achievement of Soviet objectives. This section is limited, therefore, to a more general discussion of Soviet economic performance in those sectors which have had the most bearing on the ability of Soviet decision-makers to pursue foreign policy aims.

Beginning with the first five-year plan, the Soviet economy has grown at an average rate of 4–9 per cent per annum. The index of Soviet economic development shown in Table 6.2, derived from Soviet sources using 1940 as the base year, indicates the remarkable recovery made in almost all sectors of the economy since then. It also indicates the continuing priority assigned to heavy over light industry, even in the 1970s, and highlights the very slow progress made by Soviet agriculture. The average annual growth rate of the gross national product for the years between 1955 and 1975, presented below in Table 6.3, shows a decline over the past twenty years. The bad harvests of 1963, 1972 and 1974 had a particularly detrimental effect on the economy, and reduced the growth rate of the GNP in those years to as little as 1.6 per cent. Despite the decline in the Soviet growth rate, nevertheless compared with Western countries, Soviet figures still look relatively good. Hit by inflation and recession, the West suffered in the 1971–75 period, with average annual rates of growth of 0.06 per cent in the United States, 1.6 per cent in West Germany, and 2.1 per cent in Italy.[13]

TABLE 6.2 Basic Indices of Soviet Economic Growth, 1940–77 (1940 = 100)

	1940	1945	1950	1965	1970	1975	1976	1977 (plan)
Gross social product	100	83	161	570	814	1,104	1,156	1,218
National income produced	100	83	164	597	867	1,142	1,201	1,264
Fixed productive assets of all branches of the national economy	100	86	124	503	746	1,132	na	na
Total output of industry of which:	100	91	172	786	1,183	1,694	1,775	1,874
Output of means of production	100	112	204	1,053	1,589	2,316	2,443	2,587
Output of consumer goods	100	59	122	437	654	897	924	969
Gross output of agriculture of which:	100	60	99	180	221	227	236	255
Crop products	100	57	97	161	204	190	221	na
Livestock products	100	64	104	223	265	297	282	na

na—not available

Source: USSR, Central Statistical Board, *The USSR in Figures for 1975* (Moscow: Statistika Publishers, 1976), p. 32; SSSR, Tsentral'noye statisticheskoye upravleniye, *Narodnoye khozyaistvo SSSR za 60 let* (Moscow: Statistika Publishers, 1977), p. 14.

TABLE 6.3 Average Annual Growth Rates of Soviet Gross National Product
(GNP), in Five-year Periods from 1955–80

	1956–60	6.5%
	1961–65	5.0
	1966–70	6.1
	1971–75	3.8
Plan	1971–75	5.8
Plan	1976–80	5.0

Sources: For 1956–68: Stanley H. Cohn, 'General Growth Performance of the Soviet Economy', in US Congress, Joint Economic Committee, *Economic Performance and the Military Burden in the Soviet Union*, (Washington, DC: US Government Printing Office, 1970), p. 9; for 1969–75: the figures were derived from the GNP data presented in Table 6.6 below, adjusting for inflation at a rate of between 1.5–1.8 per cent for the years 1969–72 and at 1.5 per cent between 1973–75. Inflation was calculated using the method suggested by David H. Howard, 'A Note on Hidden Inflation in the Soviet Union', *Soviet Studies*, Vol. 28, No. 4 (1976), pp. 599–609; plan figures from US Central Intelligence Agency, *Soviet Economic Plans for 1976–80: A First Look*, ER 76–10471 (August 1976), p. 3.

The figure of 3.8 per cent for the 1971–75 period is particularly affected by the two bad harvests, since in the better years the growth rate averaged at around 4.6 per cent. In 1973, when there was a record grain harvest of 222.5 million tonnes, this not only boosted agricultural production by 14 per cent but also stimulated industrial output, which went up 7.2 per cent.[14] The success or failure of Soviet agriculture continues to exert a decisive influence on the Soviet economy, since one-quarter of the labour force is employed in the agricultural sector and the one-fifth of the GNP is accounted for by agriculture, a disproportionately large figure for an advanced industrial state.

However, if Soviet agriculture exerts a particularly decisive effect on economic growth, it has also increasingly become a major domestic determinant of Soviet foreign policy. With the growth in consumer welfare, the agricultural sector has had a difficult time keeping pace with the demand for many items, including cotton, which has been imported in large quantities from Egypt and grain, imported in vast amounts since 1972, mainly from the US. While the list of agricultural imports extends well beyond these two commodities, it is these two which have exerted a particular influence on Soviet–Egyptian relations. Cotton has been the traditional commodity exported by Egypt to the Soviet Union, and although it is debatable whether the desire to increase the importation of cotton was a primary Soviet objective in the expansion of its relations with Egypt (discussed in Chapter 8) it was undoubtedly a beneficial by-product. The Soviet imports of American wheat, on the other hand, have been a major factor in East–West relations in the 1970s, both because these imports are an urgent necessity and not a luxury, and also because of the more recent American demand that grain be bought with Soviet gold and hard currency, and not on credit. People like Senator Henry Jackson have obviously appreciated the political advantages to be gained for the United States by Soviet grain dependence, and it is probably for this reason that unprecedented resources are being allocated to agriculture in the tenth Five-Year Plan. The weakness of the agricultural sector is therefore not only a continued impediment to balanced growth but also an obstacle both to the successful fulfilment of any plans to improve the standard of living and to increase Soviet flexibility in its relations with the USA. The poor performance of agriculture generally undermines the rather more impressive growth records of other sectors.

With very few exceptions, the Soviet Union is self-sufficient in raw materials, and is certainly in a better position to support a high level of industrial growth than most other countries. There are, however, several problems which prevent the full utilisation of these resources, such as their frequently inaccessible location, the absence of a fully developed road and transport system which would allow their full exploitation and the lack of skilled manpower and advanced technology. Nevertheless if one compares the Soviet and American output of four key raw materials (coal, oil, iron ore and natural gas), presented in Table 6.4, it is immediately apparent that despite these problems, Soviet output has increased much faster than that of the United States since 1955. By 1976 the Soviet production of oil and iron ore was far in excess of US levels, while the output of coal and natural gas, although not surpassing the US, has still shown a considerable increase since 1955.

Of all the raw materials, the production and demand for oil and natural gas have grown the fastest; and it is these same materials which have exerted such an important influence on the formulation of Soviet policy for the Middle East. Gas is now imported in large quantities from Iran; and oil has recently been imported from several Arab states, including Egypt. However, given the quantity of oil produced within the USSR, the extent to which the desire for Arab oil has been an important determinant of Soviet policy is a subject which needs rather closer scrutiny.

TABLE 6.4 Average Annual Output of Key Raw Materials in Periods from 1955–77, USSR and USA.

	1955–59	1960–64	1965–69	1970–74	1975	1976	1977
Coal[a]							
USSR	325,464	365,146	412,076	451,969	484,668	494,376	498,180
USA	432,974	410,174	458,062	531,862	568,158	585,684	585,864
USSR as per cent USA	75	89	90	85	85	84	85
Growth in Soviet production Column 1 = 100	100	112	126	139	149	151	153
Growth in USA production Column 1 = 100	100	95	106	123	131	140	135
Oil							
USSR	99,150	185,968	286,721	404,908	491,000	519,677	545,790
USA	344,394	362,509	426,862	459,187	413,090	400,600	403,443
USSR as per cent USA	29	51	67	88	119	130	135
Growth in Soviet production Column 1 = 100	100	188	289	408	495	524	551
Growth in USA production Column 1 = 100	100	105	124	133	120	116	117
Iron Ore							
USSR	48,428	65,412	90,648	114,234	127,483	129,062	129,600
USA	45,814	43,173	50,752	50,459	48,881	48,326	34,052
USSR as per cent USA	106	152	179	226	261	267	380
Growth in Soviet production Column 1 = 100	100	135	187	236	263	267	268
Growth in USA production Column 1 = 100	100	94	111	110	107	105	74

TABLE 6.4 (*Continued*)

	1955–59	1960–64	1965–69	1970–74	1975	1976	1977
Natural Gas							
USSR	20,620	75,241	155,659	225,722	289,268	320,953	346,000
USA	301,541	395,383	517,852	624,708	567,336	567,438	571,721
USSR as per cent USA	7	19	30	36	51	56	60
Growth in Soviet production Column 1 = 100	100	365	755	1,095	1,402	1,541	1,678
Growth in USA production Column 1 = 100	100	131	172	207	188	188	189

[a] Coal, oil and iron ore in thousand metric tonnes; natural gas in million cubic metres.

Sources: UN, *Statistical Yearbook, 1960* (New York, 1960); UN, *Statistical Yearbook, 1969* (New York, 1970); UN, *Monthly Bulletin of Statistics*, Vol. 32, Nos 8 and 9 (August–September, 1978); UN, *Statistical Yearbook, 1976* (New York, 1977). SSSR, *Narodnoye khozyaistvo SSSR za 60 let* (1977); *Izvestya* (28 January 1978).

If one examines the production and consumption figures for oil, it is clear that the greatest proportion of oil is required for the domestic market, where Soviet planners are faced with growing demand in three areas. The first is for the automotive industry, where rapid expansion is absorbing a greater proportion of oil output than previously. The second is for the switchover from coal to natural gas and petroleum. During the 1950s, the Soviet Union pursued a coal-based energy policy, with coal accounting for 63 per cent of total energy consumption in 1955.[15] The shift to oil began under Khrushchev but has proceeded slowly, and in 1970 oil accounted for only 34.7 per cent of total energy consumption, as compared with 20.5 per cent in 1955.[16] However, the switchover continues, with the prospect that the domestic demand for oil will continue to increase at a much higher rate than in those Western economies which are already petroleum-based. The third area affecting the demand for oil is in Soviet industrial growth, which has traditionally tended to be extensive rather than intensive. In other words, expansion has been achieved primarily by building new factories rather than by improving the productivity of existing works through automation or rationalisation. As a result, despite the efforts of Soviet leaders to boost productivity by importing advanced technology and promoting 'socialist emulation' campaigns, Soviet industrial growth continues to require a proportionately higher energy input than in the West.

The Soviet Union requires oil not only for domestic consumption but also for its large export markets in both Eastern Europe and the West, as illustrated in Table 6.5. The Soviet Union has traditionally supplied up to 98 per cent of the oil imported by its CEMA allies.[17] In the past this monopoly provided a source of political leverage over East Europe as well as a market for surplus Soviet output. However, Soviet domestic consumption has increased, as have Soviet exports of oil to the West in return for hard currency and vital advanced technology. As a result, the Soviet Union raised crude oil prices to its East European allies by 130 per cent and advised them to seek supplemental sources of oil in the Middle East. They avidly pursued this opportunity, and by the end of 1975 approximately one-third of the petroleum consumed in Eastern Europe emanated from the Middle East.[18]

There are certain indications of future shortfalls in Soviet oil production. Soviet writers in the past have observed that while Middle Eastern oil will increase six-fold in coming decades, Soviet

TABLE 6.5 Soviet Oil Production, Consumption and Trade 1955–77 in millions of tons*

	1955	1960	1965	1970	1975	1976	1977
Soviet oil production	70.8	147.9	242.9	353.0	491.0	519.7	546.0
Soviet oil consumption	58.0	100.0	150.6	217.4	na	na	
Imports of oil and oil products of which	4.4	4.4	1.9	3.5	7.6	7.2	
Egypt	–	–	–	2.0	0.2	0.2	
Algeria	–	–	–	0.5	1.0	–	
Iraq	–	–	–	–	5.3	5.8	
Syria	–	–	–	–	–	0.5	
Exports of oil and oil products	8.0	33.2	64.4	95.8	130.4	148.5	
of which Egypt	0.2	1.3	0.8	1.6	0.2	0.2	

* Includes both crude and refined oil
na: data not available
–: zero or negligible
Sources: SSSR, Ministerstvo Vneshney Torgovli SSSR, *Vneshnyaya torgovlya SSSR zá—god, statisticheskiy sbornik* (Moscow: Statistika Publishers) (annual); SSSR, Ministerstvo Vneshney Torgovli SSSR, *Vneshnyaya torgovlya SSSR,1918–66, Statisticheskiy Sbornik* (Moscow: Statistika Publishers, 1967; *SWB*, SU/5693/C/5 (14 December 1977); *Izvestiya* (28 January 1978).

reserves will allow only a four-fold increase.[19] Barring the unlikely discovery of major new fields in western Russia, it is thought by US government officials that the new Siberian deposits will not come in to production at a rapid enough rate to maintain acceptable 'reserves-to-production' ratios.[20] Moreover, the difficulties of expanding existing fields are exacerbated, according to one Soviet account, by 'the high frequency of accidents, prolonged stoppages, inferior quality of material and technical provisions and shortages of qualified workers and engineering and technical cadres'.[21] These fields are also evidently experiencing severe water encroachment, making recovery more difficult and requiring costly Western equipment.[22] For these reasons, it is thought that Soviet oil production may peak in the early 1980s.[23] Soviet planners themselves are taking measures to cut back energy consumption. A leading editorial in *Pravda* on 21 November 1977 called for energy conservation, stating that the 1976–80 five-year plan calls for a reduction in the consumption of boiler and furnace fuels by 3 to 4 per cent, of electricity and thermal energy by 5 per cent and of petrol and diesel fuel for goods vehicles by 8 per cent.

Although the Soviet Union could probably continue to meet all of its domestic requirements for some time to come, there are obvious advantages to be gained by importing oil from the Arab states. There is first of all the political consideration that by importing oil from these countries, the Soviet Union is at the same time denying this commodity to the Western states, thus further straining their economies. Moreover, the export of oil to the Soviet Union allows the Arab producers to diversify their trading links, thereby weakening the political influence which the oil companies had previously enjoyed. While these political objectives tended to dominate Soviet writing on Arab oil until the mid-1960s,[24] economic advantages have been more frequently stressed in recent years. Arab oil generally tends to be of much higher quality than the Soviet oil currently produced in the western regions of Russia and the Ukraine; and while Siberian oil is of a high quality with a low sulphur content, the cost and difficulties in production and transportation only reinforce the economic benefits of trading with the Middle East. These benefits were increased following the 1967 closure of the Suez Canal when the USSR bought oil from Egypt, receiving it on the Gulf of Suez and immediately reselling it to its Asian partners. Thus much of the trade in oil with Egypt in the late 1960s and early 1970s, by which time Egypt was nearing self-sufficiency in oil production, was really a switching operation between the Mediterranean and the Gulf of Suez.[25]

Two final advantages must be mentioned. In the first place, oil is imported from the Arab states not primarily on a commercial basis but in remuneration for long-term credits extended by the Soviet Union to finance industrial projects and petroleum development in these countries. Previously, the Soviet Union received in repayment such commodities as cotton, wool, hides, dried fruits, rice and semi-manufactured goods which, with the exception of cotton and wool, were not of vital importance to the Soviet economy. Now that the Soviet Union's major Arab trading partners—Egypt, Iraq, Syria and Algeria—all have nationalised oil industries, the Soviet Union is able to replace the non-vital items with oil. Finally, as stated by Professor P. A. Reynolds:

> Influences on foreign policy are relevant not merely in terms of their present and actual nature, but in terms of their future or potential . . . In judging the action that is appropriate in relation to desired trading relationships or to compensate for some deficiency, for example, the decision-maker should always

take into account not merely the actual but also the potential economic strength or weakness of his state.[26]

This observation is particularly relevant to the case of oil, since as it is a finite and non-replenishable resource decision-makers must constantly be aware of future sources and supplies. In this respect both the Soviet and American governments appear to be pursuing an energy policy designed to deplete foreign oil supplies which are presently available, while maintaining more secure domestic reserves at their highest possible level. The figures presented in Table 6.5 showing the growth in Soviet oil imports and the corresponding decline in exports since 1970 reinforce the argument that not only are real advantages to be gained by importing oil from the Middle East, but also that Soviet decision-makers are fully aware of these benefits and are seeking to enhance them. That the Soviet Union is interested more in the economic advantages of oil imports rather than their political by-products is further illustrated by the fact that while supporting the Arab oil embargoes of 1967 and 1973, the Soviet Union continued to sell oil, and reportedly even some Middle Eastern oil, to West Europe and the United States.[27] The apparent willingness of the Soviet company Neftexport to maintain supplies whatever the political repercussions evidently persuaded the Japanese to invest heavily in Siberian oil, thus decreasing their former reliance on Middle East supplies.

The continuing growth in the output of oil and other raw materials is a reflection of the general expansion of Soviet industry as a whole. Although the Soviet GNP is only about 50 per cent of the American GNP, nevertheless the Soviet output of heavy industrial products often matches and even exceeds the American levels. The production of capital equipment has traditionally been given priority over other sectors in the five-year plans. However, after 1967, the Soviet leaders projected a faster rate of growth for the consumer goods and agricultural sectors than for heavy industry, although heavy industry was still to receive a far greater share of the budget in absolute terms. Contrary to the forecast, these sectors did not in fact grow faster than heavy industry, largely due to crop failures and to their lower labour productivity. As a result, a more sober approach was adapted for the tenth five-year plan, which began in 1976. Production growth for light industry was set at between 26 and 28 per cent for the five years and for heavy industry at between 38 and 42 per cent.[28] This would produce growth consistent with the trends shown in Table 6.3.

A very large proportion of the output of industry and of the GNP as a whole is devoted to defence spending. Debates over the division of a tightly stretched budget between the four main sectors of agriculture, light industry, heavy industry and defence have been a feature of Soviet politics since the 1920s. However, since the 1950s the debates over budgetary allocation have been dominated by two diametrically opposed groups; those who have supported the improvement in consumer welfare and agriculture and those 'steel eaters' who have favoured the continued rapid growth of heavy industry and defence. The division between these groups has been reflected in the major foreign policy debates in which those favouring consumer welfare at home generally have supported peaceful coexistence and *détente* abroad, while those supporting the growth of heavy industry and defence have argued for a high stage of military preparedness and against any relaxation of international tension.

The outcome of these debates has exerted an important influence not just on Soviet foreign policy but also on the Soviet economy. If the Soviet Union is to maintain its status as a Great Power, to some extent it must match, and even seek to surpass, the military capability of its rivals. The difficulty is that because the Soviet GNP is roughly one-half that of the USA, to match American expenditure puts a much heavier burden on the Soviet economy than it does on the American. Brezhnev himself, in a particularly straightforward observation on the sacrifices which the Soviet Union must make to maintain its Great Power position, stated:

> The international situation prevents us from using all of the country's resources for economic development, improving the working people's living standard and promoting culture. Large resources have to be appropriated for defence. And I can assure you that we maintain it at the highest level.[29]

A comparison of Soviet and American GNP levels and defence spending is set out in Table 6.6. Because of the difficulty of deriving the Soviet GNP, the figures are estimates; and where two or more analysts differ on GNP levels the figures for that year are presented as a range. This also applies to the estimates for defence expendi-

TABLE 6.6 Soviet and American Gross National Product (GNP) and Defence Spending, 1955–75 (in billions of current dollars and roubles)

	USSR[a] GNP BR	USSR[b] Defence spending BR	USSR Defence % of GNP	USA[c] GNP B$	USA[d] Defence spending B$	USA Defence % of GNP
1955	121.6	11.0–13.5	9–11	398.0	40.2–40.4	10
1956	131.6	10.5–12	8–9	419.2	41.5–42.1	10
1957	143.2	10.5–12	7–8	441.1	44.0–44.2	10
1958	157.4	10.7–13	7–8	447.3	45.1–45.8	10
1959	171.6	10.9–14	6–8	483.7	45.8–46.6	9–10
1960	174–179	11.1–15.5	6–9	503.7	45.4–46.9	8.5–9.5
1961	185–191	13.6–17.5	7–9	520.1	47.8–50.2	9–10
1962	199–205	14.9–20	7–10	560.3	52.4–53.7	9–10
1963	210–220	16.5–22	7–10	590.5	52.3–56.6	9–10
1964	226–240	16.3–23	7–10	632.4	51.2–55.9	8–9
1965	244–253	16.0–24.5	6–10	684.9	51.8–57.5	7.5–8.5
1966	262–280	16.8–27.5	6–10	749.9	63.6–69.0	8–9
1967	284–309	18.2–32.5	6–11	793.9	75.4–81.2	9–10
1968	307–337	20.8–38.5	6–13	864.2	80.7–86.1	9–10
1969	332–357	22.1–42	6–13	929.1	81.4–85.0	8.5–9.5
1970	365–392	22.8–46.5	6–13	974.1	77.9–81.8	7.5–8.5
1971	394	23.2–52	6–13	1,072.9	74.9–81.4	7–8
1972	407	23.4–58	6–14	1,151.8	77.6–80.5	6.5–7
1973	439.9	23.8–63	5–14	1,289.1	78.5–81.6	6–6.5
1974	463.4	23.8–69	5–15	1,397.4	84.0–86	6–6.5
1975	492.4	26.2–73	5–15	1,498.8	89.0	6

[a] 1955–59 figures are taken from Lee and represent the upper end of the range. 1960–66 figures represent the range between the findings of Lee, Campbell and Rand; 1967–70 figures represent the range between the Lee and Campbell figures; 1971–75 figures were derived by Paul Cockle of the International Institute of Strategic Studies, using Campbell's techniques, which for the period 1960–70 produced estimates appreciably below Lee's.
[b] Figures represent the range presented between *Military Balance* (almost always the lowest figure), Cohn and SIPRI (middle figures), and Lee's estimates of total National Security Expenditure, which include outlays for arms exports and for the Soviet space programme.
[c] From Lee and *The Military Balance*.
[d] Figures represent official defence expenditure cited by SIPRI and the higher figures for total National Security Expenditure cited by Lee.

Sources: SIPRI, *World Armaments and Disarmament SIPRI Yearbook 1974* (Cambridge, Mass.: MIT Press, 1974); *The Military Balance* (London: The International Institute of Strategic Studies) (annual); Stanley H. Cohn, 'General Growth Performance of the Soviet Economy', in US, Congress, Joint Economic Committee, *Economic Performance and the Military Burden in the Soviet Union* (Washington, DC: U.S. Government Printing Office, 1970), pp. 9–18; Stanley H. Cohn, 'The Economic Burden on Soviet Defence Outlays', ibid., pp. 166–89; W. T. Lee, *Soviet Defence Expenditure for 1955–1975*, Tempo GE 75 TMP-42 (Washington, DC 31 July 1975); R. W. Campbell, 'A Shortcut Method for Estimating Soviet GNP,' *Association for Comparative Economic Studies*, Vol 14, No. 2, (Fall 1972).

ture, which vary widely because the lowest figure generally only includes the official defence budget plus three-quarters of the science budget (for defence research and development), while the highest figure includes these two elements plus military construction, personnel, arms exports and the Soviet space programme. Some analysts believe that if allowance were made for all the industrial output which is geared for defence, the figure would be even higher.

If one examines the columns which present defence spending as a percentage of GNP, several interesting points emerge. First, not only is there a wide disparity between the percentages obtained through using the official Soviet figures and the estimates of 'real' expenditure, but also this disparity has grown over the years, perhaps reflecting the increasing allocations to defence-related high technology developments and space, which would not be included in the lower set of figures. A second important observation is that while American defence spending has declined (as a percentage of GNP) since Vietnam, the economic burden of Soviet defence spending has apparently increased.

The extent to which the increased levels of defence spending are responsible for the slowdown in Soviet economic growth is a matter of contention among Western analysts. Some would point to harvest failures, diminishing returns on capital, labour shortages and inefficient management as the primary economic problems currently facing the Soviet economy. While these factors must of course be taken into account, nevertheless it is undoubtedly true that increases in defence spending are also likely to adversely affect growth, in so far as defence-related industries tend to absorb a high proportion of sophisticated technology, skilled manpower and vital raw materials, in order to produce finished products, which unlike capital goods, do not stimulate further growth.

All of these factors—perennial agricultural failures, the desire to husband reserves of raw materials, the low productivity of the agricultural and light industry sectors compared to the better record of heavy industry and the economic burden imposed by increasing defence expenditure—have exerted a decisive influence on the formulation of Soviet foreign policy. The demands on a limited budget have been growing sharper and more intractable, with the Soviet leaders seeking a solution to their economic problems in two ways; first by increasing efficiency and productivity and secondly by abandoning autarchy and adopting comparative economic advantage as the principle underlying Soviet foreign economic relations. Both solutions have involved an increased reliance on trade and contacts with both the Third World and the West, solutions which have shaped the Soviet Union's economic objectives in Egypt, the subject of Chapter 8.

IDEOLOGICAL INFLUENCES

Decision-making involves the constant interaction between the psychological and operational environments or between the image the decision-makers hold of a situation, and how that situation in fact is. As noted by Joseph Frankel, the image of the decision-maker 'does not act as a passive filter which lets through a certain proportion of the whole, but it actively selects a small portion of the facts as relevant, excludes others, and often distorts some. The omission and the distortions result in a psychological environment vastly different from the operational one'.[30] A number of factors interact to produce the image which the decision-makers hold of their enviornment—including the amount and accuracy of information at their disposal, personality factors, that society's political culture and historical traditions, and ideology.

The actual form and function of Soviet ideology is a continuing subject of heated debate both inside and outside the communist world.[31] Not only is there a considerable lack of agreement on the extent to which contemporary Soviet ideology continues to adhere to the fundamental tenets of Marxism-Leninism, but there is also a variety of differing opinions on whether Soviet ideology fulfils a motivational role in the formulation of foreign policy, or whether its function has been restricted to justification and communication. Before examining the role which ideology has played in Soviet–Egyptian relations, it is first necessary to elucidate those components of Soviet ideology which have had the greatest influence on the formulation of Soviet foreign policy generally.

One of the most frequently repeated assertions of Soviet leaders is that Soviet foreign policy is 'scientifically' based, that it proceeds from the fundamental laws of history elucidated by Marx and Engels. As a result, Soviet foreign policy is characterised as being principled and consistent, while Western foreign policy, formulated by leaders ignorant of the tenets of dialectical materialism, is condemned by the Soviets as a series of pragmatic and short-term expedients designed to deal with situations as they arise. This point is made in a Soviet text on foreign policy:

> Socialist foreign policy is intrinsically scientific, in other words, it is founded on a knowledge of the objective laws governing the development of society and international relations. Underlying it is a creative Marxist analysis of the balance of strength in the world and of the obtaining situation. This knowledge of the laws of social development allows Soviet foreign policy to look confidently to the future and gives it the strength of scientific prevision.[32]

The inevitability of struggle between the socialist and capitalist systems is another component of Soviet ideology which purports to be a basic historical law governing the development of international relations. The fundamental division of the world into two main camps is an extension of Marx's theories on the inevitability of conflict between the proletariat and the bourgeoisie, with the Soviet Union now representing the vanguard of the proletariat and the United States as the bourgeoisie. As stated by one Soviet theorist, 'the foreign policy of socialist states is fundamentally opposed to that of capitalist states, as a result of the opposition between the positions and interests of the proletariat and the bourgeoisie . . .'[33]

An intrinsic part of this world-view is the indivisibility of proletarian internationalism and the interests of the USSR. All the Soviet leaders since Lenin have held the view that the Soviet Union, as the first and strongest socialist state, is the mainstay and inspiration for the world communist revolution. Thus the dictum that 'whatever aids the Soviet Union also aids the international communist movement' has been both a fundamental feature of Soviet ideology since Brest-Litovsk, and a basic cause of friction between the Soviet Union and other communist parties, including and especially the Chinese. This aspect of Soviet ideology was not seriously questioned in the interwar period when the Soviet Union was the only socialist state (except for Mongolia) in a hostile capitalist world. Nor was it challenged by any state except Yugoslavia in the immediate postwar period when the Soviet Union's hegemony over the newly established and pliant people's democracies was still intact and when relations between the socialist and capitalist camps were at their worst. However, in the mid-1950s, Khrushchev not only made it quite clear by invading

Hungary that no anti-Soviet developments in the international communist system would be tolerated, but he also promulgated the theory of 'peaceful coexistence' with the West. As a result of these two actions, many communists outside the Soviet Union have taken the stand that the balance in Soviet ideology between internationalism and Soviet national interests has tipped in favour of the latter. However apparent the contradication between these two components may seem to critics, nevertheless the Soviet belief in the indivisibility and complementarity of Soviet state interests and internationalism continues to constitute both a major feature of Soviet ideology and a frequent subject of articles on the basis of Soviet foreign policy. A typical extract from one of them reads:

Every achievement of the Soviet Union strengthens it as the backbone of the revolutionary and liberation movements, provides further irrepressible inspiration for millions of people, enhances the might of the socialist system as a whole and smooths the way to communism for the countries of that system. Developments have fully borne out Lenin's conclusion that a strong Soviet state is needed 'for the world communist proletariat in its struggle against the world bourgeoisie and its defence against bourgeois intrigues'.[34]

Lenin's belief not only in the irreconcilable conflict of interests between the socialist and capitalist camps, but also in the inevitability of wars among capitalist states and between the capitalist and socialist systems is a feature of Soviet ideology which has been particularly subjected to 'creative development', as the Soviets call it. Lenin wrote in *Imperialism, the Highest Stage of Capitalism* that wars between capitalist states had become inevitable as a result of the desire of the bourgeoisie to seek out new foreign markets and settle new colonies. Once all the available territory had been claimed, he said, the expansionist aims of the bourgeoisie could only be achieved by the armed conquest of already colonised territory, thus resulting in war. On the subject of the inevitability of war between the socialist and capitalist systems, Lenin stated: 'It is inconceivable for the Soviet Republic to exist alongside the imperialist states for any length of time. One or the other must triumph in the end. And before that end comes there will have to be a series of frightful collisions between the Soviet Republic and the bourgeois states'.[35] However, even during Lenin's time, it was conceived that while these two systems were inherently incompatible in the long-term, in the short-term, 'peaceful coexistence' was both possible and desirable.

Stalin followed Lenin by continuing to stress the internal instability of the capitalist camp, and the dangers to world peace caused by this instability. He also stressed that the success of the Soviet Union in establishing its primary objective of 'socialism in one country' very much depended upon 'whether we succeed in postponing war with the capitalist world, which is inevitable. . . . Therefore, the maintenance of peaceful relations with the capitalist countries is an obligatory task for us.'[36]

All the Soviet leaders since Stalin, fully aware of the destructive capabilities of a nuclear holocaust, have re-examined the tenet of ideology pertaining to the inevitability of war between the two systems. Khrushchev, in his famous address to the 20th Party Congress, claimed that because the forces of socialism had finally become the dominant ideological power in the world, they could actually prevent capitalism from unleashing aggression, meaning that wars were no long inevitable.

Under Brezhnev and Kosygin, peaceful coexistence has been transformed from a general 'spirit' (the 'spirit', for example, of Geneva or Camp David, among others) characterising East–West relations into a series of concrete accords and agreements. *Détente* is not a breathing spell between inevitable wars but is rather a long-term and semi-permanent feature of relations between the two camps. G. Arbatov, the influential head of the Institute for the Study of the USA and Canada, posed the question in *Kommunist* whether *détente* would last or whether it would be just another transient episode in East–West relations. He answered that because of the American realisation that war is no longer a cost-effective instrument for achieving political objectives, *détente* 'has a solid objective foundation and hence a future'.[37] However, *détente* should not be conceived of as the final acceptance by the USSR of a permanent *status quo* between East and West. Nor should it be viewed as constituting the 'end of ideology'. Rather it represents the Soviet belief that objective conditions have been created for coexistence between two social systems whose short-term cooperation is mutually beneficial, but whose fundamental and long-term interests and objectives remain irreconcilable. Soviet analysts maintain that *détente* works in the interests of the USSR, both because it facilitates the construction of communism inside the socialist camp and also because it allows the national liberation movements to operate freely without fearing intervention from the West. As stated in *Pravda*, in an article which appeared at the end of 1975:

> International tension serves as camouflage for imperialism to use the crudest and most violent forms in supressing the national-liberation movement. All the colonial wars and acts of imperialist aggression in the past few decades were justified by references to the need to . . . oppose the 'penetration of communists' etc. *Détente* significantly expands the possibilities that the forces of national and social liberation have to resist imperialist pressure. . . .[38]

According to the current formulation, therefore, while the class basis and interests of the socialist and capitalist camps remain irreconcilable, and while the victory of socialism over capitalism is ensured, nevertheless 'the fate of capitalism will be decided not by a war between the two systems but by 'the development of its own internal contradictions'.[39]

The main components of ideology discussed thus far have been the belief in the scientific basis of Soviet foreign policy; the indivisibility of proletarian internationalism and the national interests of the Soviet state; and the inevitability of the ultimate triumph of socialism over capitalism, coupled with the non-inevitability of wars between the two systems. To this list must be added that component which has exerted the most direct impact on Soviet policy with Egypt—anti-imperialism.

It was Lenin who first wrote that capitalism had found a way out of its internal contradictions by expanding world-wide in search of markets, capital and cheap labour. As a result, Western capitalism would not collapse unless it was first deprived of its international and imperialist holdings. Communists were advised therefore to wholeheartedly support those national movements in the colonies which were seeking liberation from imperialism. This has remained a feature of Soviet ideology since Lenin's time. However, anti-imperialism has often been in apparent contradiction with other tenets of that ideology, including both proletarian internationalism and *détente*.

In countries where movements for national liberation are strong, these movements are often dominated not by the proletarian class, which tends to be weak and ill-formed, but by the national bourgeoisie. In such cases, any nascent communist party which does exist is advised to work with the national bourgeoisie to achieve a common anti-imperialist programme. The difficulty arises when the national bourgeoisie begins to suppress the communists, thus bringing into conflict the two principles of proletarian inter- nationalism and anti-imperialism. However, since Lenin Soviet leaders have almost always resolved the contradiction in favour of anti-imperialism. In other words, as long as the national bourgeoisie was pursuing a consistently anti-imperialist and pro-Soviet line, the Soviet Union would continue to support it, irrespective of whether the indigenous communist party was allowed to operate or not. Such was the ideological reasoning behind Soviet support for Kemal Ataturk in Turkey, and Reza Khan in Persia during the 1920s as well as for Qassem in Iraq and of course Nasser in Egypt during the 1960s.

A rather more difficult dilemma has been presented by the Soviet Union's simultaneous espousal of anti-imperialism and *détente*. Analysts both in the West and in the developing countries question the Soviet Union's adherence to what appears to them to be mutually exclusive principles. Soviet involvement in Angola and the Horn of Africa led many Western experts to conclude that the Soviet Union was using *détente* as a smokescreen to weaken the West's preparedness. On the other hand, the Soviet Union's attempt during the 1973 Middle East war to establish a con- dominium with the United States convinced many Arabs that *détente* took precedence over anti-imperialism in the Soviet leaders' global calculations. However, the Soviet leaders regard *détente* and anti-imperialism as complementary components of their ideology, since, as previously stated, only under conditions of world peace can the national liberation movements develop without the constant threat of imperialist intervention. All efforts must thus be made to safeguard *détente* and prevent a direct military confrontation between the USSR and the USA which would not only impede the progress of the anti-imperialist movement, but might also slow the rate of domestic economic growth inside the USSR and increase the risk of nuclear war.

While Soviet ideologues would be the first to agree that ideology has been subject to 'creative development', they would not agree with the contention that ideology is no longer a powerful influence on Soviet foreign policy. Soviet leaders have always upheld the view, as stated here by Brezhnev, that 'we Soviet Communists see

Lenin's ideas and the principles he worked out as a reliable guiding thread. Loyalty to these principles . . . constitutes an inexhaustible source of strength for our foreign policy course'.[40] However, this is not to say that 'Soviet ideology' is synonomous with 'the works of Marx and Lenin'. Rather, ideology is imparted by Soviet leaders themselves who have a full understanding of the Marxist laws of historical development and who are thereby able to fully comprehend the nature of the present epoch and establish the concrete ideological foundations which underpin Soviet foreign policy. This point is made by a Soviet text:

> On foreign policy the CPSU Central Committee and the Soviet Government are steadfastly guided by the theoretical propositions and basic principles worked out by Lenin, creatively enlarging upon them and applying them in the new conditions. Soviet foreign policy is thus Leninist.[41]

However, it is interesting that in listing the reasons why Soviet foreign policy has been an increasingly effective force in international relations, this same text maintains that it has been not only because of the Soviet leaders' strict adherence to ideology but also because of their 'flexibility, realism and willingness to accept reasonable compromises'.[42]

This quotation would seem to express the admission that the influence of ideology must be moderated on occasion by a more pragmatic approach, and it must be asked therefore whether in the formulation of Soviet policy, ideology has not variously acted as both a capability and a constraint. In a general sense, the adherence to a defined and universally accepted ideology would act as a capability in so far as it presents a single world view which both demands and promotes long-term planning and short-term patience. Soviet leaders do tend to regard all international events as part of the same jigsaw puzzle, which when completed will reveal a picture of the ultimate triumph of socialism. Needless to say, there are many who would disagree with this world view. The point is, however, that because all Soviet leaders basically adhere to this *Weltanschauung*, long-term planning is facilitated. This is in marked contrast to the situation in countries such as Great Britain or Italy, for example, where frequent changes of government and the constant need for consensus building, two basic components and virtues of a pluralist system, also result in the near impossibility of formulating a national long-term strategy on domestic or foreign policy.

A second capability which might accrue to the Soviet Union as a result of adherence to a determinist view of history is the belief that history is inevitably on their side, a belief which has tempered the Soviet reaction to setbacks and has perhaps made the Soviet leaders more patient and even-handed in their approach. For example, in the last two decades of Soviet–Egyptian relations, despite frequent disputes, the Soviet Union has always adhered to the view that any setback is temporary and that every effort must be made to continue relations, even if at a low level. The steady flow of Soviet economic aid and trade in the period preceding the abrogation of the Soviet–Egyptian Treaty in the spring of 1976 was an example. This attitude is rather different to the Anglo-American policy pursued throughout the previous two decades in which every issue was regarded as a major one and every slight to Western prestige was met by an appropriate and maximum response. In writing of the effect which ideology has in promoting a long-term strategy, one is tempted to contrast Mao Tse-tung's observation that 'the first century of a new regime is always the most difficult' with the celebrated remark by Harold Wilson that 'one week is a long time in politics'. In the realm of Soviet–Egyptian relations, ideology has acted in some respects as an important capability for the achievement of Soviet policy. In particular the anti-imperialist component of Soviet ideology was certainly shared by the Egyptian leaders who throughout the 1950s and 1960s pursued a consistently anti-Western policy.

In other ways, however, ideology has acted as a constraint. Because ideology is one of the factors shaping the image which Soviet decision-makers hold of a situation, and also since ideology forms the parameters within which policy options are formulated, it can be argued that adherence to this ideology has produced a number of misperceptions about the situation in the Middle East, as well as a certain policy inflexibility which might have been less apparent had ideology not been a motivating force. Furthermore, the continual debates within the Soviet leadership over the 'correctness' of any particular policy exposes that policy to scrutiny and criticism from observers outside the regime. The ideological dimension of Soviet–Egyptian relations has often been the subject of disputes between the two governments—disputes which were often far removed from the day-to-day running of affairs.

For example, while the Egyptian and Soviet leaders may have

shared a common interest in seeking an end to Western influence in
the Middle East during Nasser's time, their respective strategies and
long-term goals were motivated by entirely different ideological
perspectives. For the Soviet decision-makers, the national liberation
struggle was but the first step towards the ultimate and inevitable
transition to communism, a transition which would take each
country through the various stages of 'National Democracy' and
'People's Democracy' until it reached first socialism and then
communism. However, the Egyptian leaders had no such historical
progression in mind. For them, Western domination should
certainly not be replaced by Soviet domination. Neither did they
see non-alignment as a mere bridge between the ideologies of East
and West. Rather, independence from Western influence was
sought in order to reassert their own indigenous culture, values and
ideology. As stated by Anwar al-Sadat in a famous letter to
Khrushchev in 1961: 'As regards capitalism and communism, we do
not [believe] that the historical development of man runs along the
blind alley, of which capitalism is the beginning and Communism is
the imperative end . . . Our people refuse to be limited to this
choice'.[43] Although the Egyptian leaders have been willing, and
even eager, to accept Soviet assistance in the 'common fight against
imperialism', they have remained adamantly opposed to communist ideology, denouncing it as Nasser did on one occasion early
in his career as 'atheism [and] the bitter enemy of spiritual values,
serenity of soul, sincerity, high-mindedness, self-respect, fraternity,
love and peace'.[44]

Ideology has further affected Soviet relations with Egypt in so far
as the Soviet leaders' adherence to Marxism–Leninism has precluded their unqualified support for nationalist movements, such as
Arab nationalism, Pan-Islam and Arab unity. The Soviet leadership regard nationalist movements as progressive only when they
are directed against Western imperialism. For example, when
Nasser consented to the formation of the union between Egypt and
Syria, a union which was to result in the suppression of the Syrian
Communist Party, it was not surprising that the Soviet Union did
not immediately welcome the action (see Chapter 2). Yet when
anti-imperialism has come into conflict with proletarian internationalism, the former has usually taken precedence, particularly when applied to developing countries. This priority has
been questioned on numerous occasions by Soviet ideologues, by
leaders of the communist world and by the Arab communists

themselves. Many of them see no necessary link between the Soviet support for the 'national bourgeoisie' and the ultimate transition to socialism in these countries, and they demand a reappraisal of Soviet policy in the Middle East. As a result, Soviet leaders often feel constrained to lend some measure of support to the Arab communist parties, which on several occasions has produced an open split between the Soviet and Egyptian governments. Such disputes were frequent in the late 1950s and early 1960s when communist influence in Syria and Iraq was high. The 1975–76 Lebanese civil war forced the Soviet Union to choose between a progressive and anti-Western Syrian regime and the leftist elements in the Lebanon. The Soviets protested to the Syrians, but did not stop supplies.

It has been said that international relations are 'in some senses relations between beliefs, beliefs about the nature and component elements of situations, and about the effects in these situations of the adoption of various courses of action'.[45] The Soviet belief that the situation in the Middle East can be explained almost entirely in terms of the struggle of the newly independent Arab states against imperialism and its manifestations is a view only partially shared by the leaders of the Arab radical regimes. While the 'struggle against imperialism' is an important variable in the belief-system of these Arab leaders, other variables relating to the domestic and regional environment have played and continue to play an equally important part in shaping Arab perceptions. These factors include the Arab–Israeli conflict, inter-Arab rivalries, and purely domestic considerations. The constraining influence of ideology has led to the Soviet failure to appreciate fully the strength of the movements for Arab unity; the Arab aversion to communism; the intransigence of Islam; the depth and vehemence of Arab hostility toward Israel; and the importance of domestic, personality and power-political factors. To return to the remarks quoted at the beginning of this section, it would seem that ideology did play an important part in shaping the psychological environment of the Soviet decision-makers, and that the resultant 'omissions and distortions' may indeed have produced 'a psychological environment vastly different from the operational one'.[46] Finally, the importance of ideology as an influence on Soviet foreign policy in the Middle East was stressed by Walter Laqueur when he said:

All attempts to account for Soviet foreign policy without due regard to the ideological factor are ultimately sterile; their only effect is to make a complicated phenomenon even more incomprehensible. . . . If the importance of the 'professional ideologies' has declined over the years in the field of foreign policies as elsewhere, all that has happened is that their monopoly has vanished. It does not mean that ideological motivation had disappeared.[47]

INFLUENCES FROM THE EXTERNAL ENVIRONMENT

In the formulation of a state's foreign policy, decision-makers must take into account not only variables in their internal environment, such as geography, demography, economic factors and ideology but also factors in the external, international environment. Specifically, decision-makers must assess both their own capabilities in relation to the capabilities of those states whose behaviour they seek to influence, and the likelihood and nature of external responses to actions taken. In the formation of Soviet foreign policy towards Egypt, the main influences from the external environment emanated from the West, from the Communist world, and from the other states of the Middle East.

The West

The 'West', as the so-called 'base of imperialism', the creator of NATO and the Baghdad Pact, and the primary supporter of Israel, has exerted both an ideological and a geostrategic influence on Soviet decision-making, as discussed in previous sections. However, the specific influence which Western industrialised states have exerted both on Soviet–Egyptian relations and on the dominant Soviet and Egyptian images of Western intentions and interests in the Middle East requires further elucidation.

It must first be reiterated that the Soviet leaders tend to view the conflicts in the Middle East as an extension of the wider relationship between the socialist and capitalist systems. For example, Khrushchev, in an interview with the Egyptian newspaper *al-Ahram*, once stressed that Soviet relations with the Arab states would be kept within the limits of the broader policy of 'competitive but peaceful coexistence with the Western powers'.[48] Until the Soviet naval buildup in the 1960s, the USSR could not begin to match Western military capabilities, particularly in the Middle East where the presence of the Sixth Fleet and the continued control of military bases in Bahrain, Libya, Aden, Tunisia, Iran, Greece and Turkey gave the West a considerable strategic advantage.

The Soviet perception of the Western ability and motivation to adopt a more 'aggressive' stance in the Middle East, as elsewhere, thus acted as a constraint on the formulation and implementation of a more activist foreign policy. This constraint was apparent particularly in the 1950s, in the Soviet Union's belated and qualified support for Egypt during the Suez Crisis in 1956; her proposal in that same crisis for joint Soviet–American action; and the Soviet sponsorship of a multilateral Great Power arms embargo to all states in the Middle East following the 1957 Syrian crisis and the 1958 Lebanese civil war.

While Soviet options in the Cold War may have been limited by perceptions of Western 'aggressiveness', Soviet policy benefited from the dominant, negative image of the West held by large sections of the population in Egypt. Britain and France in particular were distrusted because of their former colonial status in the region. This distrust was perpetuated through the poor record of Western diplomacy in the post-independence era, a record which included Western support for the creation and perpetuation of the state of Israel (the USSR's role in the creation of Israel was not often mentioned), the alleged maintenance of the military balance in Israel's favour following the Tripartite Declaration of 1950, the abrupt withdrawal of American aid for the Aswan Dam Project, the creation of the Baghdad Pact, the Suez Crisis, the Eisenhower Doctrine, and the American and British interventions in the Lebanon and Jordan. Writing of the reasons for the failure of Western diplomacy in the area during the period, Patrick Seale stated:

> To many Arabs, the West seemed the main obstacle to the independence, unity, and reform of their homeland. A defence pact directed against Russia such as the West was insistently advocating, seemed both a distraction from their local quarrel with Israel and a new form of veiled colonialism.[49]

Both Nasser and many Western analysts were to assert repeatedly that these Western-created military pacts, by splitting the Arabs and forcing them to take sides for or against the West, were the primary reasons why many Arab governments sought closer relations with the Soviet Union, an alignment which in any other circumstances would probably not have occurred.[50]

Since the mid-1960s, however, Soviet–American relations have undergone a marked change. In the first place, the USSR has achieved military parity with the USA, particularly in the area of strategic nuclear weapons. This has had the effect of reinforcing the Soviet Union's self-image as a Great Power with legitimate global interests. It has also had the effect of convincing both the USSR and the USA of the necessity of cooperation both to control the arms race and to prevent the outbreak of local wars which might threaten superpower involvement. In economic relations too, confrontation has been replaced by limited cooperation, and the Soviet Union has become increasingly dependent upon imports of Western grain and advanced technology. It has been these aspects of East–West relations which have figured so prominently in the SALT talks and the summits in Moscow, Washington, Helsinki and Vladivostok.

If Soviet–Egyptian relations under Khrushchev were framed within the limitations imposed by peaceful coexistence with the West, this is even more the case with *détente*. The enhancement of the Soviet Union's military capability has led to a corresponding increase in its military involvement in the Arab world. However this involvement always has been strictly determined by the Soviet assessment not only of Western levels of support for her clients but also of the possible Western reaction to Soviet moves. For example, the decision to meet Nasser's request for Soviet pilots during the 1970 War of Attrition was taken, according to Egyptian sources, with the American response uppermost in Soviet calculations.[51]

The 1971 talks between Soviet and Syrian Communist Party leaders was another instance when the Soviets stressed the primacy of *détente*. The transcript, leaked by a dissenting member of the Syrian delegation, contains a passage in which the Soviet side unequivocally states that a new Middle East war must be averted because it could 'lead to a confrontation between the Soviets and the Americans. We do not conceal the fact that we are not in favour of this except in the case of extreme necessity'.[52] Of course, the best example of the extent to which *détente* has taken priority over Soviet relations with Egypt was the Soviet behaviour during the October 1973 war. When the Soviet attempt to use *détente* to form a condominium arrangement with the United States failed, the Soviet Union threatened unilateral action to save the beleaguered Egyptian Third Army. However, the American nuclear alert signalled to the Soviet leaders that such action would be met with American escalation; and the Soviets were forced to shelve any plans for direct involvement which they may have had.

The Egyptians for their part have often criticised the Soviet Union's adherence to *détente*. Whereas non-aligned states such as Egypt had been able to exploit Great Power rivalry during the Cold War, in conditions of Great Power cooperation, the Egyptians felt that the Soviet interest in *détente* took precedence over Soviet support for the progressive Arab regimes. In particular the Soviet reluctance to supply Egypt with the offensive weapons which would ensure victory against Israel led Egyptian observers to conclude, as Heikal did in the aftermath of the 1967 defeat, that the two major facts governing Soviet–Arab relations were the Soviet desire to prevent a military clash with the United States and the Soviet interest in strengthening *détente*, because of the need for technology and because of the Sino–Soviet conflict.[53] That Heikal was able to make this statement as early as 1967 is both a tribute to his insight and an indication of the constancy of the external influences on Soviet foreign policy emanating particularly from the United States and China.

The Communist World

In the formulation of its policy towards Egypt, the Soviet leaders have often been influenced by considerations relating to their hegemonial position in the international Communist movement. Such a position has great advantages as well as undisputed responsibilities, for if hegemony is to be maintained primarily by consensus, with the threat of force present but not paramount, then that hegemonial power must constantly be responsive to the demands and requirements of the subsidiary states.

The Soviet Union's policy towards the Middle East has not always met with the unanimous approval of its East European partners. Although they have usually fallen in with the Soviet line and have provided economic and military aid to Arab regimes within the framework of a Soviet-orchestrated policy, there have been notable exceptions. The first was Tito's attempts in the mid-1950s to form a neutralist 'camp' along with Nasser and Nehru which would rival and balance Soviet and American predominance. The second act of independence from Moscow was Rumania's refusal to sign a joint declaration condemning Israel's actions during the 1967 war. Rumania was the only socialist state not to break off diplomatic relations with Israel following the war, with the result that Rumania has been able to play an important mediating role in the Arab–Israeli dispute. Indeed, Sadat has claimed that his decision to visit Jerusalem in December 1977, a decision vehemently denounced in Moscow, was taken only after receiving President Ceausescu's assurances that Prime Minister Begin was strong enough domestically to enable a positive response to the Sadat initiative.[54] The third example of East European dissent from the Soviet position also occurred following the 1967 war. In Prague, the first signs of the reform movement were making themselves felt. The break in diplomatic relations with Israel caused considerable dissatisfaction in Czechoslovakia where this issue assumed importance both as a symbol of the inability to formulate an independent foreign policy and as an issue in intellectuals' discontent over the treatment of Jews at home. In May 1968, a petition with over 13,000 signatures calling for the restoration of diplomatic relations with Israel was presented to the Czechoslovak Ministry of Foreign Affairs, but with no result.[55] Far from persuading the Soviet decision-makers of the need to revise their policy towards Israel, such actions, if anything, only further convinced them of the threat which a continuation of the reform movement posed to Moscow's position.

Of all the socialist countries, China has exerted the greatest influence on Soviet policy. As the second most powerful socialist state, China's influence was bound to be important, although the nature of that influence varied considerably according to the state of Sino-Soviet relations.

During the early and mid-1950s the Soviet Union encouraged and received Chinese support for her Middle-Eastern policy, support which included the establishment of Chinese diplomatic relations with Egypt, Syria, Iraq, and the Yemen; adherence to the Soviet 'line' at Afro-Asian and non-aligned conferences from which the Soviet Union was occasionally excluded; and even Chinese intervention on Nasser's behalf in the dispute between Molotov and Khrushchev on the advisability of supplying arms to Egypt in 1955.[56] The importance of the Chinese Revolution as an example for other national liberation movements was a frequent topic in Soviet speeches and articles. For example, Yevgeny Zhukov once wrote:

Of particular significance for the national liberation movements in the Afro-Asian countries is China's wealth of practical experience in uniting the people and rallying them first for the anti-imperialist and anti-feudalist struggles, and later for the common struggle for Socialism. . . . [Also] of exceptional significance for most Afro-Asian . . . countries is the Chinese example of the cooperation between the working masses and the national bourgeoisie.[57]

However, following the Iraqi Revolution in July 1958, the Chinese and Soviet views of the situation in the Middle East began to diverge, and China began to exert a constraining rather than a supportive influence on Soviet policy-making.[58] The Chinese began to lend their full support to the communist parties of Iraq and the UAR, while the Russians continued to advocate united front tactics.[59] When the Secretary-General of the Syrian Communist Party, Khalid Bagdash, made a speech at the Tenth Anniversary of the Chinese Revolution in Peking labelling the UAR as a 'terroristic and dictatorial regime which applies fascist tactics',[60] Khrushchev reportedly sent a letter to Nasser dissociating the Soviet Union from these attacks.[61] However, Chinese radicalism continued, and at a joint Sino-Soviet academic symposium held in 1959 on wars of national liberation, the Chinese were openly critical of current Soviet policy, noting that anyone who failed to lend their full support to such wars lacked a 'sincere desire for the preservation and strengthening of peace'.[62] When the Soviet representatives stressed that such an adventurist policy might result in a war with the West, the Chinese retorted that aid to national liberation movements would strengthen peace because it 'would weaken imperialism and its capabilities for war'.[63]

Moreover, at the Moscow Meeting of Representatives of Communist and Workers' Parties in November 1960, the Soviet leaders were under considerable pressure to accept a major ideological re-evaluation of the roles of the national bourgeoisie and the indigenous communist parties. In the statement issued at the end of the conference, certain sections of the national bourgeoisie were characterised as being 'inherently unstable . . . and inclined to compromise with imperialism and feudalism'.[64] On the other hand, non-ruling communist parties were directed to continue their work with progressive elements in the anti-imperialist struggle, while at the same time 'exposing attempts by the reactionary section of the bourgeoisie to represent its selfish, narrow class interests as those of the entire nation'.[65] The major product of the conference was the revision of the communist attitude toward domestic politics in the developing countries. Whereas previously support had been given to any state pursuing an anti-Western foreign policy, regardless of its domestic programmes, henceforth the fullest support would only be given to those 'National Democracies' which pursued a progressive policy in both domestic and external affairs. This new 'State of National Democracy' was defined as:

A state which consistently upholds its political and economic independence, fights against imperialism and its military blocs . . . a state which fights against the new forms of colonialism and the penetration of imperialist capital; a state which rejects dictatorial methods of government; a state in which the people are assured broad democratic rights and freedoms . . . the opportunity to work for the enactment of agrarian reforms and other domestic and social changes and for participation in shaping governmental policy.[66]

At the 1963 Afro-Asian Solidarity Conference in Tanganyika, the Chinese for the first time tried to win support away from the USSR by forming a bloc of all non-white races. The attempt failed, but the conference broke up without success, leading the Soviets to condemn China's divisive influence.[67] In the same year the exchange of open letters between the Chinese and Soviet Central Committees led to splits in many of the Third World Communist parties who were forced to declare their allegiance to either Moscow or Peking.

In the late 1960s, Chinese foreign policy went through a period of extreme radicalisation, as a result of the internal upheavals of the Cultural Revolution. The Chinese began to divide the world into rich and poor nations, into the countryside and cities of the globe, advocating that the peoples of the under-developed states should surround and capture the advanced industralised areas. This thesis naturally included the USSR as part of the industralised sector and was seen by the Soviet leaders as an attempt to isolate the USSR from the national liberation movement. As Soviet theorists were to repeatedly assert, 'contrary to the allegation of Peking revisionists of the Mao Tse-tung group, the national liberation movement of the peoples can triumph only with support of the international working class'.[68] One of the more amusing episodes of this period of Chinese radicalism occurred after Nasser accepted the ceasefire following Egypt's overwhelming defeat in the June 1967 war. Evidently, Nasser received a message from Mao Tse-tung encouraging him not to allow the Israelis to occupy Sinai and instead to enter into a Chinese-style people's liberation war, establishing base areas among the local population and engaging in guerrilla activities behind enemy lines. Heikal relates that

> Nasser had to send him back a complete description of the Sinai. 'It is a desert and we cannot conduct a people's liberation war in Sinai because there are no more than thirty thousand people in the whole of Sinai,' he told the Chinese. 'The whole area is arid and you can see for thirty and forty miles. The independent brigades would stand no chance.' But still the Chinese were not convinced.[69]

During the first half of the 1970s, following the Cultural Revolution, China's foreign policy was in some ways not so disruptive. China had become a permanent member of the UN Security Council and had welcomed an improvement in her relations with both the United States and Europe. However, if anything, Sino-Soviet relations deteriorated and their competition for influence amongst the Third World states and national liberation movements increased. China began to pursue the policy laid down by Mao that 'we should support whatever the enemy opposes and oppose whatever the enemy supports'. This policy meant that the USSR and China found themselves on opposing sides in the 1970 Jordanian civil war (when the Russians openly criticised the Chinese for encouraging the Palestinians to commit certain 'ill-considered actions');[70] in the attempted communist coup in Sudan in 1971 (the Chinese supported the return of President Jaafar al-Numeiri); in the Indo-Pakistani war in 1971; and in the Angolan and Rhodesian conflicts, when they supported different African factions.

While attacks from the Chinese press in the 1960s may have been responsible for a leftward shift in the Soviet analysis of the national liberation movement, in the 1970s such attacks have had quite the opposite effect. Now the Soviets tend to criticise the Chinese for detracting from international stability. As one *Izvestiya* article stated, the Chinese can no longer legitimately consider themselves to be a 'poor' country, since they have become 'vested with the extensive responsibility of a great power'.[71] However, Chinese policy has remained firmly based on the resolute support of all the Soviet Union's enemies. Thus the Chinese favour the establishment of a strong Europe and a Middle East devoid of Soviet influence. They welcomed Sadat's decision to abrogate the Soviet–Egyptian Treaty and have provided MiG-17 engines and military hardware to offset the loss of Soviet shipments. Even after Mao's death, the new leaders have continued to denounce the 'detestable sabre-rattling revisionists' of the Soviet Union, who have received 'defeat after defeat' in the Middle East. The Chinese leaders' stated intention to 'carry the struggle against imperialism, social imperialism and modern revisionism through to the end' and their apparent determination to 'never seek hegemony and . . . never be a superpower'[72] would seem to indicate that the state of Sino-Soviet relations is going to continue to be a major determinant of Soviet foreign policy for some time to come.

The Middle East

A further determinant of Soviet policy towards Egypt has been the state of relations not only between the Soviet Union and the other Middle Eastern states, but also between the Middle Eastern states themselves. The Soviet Union is severely constrained from pursuing a coherent and long-term Middle Eastern policy by the continual rivalries and conflicts amongst the regional actors. The formulation of Soviet policy towards Egypt therefore has been very much influenced by the state of Soviet and Egyptian relations with the rest of the Middle East. For example, in the two years following the 1958 Iraqi revolution when communist strength was high in that country, Soviet–Egyptian relations deteriorated due to the Soviet leaders' firm support for Qassem and the Egyptian leaders' equally firm condemnation of him. In another instance, the conflict between Egypt and Libya, in the early 1970s, precluded the Soviet Union from improving its relations with Libya's President Muammar al-Qadhafi. However, once Soviet–Egyptian relations deteriorated after 1974, the Soviet Union soon found the Libyans more amenable to increased Soviet activity in that country, including shipments of arms that were being denied to Egypt. When *al-Ahram* protested that Libya was receiving arms which she could only use against Egypt, *Pravda* issued a vehement denunciation of the article, saying that it was surprising to see 'press organs of an

Arab country which officially has friendly relations with the Soviet Union, joining suddenly in the chorus of imperialist and Zionist propaganda'.[73]

A further example is provided by the reaction to Egypt's attempts to achieve a Middle Eastern settlement. When Syria, Jordan and the Palestinians denounced Egypt's decision to sign an interim agreement with Israel in 1974, Sadat alleged that these protests and attempts 'to split the Arab ranks' were being orchestrated in Moscow. The Soviet leaders were indeed against the interim agreement and all such American-sponsored partial settlements;[74] and this coincidence of views between the Soviets on the one hand and the Syrians, Palestinians and Jordanians on the other, led to a temporary improvement of relations between all of these anti-Egypt forces, before the Lebanese civil war once again reintroduced old rivalries. Following Sadat's visit to Jerusalem, these forces once again found common cause with the Soviet Union, who took active measures to strengthen the unity of this group by mediating between the Syrians on the one hand and the Libyans, Iraqis and the PLO on the other, although not with complete success.

All these examples, therefore, illustrate the balance which the Soviet leaders have had to maintain between their various interests in the Middle East. This balance was relatively easy to keep while Nasser was alive and Egypt was the leader of the Arab world and the linchpin of Soviet policy. After President Sadat came to power, however, Egypt's primacy in Arab politics was undermined and Soviet policy-makers were forced to let the balance tilt away from Egypt towards the Fertile Crescent states.

As the foregoing discussion illustrates, Soviet policy towards Egypt was not formulated in a vacuum. Soviet decision-makers were constantly made aware of the impact of both the domestic and external environments on their policy towards Egypt. Equally, the formulation of Soviet policy was the outcome of a dynamic process involving the interaction between the domestic and external environments and the impact of this interaction, through feedback effects, on the formulation of future policy towards Egypt. However, the ability of any decision-making elite not only to maintain the homeostatic balance between these various contending influences, but also to formulate clear and reasonable objectives, and to achieve these objectives with the minimum commitment of resources, is very much dependent upon the structure and efficiency of the decision-making process itself, the subject of the next chapter.

7 Soviet Decision-making Structures and Processes

In the analysis of foreign policy, it has always been recognised that one of the most important influences on policy outcomes is the nature and structure of the decision-making process itself. When examining this process, it is necessary first of all to locate the centres of authority in the system. This is important not only because it reveals the institutional context of decisions but also because it leads to the consideration of wider issues such as the development of the decision-making process over time and the stability and regularity of that process during any given period. It is also important, secondly, to discover the impact of other factors outside the formal institutional setting which may affect both the structure of the decision-making process and the foreign policy decisions themselves. In particular the character of the political leadership and the role of interest groups and bureaucratic politics are variables which interact with the political institutions to produce a decision-making process which is often operationally quite different from formal or constitutional arrangements.

Brecher and other theorists, such as James Rosenau, David O. Wilkinson, Joseph Frankel, and K. J. Holsti, have long asserted that an important source of foreign policy emanates from the nature of the political system itself.[1] Analysts of Soviet foreign policy, however, have long complained of the apparently intractable problems involved in the study of the policy process, problems which one observer sees as 'the puzzling duplication of state and Party institutions, the perplexing fluctuations in their relationship, . . . the bewildering profusion of constitutional and institutional changes, the arbitrary tendency to ignore or short-circuit elaborately detailed institutional channels, and . . . the capricious and convulsive turnover of personalities'.[2] If these are some of the problems faced in the general analysis of the policy process, these difficulties are increased when the analyst seeks to examine the effect of that process on any particular foreign policy outcome. Yet the paucity of data does not diminish the importance of considering the formal institutional structure of Soviet foreign policy as well as the role which interest groups and bureaucratic coalitions have played in the formulation and implementation of Soviet policy towards Egypt.

THE POLITICAL STRUCTURE

The Soviet state and government organs shown in Figure 7.1 are constitutionally responsible for the formulation and conduct of Soviet foreign policy. The fact that they have not been allowed by the Party to exercise their constitutional powers fully does not, however, mean that they play no part in the policy process.

According to the Soviet Constitution, the *Supreme Soviet* is empowered to enact all basic legislation and to make all constitutional amendments; to examine and ratify all treaties; to declare war and peace; and to authorise all the decisions and decrees of the Praesidium and the Council of Ministers. However, because of its short sessions, the opportunities for open and free debate on foreign policy issues are severely attenuated. Rather, the formal sessions of the Supreme Soviet serve primarily as forums for announcing changes in foreign policy and soliciting support amongst both domestic and foreign audiences for the current line in international relations. In 1955, the Supreme Soviet gained entry to the Inter-Parliamentary Union and since then has engaged in a large number of parliamentary exchanges with other countries. In the case of Egypt, parliamentary delegations were exchanged frequently, especially during Nasser's time, including in 1961, 1964, 1967, 1969, 1970, and 1974. A special Soviet–Arab section of the Supreme Soviet Parliamentary Group has even been established. However, these activities have been important only in so far as they have provided those top Party officials who are also Supreme Soviet delegates with the opportunity to take part in formal intergovernmental exchanges.

Praesidium of the Supreme Soviet

The Praesidium of the Supreme Soviet carries out most of the day-to-day functions of the Supreme Soviet when that body is not in

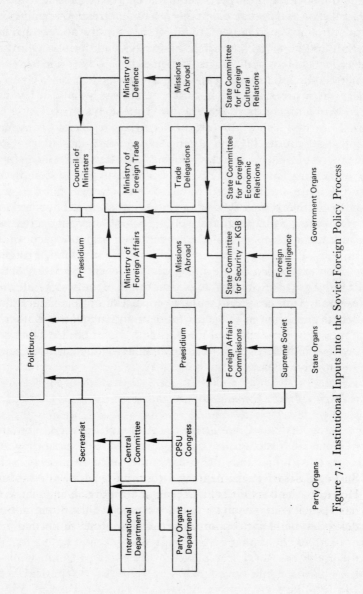

Figure 7.1 Institutional Inputs into the Soviet Foreign Policy Process

session, including the supervision of the Standing Committees of the Supreme Soviet and the preparation of reports. Its president acts as head of state and as such is empowered to sign treaties, appoint and recall diplomatic representatives of the USSR, and award all medals and honours. Khrushchev's split-second decision to award the orders of Hero of the Soviet Union to both Nasser and Marshal Amer, the Egyptian Minister of Defence, during his visit to Cairo in 1964, was criticised severely by Suslov and others because he had not been within his constitutional rights to issue such awards.[3] After his ouster, the new leadership took the decision at a specially convened Central Committee Plenum to define more clearly, and to separate, the powers of General Secretary, Prime Minister and President: and for some time after that President Podgornyy was seen to be playing quite an active and public role in foreign policy. It was Podgornyy for example who headed the delegation to Egypt in May 1971 to secure Sadat's signature on the Soviet–Egyptian Treaty of Friendship and Cooperation. However, even before his removal in June 1977, Podgornyy's constitutional right to sign foreign treaties was often superseded by Brezhnev, who as General Secretary of the CPSU did not have the right to sign on behalf of the Soviet state, but who was nevertheless frequently given special authorisation to do so.[4] This gap between the constitutional and actual powers of the Presidency was closed when the Supreme Soviet elected Brezhnev to replace Podgornyy, thus once again merging the Party and state at the highest levels.

The Foreign Affairs Committees

The Foreign Affairs Committees of the Council of the Union and the Council of Nationalities (the two houses of the Supreme Soviet) have increased their activities considerably since the passage of the 1967 Legislative Reform Act. As a result of this act, all standing committees now have the right to require any government official to give testimony; to subpoena any government documents; and to make recommendations to any government ministry for action.[5] In his report to the 25th CPSU Congress, Brezhnev stated that 'a considerable role [has] been played by the standing commissions of the USSR Supreme Soviet, whose activity has in general been markedly invigorated in recent years'.[6] The two Foreign Affairs Committees have been headed for some time by Mikhail Suslov and Boris Ponomaryov, both powerful CPSU Secretaries, perhaps indicating the inability of the Committees to formulate policy options independent of the Party. However, it is interesting that commensurate with the growth in the formal functions of the Committees, more publicity has been given to their activities and status. For example, in official communiqués, Ponomaryov is now listed as being a candidate member of the Politburo, a Secretary of the Party's Central Committee, and the Chairman of the Standing Committee for Foreign Affairs of the USSR Council of Nationalities.[7] In the absence of stenographic reports of their sessions, it is still difficult to judge the extent to which the Foreign Affairs Committees are making any real impact on the formulation of policy. However, a recent Soviet book on the workings of the Supreme Soviet hinted at the limited parameters within which the Committees work when it stated that they 'take an active and regular part in the diverse foreign policy activity *of the USSR Supreme Soviet*' (italics added).[8] This view is supported in another article which maintained that although the Council of Ministers is able to deal with 'the most important questions of government in all areas of the economic, political and cultural life of the country, . . . the standing committees operate only in the special areas of activity of the USSR Supreme Soviet'.[9]

Council of Ministers

The Soviet Constitution draws the distinction between the organs of state *power* (which consist of the Supreme Soviet and its subsidiary structure in the Union Republics) and the organs of state *administration* which are theoretically appointed by and responsible to the organs of state power. At the apex of the administrative pyramid is the Council of Ministers and its Praesidium. The new Soviet Constitution empowers the Council of Ministers to exercise 'general direction in the sphere of relations with foreign states',[10] and more specifically to supervise diplomatic, economic, cultural, and scientific cooperation with foreign countries. Unlike the Supreme Soviet, the Council of Ministers and its subordinate ministries and state committees do exercise much of the power invested in them by the Constitution. The Council of Ministers, along with the Ministries of Defence, Foreign Affairs and Foreign Trade and the State Committees for Security (KGB) and Foreign Economic Relations, are the primary bodies in charge of the day-to-day administration of Soviet foreign policy with non-communist countries. They also supply information and technical expertise to those in the highest echelons of the Party who are actually responsible for the formulation of policy. The State Committee for Foreign Cultural Relations which is also included in Figure 7.1 was incorporated into the Ministry of Foreign Affairs in 1968.

After the death of Stalin, the top Party organs began to reassert their traditional and pre-eminent role in the making of foreign policy. Even Foreign Minister Molotov, speaking at the 20th Party Congress, was forced to concede that 'never before has our Party Central Committee and its Praesidium [the Politburo] been engaged so actively with questions of foreign policy as during the present period'.[11] While the main function of the *Party Congress*, which meets on average once every four years, is to announce and adopt the current line on foreign policy for the Middle East and other areas, as set out by the leadership, the Central Committee and the Secretariat, which are nominally elected by the Congress, do have a more active role.

The Central Committee

The Central Committee meets in formal session at least twice a year and frequently considers questions of foreign policy. However, as with the sessions of the Supreme Soviet and the Party Congress, unanimity is the rule rather than the exception (as discussed below, the plenum which debated the 1967 June war was apparently one such exception). Foreign Minister Gromyko stated in 1971 that the plenary sessions of the Central Committee have 'invariably approved the Politburo's foreign policy activity'.[12] Although the plenary sessions may fulfil little more than a 'rubber stamp' function, the Central Committee itself, as a body of full-time paid officials or *apparatchiki* responsible for the day-to-day affairs of both the Party and the state, has very considerable power indeed. The Central Committee is divided into a number of functionally defined departments which are supervised by the Party's *Secretariat*. The *International Department* is in charge of Soviet relations with all the non-ruling communist parties, the national liberation movements and the non-communist states, including Egypt. Boris Ponomaryov, a candidate member of the Politburo and a Central Committee Secretary, has been in charge of the International Department since 1961. When it comes to relations with the national liberation movements and communist parties, matters thought to be normally outside the jurisdiction of the Foreign Ministry, the International Department has considerable power both to enter into direct relations with these groups and to provide them with the necessary support. Thus for example, Heikal claimed that after one of Yasser Arafat's trips to Moscow in 1969, 'the Soviet Central Committee . . . decided to give the Palestine resistance movement arms worth $500,000'.[13]

The *Party Organs Department* is responsible for the control of the *nomenklatura* lists for all diplomatic appointments abroad and for the important positions in the foreign policy apparatus in Moscow.[14] Although the *Department for Liaison with Communist and Workers' Parties of the Socialist Countries* is not responsible for Soviet relations with Egypt, nevertheless its head (K. Katushev until 1977) forms part of the triumvirate of Party Secretaries along with Ponomaryov and Suslov who are responsible for the ideological thrust of Soviet foreign policy, and for ensuring ideological coherence and consistency in policy formulation.[15] It was these departments of the Central Committee and the Secretaries who head them that Valerian Zorin, a Soviet diplomat, was referring to when he stated that 'the Central Committee of the CPSU provides day-to-day direction of the foreign policy measures and of the diplomatic moves implemented by the Ministry of Foreign Affairs of the USSR, ensuring successful attainment of the foreign policy objectives of the Soviet state which have been established by the Party'.[16]

The Politburo

By 'the Party' Zorin meant 'the Politburo' for it is this body which has the ultimate authority for the formulation of Soviet policy. Although minutes or reports of its deliberations do not exist, nevertheless quite a lot is known about its 'operational code', its sphere of competence and, of course, its composition. In his report to the 25th Party Congress, Brezhnev stated that the Politburo had met 215 times since the last Congress, or about once a week.[17] The scant information available suggests that the emphasis has always been on the desirability of obtaining unanimity within the Politburo before a decision is taken, but that matters are discussed fully and openly prior to any decision.[18] In accordance with Lenin's rules of democratic centralism, which govern decision-making and Party organisation in the Soviet Union, once a decision is taken, it is final, with the views of the majority binding on the minority. It seems that since no official or individual is an automatic member of the Politburo, continued refusal to comply with the decisions reached by the majority would result in demotion.

Turning to the question of the Politburo's sphere of competence, or the extent of its monopoly over Soviet policy-making, in the realm of Soviet foreign policy and Soviet–Egyptian relations, the Politburo does seem to have involved itself in a surprising amount of detail. Brezhnev stated at the 25th Party Congress that the Politburo has given 'a great deal of attention to various aspects of the country's external political activity and the strengthening of its defences'.[19] It certainly seems clear that the Politburo, and especially its General Secretary, is involved in drawing up the general line of Soviet foreign policy on such important matters as East–West relations and Soviet policy toward the socialist bloc and the national liberation movements. Although one would not have expected Politburo members to be actively involved in the minutiae of Soviet–Egyptian relations, nevertheless on several occasions they did concern themselves with the actual direction of Soviet policy. In 1958, when the Iraqi revolution and the Lebanese civil war seemed poised to spark off a major Western intervention to prevent the overthrow of the remaining pro-Western regimes, Nasser flew to Moscow to appeal for direct Soviet aid. Heikal, who accompanied the Egyptian President, relates that Nasser had private talks for two hours with Khrushchev who steadfastly refused to intervene. When Nasser persisted, Khruschchev 'went off to discuss Nasser's request with members of the Politburo who were waiting in a nearby *dacha*'. They agreed to hold strictly limited manoeuvres on the Bulgarian–Turkish border, but made it clear that Nasser could expect nothing more.[20] Moreover, although the Party Organs Department controls the *nomenklatura* for the position of Soviet ambassador to Cairo, it would seem that the Politburo actually chooses the candidate. This was confirmed by Vladimir Vinogradov, the Soviet ambassador to Cairo, who told Heikal in 1970 that 'before I came here there was a meeting of the Politburo and they decided to nominate me for the Cairo Embassy'.[21]

A further instance of top-level activity in Soviet–Egyptian relations is provided by the account of Nasser's meeting with the

Soviet leadership in January 1970, at the height of Israel's 'deep penetration' bombing of targets near Cairo. The Soviet side consisted of Brezhnev, Kosygin, Podgornyy, Grechko, Sergei Vinogradov, (the Soviet ambassador in Egypt at that time, not to be confused with his successor Vladimir Vinogradov) and General Katyshkin, the head of the Soviet military mission in Cairo. When Nasser demanded that the Soviets send their own pilots and missile crews to Egypt to participate actively in its defence, it was decided that this 'was such a critical step that it should be put before the whole Politburo'. The Politburo, and twelve Soviet marshals to represent the military's point of view, were summoned from all over the country to make their decision.[22] A final example which Heikal provides about the workings of the Politburo does not relate specifically to Soviet–Egyptian relations, but is an excellent example of the extent to which Brezhnev, Podgornyy and Kosygin appear to have been collectively responsible for much of the running of foreign policy. The incident occurred in June 1970, during a meeting between Nasser and the Soviet leadership, at which Heikal was also present:

> At one point the door opened and a senior official from the Ministry of Foreign Affairs came into the room and gave a piece of paper to Vladimir Vinogradov . . . Vinogradov gave the paper to Gromyko . . . who read it, got up and took it to Kosygin. Kosygin read it . . . Brezhnev read it . . . Podgorny read it . . . Then Brezhnev signed it and gave it to Kosygin, who signed it too. Then Podogorny signed . . . When it was all over, Brezhnev saw that the whole Egyptian delegation was staring at him, and presumably felt that he ought to give some sort of explanation . . . 'We have received information that there will be an attempt at a coup against General Siad in Somalia tonight. We have accordingly decided to send him a telegram of warning. We have now seen this telegram and approved it'.
> Later, as we were going out of the meeting Nasser said to me ' . . . it is too bureaucratic. If a telegram to General Siad in Somalia needs the signature of all those three, then we are in trouble. Now I understand why our requests take such a long time to produce results'.[23]

These tentative insights into the actual working of collective leadership are particularly interesting because they suggest first of all that the Politburo as a whole is collectively responsible for making decisions; that in some instances the top Soviet leadership has felt constrained to elicit the views of groups outside the Politburo; and finally that the triumvirate of Brezhnev, Kosygin and Podgornyy as representatives of the Party apparat, the Council of Ministers and the Supreme Soviet Praesidium respectively, appeared to act as an interdependent unit in the foreign policy sphere. This last point supports the contention that at least until Podgornyy was ousted, there was greater collective leadership and institutional diffusion of power at the top. It also coincides with the views put forward in a recent book on Soviet foreign policy to which Foreign Minister Gromyko was a key contributor:

> In the interests of implementing the foreign policy line charted by the 24th Congress, it has become the practice for the key talks conducted by delegations and leaders of the USSR with representatives of foreign countries to be examined collectively by the leading organs of the CPSU and the Soviet state, namely the Political Bureau of the CPSU Central Committee, the Praesidium of the Supreme Soviet of the USSR and the Council of Ministers of the USSR.[24]

Although these joint meetings apparently do still take place,[25] there has also been a steady increase in Brezhnev's power following, and even before, his election as President of the Praesidium of the Supreme Soviet. It is now common for other Soviet leaders to refer deferentially to his central role in foreign policy-making, as Gromyko did in a speech delivered during the visit by Syria's Foreign Minister Abd al-Halim Khaddam at the end of November 1977, when he said that 'expressing the will of the whole Soviet people, the Soviet leadership and Leonid Brezhnev personally, are determined to continue to strengthen cooperation with Syria'.[26] Brezhnev, as General Secretary of the Party, has a large staff of researchers and advisers who fill a function similar to the US President's White House staff. They prepare briefs, take charge of appointments and are sometimes even present during negotiations with other heads of state. During the visits to Moscow of Libyan leader Major Abd al-Salam Jallud in February 1978 and Yasser Arafat in March, Moscow Radio reported that Brezhnev's personal assistant, Yevgeniy Samoteykin, was also present at both sets of meetings between Brezhnev and the two Arab leaders.[27] This inner core of personal advisers within the apparat certainly puts Brezhnev in an advantageous position *vis-à-vis* other Politburo members, who do not appear to have such wide access to information over the whole range of domestic and foreign policy issues.

In Soviet–Egyptian relations, the personal style of the General Secretary has had an important bearing on the state of relations at any given time. As has been discussed in Chapter 2 Khrushchev's flamboyant personality and his ill-considered statements frequently caused a rift in relations. On the whole, Brezhnev's style has been more pragmatic and cautious and his personal involvement in the troubled state of Soviet–Egyptian relations has been evaluated favourably on the whole by Egyptian leaders. Sadat, in an interview published in February 1978 offered the following, typically outspoken, appraisal of those Soviet leaders most involved in foreign policy:

> President Brezhnev is the only statesman among the Soviet leaders, and I can bear witness that he was the only one who used to intervene to resolve the crises that often occurred between me and Podgornyy and Kosygin. . . . The Soviets judged the position correctly when they removed Podgornyy. He disturbed the serenity of any relations between the Soviets and Egypt. The Soviets will undoubtedly do the same with Ponomaryov. He is the worst man there, the worst tool they use to convey incorrect information and rash judgements. His mistakes were proven dozens of times in Egypt and elsewhere. One of his mistakes was that he expected a communist coup to overthrow me [referring to the Ali Sabri group].[28]

The preceding discussion has elucidated the authority which the various state and Party institutions have in the formulation of Soviet foreign policy in general and Soviet–Egyptian relations in particular. However, many important questions remain unanswered. What are the relationships between these institutions? What are the communication flows which occur between them? Is the Politburo an independent and unitary actor or is it composed of men who represent powerful interests? To the extent that these questions can be answered with any degree of certainty, they can only be answered by examining not just the institutions but also the competition between the ruling elites and the role of interest groups.

COMPETING ELITES AND INTEREST GROUPS

Analysts of Soviet politics have long debated the exact nature of the Soviet decision-making process. Advocates of the traditional totalitarian approach contend that Soviet foreign policy is the outcome of decisions made by a highly centralised and unified elite, headed by a single dictator, acting to maximise Soviet capabilities according to a clearly defined and purposive set of values, principles and objectives.[29] Yet with the changes in the Soviet system following Stalin's death, and with the advances made in the study of comparative politics, analysts have been concentrating more on examining the extent to which outcomes are the products of competition within the ruling elite and demands on that elite by interest groups and bureaucratic coalitions.[30] In the making of Soviet policy towards Egypt, there are indications that outcomes were frequently influenced by pressures from vested interests within the system. In particular, representatives of the Foreign Ministry, the Party apparat, the Trade Unions, the Academy of Sciences, and the military have been involved on several occasions in debates over the correct nature, and future direction, of Soviet–Egyptian policy. Yet due to the continued problems of data availability, the discussion presented cannot hope to detail anything more than instances in which such debates have become public knowledge, thus precluding the possibility of drawing more general conclusions about the structures and processes of Soviet decision-making over time.

The Foreign Ministry

The Foreign Ministry, as the institution with the constitutional responsibility for the day-to-day running of Soviet foreign policy, was one of the major bureaucracies to be affected by the strengthening of the Party in the post-Stalin period. Molotov, who had been Foreign Minister almost without break since 1939, had built up a highly efficient and closely knit staff. He had assumed prime responsibility along with Stalin for both the formulation and implementation of foreign policy. When Khrushchev sought to reorient foreign policy in the mid-1950s, his efforts were impeded by Molotov and the Foreign Ministry apparat. In particular, Molotov is said to have opposed giving arms to Egypt in 1955 in recognition of Nasser's role as a leader of the growing group of non-aligned states.[31] Following his demotion, Molotov was forced to admit that 'we still suffer frequently from an underestimation of the possibilities which have opened before us in the postwar period. This shortcoming has also appeared in the work of the Ministry of Foreign Affairs which was pointed out in good time by our Party Central Committee'.[32] In negotiating with Nasser, Khrushchev had by-passed the Foreign Ministry, using his own emissary, Dmitri Shepilov, who replaced Molotov as Foreign Minister following the latter's demotion. However, Shepilov himself was dismissed in 1957 following similar charges of using the Foreign Ministry to obstruct the implementation of Party policy. Thereafter, the International Department of the Central Committee seems to have assumed greater responsibility for the formulation of policy towards Egypt, at least until April 1973, when the Foreign Minister was once again included within the Politburo as a full member.

It is difficult to assess the effect of Gromyko's promotion on the Foreign Ministry's influence in the making of Soviet policy towards Egypt. In his speech to the 25th Party Congress, Brezhnev declared that in the future, the Party would be paying even more attention 'than before to the control and verification of decisions taken'.[33] Interviews with officials in the Soviet Ministry of Foreign Affairs confirmed that the role of the Ministry in influencing the formulation and implementation of Soviet policy towards Egypt is constantly held in check by the Party. Party units within the Ministry ensure the implementation of central directives, while the activities of the Central Committee apparat largely parallel the work of the Ministry in the provision of information and the formulation of policy. Although the Ministry does now have direct access to the Politburo through Gromyko, it is not clear that this has led to a corresponding increase in the Ministry's role in policy-making. A Foreign Ministry official in charge of relations with Egypt claimed when interviewed that in the pre-decisional stage, the Ministry's role was to make proposals to the Politburo *through* the Central Committee apparat. The acceptance of any proposal, according to this official, was certainly not taken for granted; and the dependence of the Ministry on the Central Committee as a channel of access to policy formulation had not been substantially affected by Gromyko's promotion to the Politburo. This view was contradicted, however, by the Director of an Institute of the Academy of Sciences, who claimed that the role of the International Department of the Central Committee had been overemphasised in the West and that the Ministry of Foreign Affairs was clearly more important *because* Gromyko was a full Politburo member, whereas Ponomaryov had not been able to rise above candidate status.[34]

The Party Apparat

The Party apparat would seem to be the focus for the making of Soviet policy towards Egypt. Yet it cannot be assumed that it represents a single coherent body of like-minded officials whose views necessarily coincide at all times. In 1961, for example, the debate on the role of indigenous communist parties in the Third World led to a split between Khrushchev and Ponomaryov, the head of the International Department, who openly advocated communist takeovers in Egypt and elsewhere.[35] The debates which took place at the June Central Committee plenum following Egypt's defeat in the 1967 war provide a further instance of splits within the Party. In particular, there were some who reportedly questioned the benefits to be derived from continued support for the Arab states. Among them was Nikolai Yegorichev, the first secretary of the powerful Moscow Party organisation, who had headed a CPSU delegation to Cairo earlier in that year. Yegorichev made a major speech at the plenum, the text of which was inexplicably never published or quoted from. At the same meeting, Yuri Andropov, the KGB head, was promoted to candidate membership of the Politburo, while Yegorichev a week later was replaced by V. Grishin, the head of the Trade Unions. Yegorichev was made ambassador to Denmark, and subsequent reports suggest that he was demoted for his outspoken criticism of the Party leadership for 'squandering Soviet arms and prestige in support of Arab states'.[36] In addition to the views put forward by the International Department and members of the Central Committee, there is also Brezhnev's own group of personal advisers within the Party apparat. Although little is known of their views and activities, it is interesting that Brezhnev should choose to have his own adviser on Middle East affairs, Yevgeniy Samoteykin, to be present at recent negotiations with Arab leaders, rather than members of the International Department. It is possible that this may reflect a split between Brezhnev and Ponomaryov over Middle East policy. Sadat's statement, quoted earlier in this chapter, that Ponomaryov had been responsible for the attempts by Ali Sabri's group to take power following Nasser's death would support this view, although it seems highly unlikely that any direct Soviet involvement would not have been the joint policy of the entire Politburo.

Trade Unions

The leaders of the Trade Unions are another group whose views have sometimes been in conflict with established policy. The trade Unions have played a not insubstantial role in Soviet policy toward Egypt inasmuch as they have been responsible for encouraging the development of, and maintaining contacts with, the Egyptian trade union movement. That movement played an active role in organising and politicising Egyptian workers, particularly in the larger industrial complexes, such as the one in Helwan; and it was at the forefront of anti-government activity during the long periods when the Egyptian Communist Party was either proscribed or disbanded. The Soviet trade union newspaper, *Trud*, was always amongst the first to condemn any suppression of the 'progressive forces' by either Nasser or Sadat. A recent comparison of the attitudes toward the Middle East expressed by both *Pravda* and *Trud* revealed that of the two papers, *Trud* followed 'a more uncompromising "dogmatic" line towards the United States as well as towards the Arab regimes', and urged 'a more revolutionary, "party-oriented" approach' towards the Arab world, implying that support should be withdrawn to those Arab governments who continue to suppress progressive elements. The author's hypothesis that *Trud* reflected the attitudes of Shelepin, who headed the Trade Unions at the time would, if true, further support the view that Shelepin's dismissal in 1976 was due to his consistent opposition to Brezhnev's policy of *détente* and the avoidance of direct confrontation with the West.[37]

Academy of Sciences

The research institutes within the Academy of Sciences appear to be one of the few interest groups outside the Party and state apparatus which has influenced Soviet policy towards Egypt with any regularity. Interviews conducted with academics doing work on Egypt revealed that reports to the Central Committee and the Council of Ministers form a major component of their output and are encorporated into their annual plans; that working parties of experts from various Institutes draw up joint reports which are forwarded to the relevant governmental or Party department; and that experts in the Institutes play an important role in maintaining informal links between the government and Egyptian embassy officials resident in Moscow.[38] Although the constraints imposed by the centralised and authoritarian nature of the system prevent Soviet academics from acting as an organised pressure group in the same way that their Western counterparts can, nevertheless it seemed clear both that they *expect* to be consulted on policy issues and that, failing this, there are a number of channels available to them for the articulation of interests and views. One is by secondment to a government ministry or cooptation onto either the Central Committee or one of the related front organisations, such as the Afro-Asian Solidarity Committee. Many of the researchers currently engaged in work on Egypt have worked in the government and most have spent some time in Cairo. The former Director of the Institute of Orientology, R. A. Ul'yanovskiy, was promoted to the International Department of the Central Committee as Ponomaryov's deputy, thus giving his associates in that Institute a valuable contact in the highest echelons of the Party. Equally, the directors of the Institute of World Economy and International Relations (Inozemtsev) and the Institute for the Study of the USA and Canada (Arbatov) are both Central Committee candidate members, with the result that the departments for the Arab countries, which exist in both Institutes, also have a channel to top officials. The researchers in the Middle East department of the Institute of Africa have a powerful ally in their director, who is Foreign Minister Gromyko's son. An informative interview with the Deputy Director of one Institute revealed that if he wanted to put forward his views on a particular policy, he could either publish an article in the Institute's journal, or contact one of his friends or former students who occupy various Party and governmental positions. The decision on whom to contact would depend, in his words, on the nature of the proposal and 'who you knew where'. While the role of the research institutes may not be highly 'visible', nevertheless, their direct and indirect influence in the policy-making process cannot be discounted.

Military

Of all the groups which have played a part in the formulation of Soviet policy towards Egypt, perhaps it is the Military which has exerted the most consistent influence, particularly in recent years. The Soviet Union's strategic interest in Egypt and the supply of arms and military assistance have provided a strong motivation for military involvement in the formulation of policy towards Egypt. Yet the military's influence has not always been strong. In 1957, Khrushchev promoted the Minister of Defence, Marshal Zhukov, to the Politburo in return for the support which the military had given to Khrushchev in defeating the 'anti-Party group' that had sought to oust him. Zhukov took advantage of his promotion by engaging in efforts to reduce Party control within the armed forces. Moreover, during the 1957 Syrian crisis, when Baghdad Pact states threatened to invade Syria to prevent an alleged takeover by the Communist Party there, Zhukov, in an unauthorised statement over Albanian radio, declared the Soviet military's readiness 'to strike at any military adventure organised by the United States near our southern borders'.[39] Khrushchev appeared unexpectedly at a Soviet–Turkish reception a few days later, announcing that the Syrian conflict should be resolved peacefully and that Zhukov had been relieved of his posts. Following his demotion, military influence in the formulation of Soviet policy towards the Middle East waned until after the 1967 war.

With the massive Soviet involvement in the rebuilding of the Egyptian army following the Six-day War and the signature in March 1968 of an agreement allowing the Soviet navy to use Egyptian ports,[40] the role of the military in decision-making appears to have been dramatically increased. The head of the Soviet military mission in Cairo, General Katyshkin, and the Chief of Staff of the Soviet Army, M. V. Zakharov, who had taken personal responsibility for retraining the armed forces in Egypt, were almost always included along with the Minister of Defence in top-level negotiations with the Egyptians. In 1970, as stated previously, the decision to put Soviet forces in combat positions in Egypt was taken jointly by the Politburo and twelve Soviet marshals. Then in 1973, the Minister of Defence, Marshal Grechko, was included in the Politburo, thus restoring to the military the direct access to the top decision-making body which it had lost in 1957.

In addition to the Politburo, the military also has considerable representation in the Defence Council, a body which recently has been rehabilitated after losing the position of pre-eminence it enjoyed in the decision-making process under Stalin. Although little is known of its activities or composition, its existence is in fact enshrined in the new constitution which in Article 121 states that the Praesidium of the USSR Supreme Soviet 'forms the USSR Defence Council and ratifies its composition'. Reports suggest that Brezhnev is its chairman, with the chairman of the Council of Ministers (Kosygin), the Minister of Defence (first Grechko and then Ustinov), the Party secretary in charge of defence industries (Ustinov and his successor, although one has not yet been named), the Foreign Minister (Gromyko), the KGB head (Andropov), the Military-Industrial Commission head (Smirnov), the Chief of the General Staff (Ogarkov) and other senior military officers among its members.[41] It is not clear what the sphere of competence of this Council is, although it is believed to be almost a subgroup of the Politburo with authority on all the most vital military and strategic matters. Such a development would suggest a major role for the military in the formulation of foreign and defence policy generally, as well as policy towards the Middle East and Egypt.

The military's centrality in Soviet–Egyptian relations was illustrated both by the role they played as a vital communication channel between Moscow and Cairo and by the development in their own newspapers of a distinctive and independent approach to the Middle East. In examining the most frequent channels of communication between the Soviet and Egyptian leaders, an interesting and surprisingly regular pattern emerged. After 1967, with the buildup of Soviet military influence in Egypt, many of the most important communications between Moscow and the Soviet embassy in Cairo appear to have gone via the Ministry of Defence, completely bypassing the Ministry of Foreign Affairs. A direct telephone link was established between the office of the Military Mission in Cairo and the Ministry of Defence in 1970, and Brezhnev reportedly was kept informed by Marshal Grechko of events in Egypt, particularly during the War of Attrition and the October 1973 war. While the Soviet ambassador in Cairo was responsible for most of the direct dealings with the top Egyptian leaders, he often relayed messages directly from Brezhnev, the Politburo, the International Department of the Central Committee and the Ministry of Defence. It is interesting that in all of the accounts of dealings between the two sides published by Heikal and Sadat, not a single instance was cited by them in which the Soviet ambassador delivered messages from the Ministry of Foreign Affairs. Of course, the embassy in Cairo must have had dealings with that Ministry, but it would appear that these may have been of such routine detail

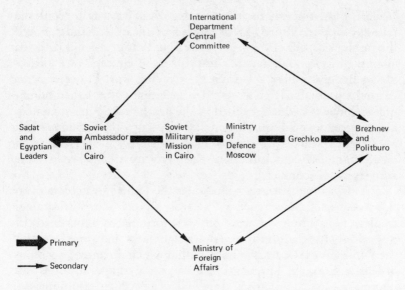

Figure 7.2 Soviet–Egyptian Action Channels 1970–76

as not to warrant reporting by the Egyptian side.[42] The primary channels used in Soviet–Egyptian relations after 1967—channels which underline the vital role of the military in these communications—are presented in Figure 7.2.

A comparison of articles on the Middle East published by both *Pravda* and *Krasnaya zvezda* revealed a clear divergence of attitudes between the two papers, a divergence which one analyst hypothesised also reflected the divisions between the Party and military leaders.[43] Firstly, *Krasnaya zvezda* devoted much more attention to the Middle East than did *Pravda*, with the former stressing more than the latter the repercussions of events in that area on Soviet security and the global correlation of forces. Equally, whereas *Pravda* attempted to discount the 'Western hysteria concerning the so-called Soviet threat',[44] the Ministry of Defence paper upheld the Soviet military presence in the Middle East which was 'in keeping with the state interests of the Soviet Union and the Arab countries'.[45] Particularly in the early 1970s, the military press favoured a strengthening of the Soviet Union's direct commitment to Egyptian defence and hailed the 1971 Treaty of Friendship with Egypt which would have 'a substantial effect on the situation in the

Middle East, since it includes Soviet commitments to continue military support of the UAR'.[46] *Pravda*, on the other hand, ignored the military aspect of the treaty, stressing that it was not directed against anyone, and that it constituted the epitome of a peace-loving Leninist policy.[47] During the October war, *Krasnaya zvezda* carried a particularly vehement denunciation of the Israeli bombing of Damascus which resulted in the death of a Soviet citizen. It also referred to an alleged Israeli plan to occupy the Syrian capital, a reference which may have been intended to persuade the recalcitrant political leaders of the necessity to intervene more actively in the conflict.[48]

The preceding discussion illustrates the variety of influences on the making of Soviet policy towards Egypt. The institutional framework within which decisions were formulated underlined the disparity between constitutional arrangements and practice, with the Politburo as the central body within which the major decisions are made. Equally, however, the discussion of competing elites and interest groups emphasised the extent to which decisions are frequently the result of a process involving consultation with interested parties, conflict within the ruling circle and compromise between divergent opinions. Outcomes were certainly not the result of decisions taken by a highly centralised and unified elite, headed by a single dictator, as totalitarian theorists would assert. Nor, however, were decisions solely the result of the free interplay of equally balanced groups and bureaucracies seeking to enhance their own institutional self-interest, as analysts who advocate the applicability of the bureaucratic politics model to the Soviet Union maintain.[49] Rather, the decision-making process was characterised by the continued centrality of Party organs working together with the other major groups which have a vested interest in influencing policy outcomes. The high incidence of interpenetration of Party and state organs, the reliance on informal contacts in the highest echelons as a channel for the articulation of demands, and the frequency of cross-bureaucratic communication suggests a decision-making process based on the necessity for continuous coalition-building and consensus-formation. Given the apparently irregular and amorphous nature of this process, it is perhaps surprising that Soviet leaders found it at all possible to formulate a relatively consistent set of objectives to guide their policy towards Egypt—the subject of the next chapter.

8 Soviet Objectives Towards Egypt

The foreign policy objectives pursued by any state are the end result of interactions between values, images and capabilities. Whereas a state's values will determine what is desirable, the capabilities, as perceived by decision-makers, will determine what is feasible. The general objectives of Soviet foreign policy are the outcome of such an interaction.

A basic value of any state, and the Soviet Union is no exception, is the continued survival of that state as a practical unit. Thus most decision-makers would regard the security of their state's territory and the perpetuation of a particular political, economic and social system as paramount and worthy of ultimate material and human sacrifices. Ever since Stalin's proclamation of 'socialism in one country', Soviet leaders have upheld both the security of Soviet territory and the protection and strengthening of socialism within it as the two basic values of Soviet foreign policy. Two further and related values also influence the formulation of Soviet objectives. One is the desire to weaken Western capitalism, not only because it threatens the security of the USSR, but also because only with capitalism's downfall can the fourth and ultimate value of Soviet leaders be realised—the victory of communism on a worldwide basis.

These values are loosely ranked in hierarchical order with the protection of territorial integrity as the core value, and the victory of communism as the ultimate value which encompasses and assumes the achievement of the three preceding values. The extent to which Soviet decision-makers will actively seek the fulfilment of the ultimate value will depend on the perceptions they hold of their own capabilities *vis-à-vis* the capabilities of the states they seek to influence. The end product of this process of balancing values with capabilities is an assessment of what the Soviets call 'the current correlation of forces' between the socialist system and the forces in opposition to it. In the realm of East–West relations, this assessment resulted first in a policy of 'peaceful coexistence' and more recently in the policy of *détente*.

POLITICAL AND STRATEGIC OBJECTIVES

The political and strategic objectives toward Egypt were also formulated within the context of this 'global correlation of forces'. In this respect, three key elements were constantly in interaction to produce shifts and reappraisals in Soviet objectives: the perceptions Soviet leaders held of Western intentions in the Middle East, the importance attached to movements for national liberation and non-alignment, and the significance Soviet leaders assigned to changes in their own economic and military capabilities.

Soviet leaders have tended to interpret Western activities in the Middle East as attempts both to use the area as a base for aggression against the Soviet Union and to retain or establish a colonial foothold in the area for the purpose of protecting their economic interests. This dominant image of Western motives was extended to include not only American, British and French activities in the area, but also the activities of Israel, Jordan, Saudi Arabia and other pro-Western governments who were variously described as 'lackeys of imperialism', 'the tools of Western monopolies', or 'hangers-on from a colonial past'. Rather than viewing the many conflicts in the Middle East as being basically region-generated, Soviet decision-makers have tended to interpret events through the much wider perspective of the global struggle between 'imperialism' and 'socialism'.

With the emergence of states whose economic base was primarily feudalist or capitalist but whose foreign policy was anti-Western, Soviet decision-makers were faced with a dilemma. They could either lend their support only to those leaders or groups actually committed to the construction of a communist society, or they could throw their weight behind those governments pursuing an anti-Western foreign policy. In the case of Egypt, and indeed in most newly independent countries, the choice was between the numerically small and politically weak Egyptian Communist Party and a 'national bourgeois' government already firmly in power. The Soviet decision to support the latter, at least while Nasser was alive, was based on the requirements of Soviet security and on a practical assessment of the strength of the Egyptian Communist Party. To use the Egyptian communists as the instrument for achieving the dual objectives of strengthening Soviet security and weakening Western imperialism would have been a long process, might ultimately have failed, and would certainly have increased Western resolve to maintain a presence in the Middle East. This argument was fully appreciated and frequently reiterated by Soviet commentators themselves.[1] The final determinant in the formulation of Soviet objectives has been the growth in Soviet military power.[2] It was these three factors—perceptions of Western intentions, attitudes toward the national liberation movements, and shifts in Soviet capabilities—that have shaped Soviet objectives towards Egypt since 1955.

1955–58

The establishment of Western bases on territory adjacent to the Soviet southern perimeter was perceived by Soviet decision-makers as a major threat to their core value of security. As a result, beginning in 1955, the Soviet government made public its willingness to commit resources to the breakup of Western military blocs in the Middle East; and from 1955–58 this objective was to dominate Soviet relations with Egypt. The primacy of the strategic objective was such that it overshadowed and even dictated the Soviet view of Middle Eastern politics. Soviet statements on the Arab–Israeli conflict, for example, especially prior to the Suez crisis, made it clear that without Western interference in the area, there would be no reason why the Arabs and Israelis should not reach an amicable agreement—a view certainly not shared by Egypt and her Arab neighbours.[3]

The single-minded pursuit of the strategic objective also resulted in the support of any Arab government willing to follow an anti-Western foreign policy, irrespective of the domestic policies pursued. Despite their persecution of communists, the Egyptian regime continued to receive massive Soviet support. A statement by Khrushchev in 1957 gives a clear indiction of the primacy attached to Egypt's anti-imperialist foreign policy:

> You know, of course, that many Arabs . . . are very remote from Communist ideas. In Egypt, for instance, many Communists are held in prison. The leaders of the Arab countries are nationalists.

They are against colonial slavery and they stand for the consolidation of their political and economic independence. . . . [In the Middle East] we do not pursue any objectives but one, that the peoples be freed from colonial dependence. . . . Is Nasser a Communist? Certainly not. But nevertheless we support Nasser. We do not want to turn him into a Communist and he does not want to turn us into nationalists.[4]

1958–67

However, the period from 1958–67 witnessed a departure from the near-monopoly which the strategic-military objective had exerted. The 1958 revolution in Iraq, which led to that country's withdrawal from the Baghdad Pact and to the end of Western hopes of establishing an Arab-centred security system, was the major event which precipitated the reappraisal. Yet, the advances in Soviet and American military technology[5], the improvements in the Soviet economic capability, the strengthening of pro-Soviet and quasi-socialist trends in Egypt, and pressure from leftist elements within the international communist movement, were all factors which influenced the reformulation.

After 1958, other objectives became more apparent. Soviet decision-makers were increasingly concerned to elicit Egypt's support for the Soviet stand on various international issues, such as the recognition of the Chinese People's Republic and the German Democratic Republic; the denunciation of Western activities in the Congo and South-East Asia; the establishment of a Soviet-proposed *troika* system for the UN Secretariat; and, of course, disarmament. While there were differences between the Egyptians and Soviets over both the Congo and the *troika* proposals, nevertheless, there was a broad coincidence of views between the two countries on most other international issues.

Moreover, pressure from leftist elements within the Communist movement, and particularly from the Chinese, forced the Soviet leaders to re-examine the question of whether the USSR should continue to expend resources on strengthening a regime which may be anti-Western in its foreign policy but which was also anti-communist in its domestic policy. After the 1960 meeting of 81 Communist and Workers' parties in Moscow, the Soviet evaluation of Nasser's regime began to include appraisals of his domestic policies. And between 1958 and 1961, during the period of the union between Egypt and Syria when the communist parties in these two countries were suppressed, these appraisals were far from complementary. Without naming any particular country, Khrushchev, at the 22nd Party Congress in 1961, reported that there were elements within the ruling classes of certain developing countries who were attempting to 'hamper the further development of the national revolution. Such forces are steering along the line of appeasement with imperialism abroad and feudalism inside their countries and are resorting to dictatorial methods'.[6] Editorial comment in Soviet newspapers did not, however, refrain from mentioning Egypt by name. One such article signed by 'Observer' described Egypt as 'a society in which exploiters rule and people make speeches about democracy, while for their political beliefs progressive people languish in torture chambers.'[7]

After 1961, however, Nasser enacted a number of progressive measures including the nationalisation of banks and industries, the promulgation of the National Charter and the release of communists from prison. All of these measures met with the broad approval of the Soviet leaders and resulted in a high degree of congruence between the domestic transformation taking place in Egypt and Soviet objectives. While this transformation was facilitated by Soviet economic and political support (and in the case of the release of the Egyptian communists, by the direct intervention of Khrushchev's son-in-law, A. Adzhubei), nevertheless it would not be true to say that it was achieved during this period as the direct result of Soviet involvement.

Of all the objectives pursued between 1958–67, primacy was still accorded to the encouragement of Egypt's anti-imperialist and anti-Western foreign policy. However, this encouragement was now being given for rather different reasons. Whereas the Soviet Union had supported Egypt's anti-Western policy during 1955–58 in order to defeat what it perceived to be a direct threat to the core value of the security and integrity of its own territory, after 1958, for reasons already given, this threat was greatly diminished. Rather anti-Western policies were being encouraged for three other reasons. First was the desire to weaken Western 'capitalism' and 'imperialism' *per se*, the third of the values listed above. This move to a more activist and aggressive posture was initially made possible by the Soviet (and American) belief in the late 1950s and early 1960s that Soviet advances in space and missile technology had given the Russians a strategic advantage *vis-à-vis* the United States.

The second reason for the encouragement of Egypt's anti-Western foreign policy resulted from the redefinition of what constituted a threat to Soviet security. Although the defence of home territory is generally regarded as the core value of any state, governments, nevertheless, often place equally great value upon controlling or defending foreign territory, either because these areas contain important economic or strategic assets or because decision-makers perceive that a major threat to their own security might emanate from these territories.[8] The defence of foreign territory to enhance the security and capabilites of one's own state represented one of the major principles underlying the decision to establish the various collective security systems such as NATO, the Baghdad Pact and the Warsaw Pact. With the expansion of the Soviet Union's world role, the growth in her maritime capability and the beginning of American involvement in South-East Asia, the Soviet Union, like the United States, Britain and France before her, was concerned not only to safeguard her own borders, but also to protect and expand the influence she exerted over foreign territory. In this respect, the Soviet Union sought to maintain good relations with Egypt not only to increase her influence within that country but also to protect navigation routes through the Suez Canal which were vital both for the extension of Soviet influence in the Indian Ocean and for the supply of communist forces in South-East Asia.

Finally, anti-Western and anti-imperialist objectives were pursued because of the Soviet Union's growing conviction that the domestic transformation of Egypt and other developing countries would be impossible so long as Western governments and multinational companies maintained their influence over economic life. Thus, for example, where Western military bases had been denounced in the 1955–58 period because of the threat which they posed to Soviet security, in the 1958–67 period, Soviet commentators claimed, as in this extract, that these military bases served a two-fold purpose:

First they protect the imperialist interests of the Western powers. With the protection of the military bases, the imperialist monopolies can plunder more crudely the national resources of the former colonies. . . . Secondly, the military bases serve as strategic bridgeheads for the imperialist aggressors.[9]

The three main objectives pursued during this period—the

enlistment of Egyptian backing for the Soviet stand on international issues, the support of Egypt's domestic reforms, and the encouragement of Nasser's anti-Western foreign policy—were all interrelated parts of the overall Soviet attempts to form a strong anti-imperialist front of all socialist and progressive forces. In stressing the continuity in Soviet policy towards the Arab world following the overthrow of Khrushchev, a Soviet commentary emphasised that 'the *main* and *permanent* feature of this policy is support for the Arab people's struggle against imperialism.'[10]

1967–72

It was not until after Egypt's defeat in the 1967 war that the Soviet Union once again redefined its political and strategic objectives. From 1967 until the expulsion of Soviet advisers in 1972, the Soviet Union committed massive amounts of resources, including arms, aid and political support, towards the achievement of its objectives in Egypt. Whereas a main objective in the previous two periods had been the elimination of Western influence, in the 1967–72 period, this objective was rather subordinate, if only because British and American influence in Egypt was already at a low ebb, following their support for Israel during the Six-day War.

After 1967 it could be said that the Soviet leaders did try to achieve their maximum objective, the establishment of a pro-Soviet socialist system in Egypt. There was never any indication that they were willing to use force to achieve this objective. Instead they relied first of all on the belief that Nasser himself was gradually moving toward adherence to 'scientific socialism'.[11] In 1965, the Egyptian Communist Party had voluntarily disbanded and its members had been allowed to join the Arab Socialist Union. Soviet writers also were optimistic that with the influence of these elements plus other pro-Soviet but non-communist leaders, the ASU could be transformed into a vanguard party which could carry out the revolution 'from above'.[12]

This goal could not be achieved without a corresponding transformation in the economic system of the country. The state sector would need to be strengthened; agricultural output should be increased at least to the level where Egypt could feed her own population; industry and the economic infrastructure needed to be developed. Egypt's hitherto strong trading links with the West had to be diversified; and the decline in her hard currency reserves had to be halted. These were all long-term aims which the Soviet leaders felt were necessary concomitants of any transformation in the political structure.

On the military side, the Soviets had decided that the Egyptian defeat in the June war was due less to any faults in Soviet weaponry than to fundamental defects in the discipline, structure and training of the Egyptian army as a whole. As a result, the task which most preoccupied Soviet decision-makers in the 1967–72 period was the complete rebuilding of the Egyptian armed forces. The massive Soviet military presence in Egypt helped not only to increase Egypt's military capabilities but also to stabilise the situation along the Suez Canal by deterring Israel from continuing its deep penetration bombing of Egyptian cities and by restraining the Egyptian military from starting a war in which victory was not assured.

The Soviet Union's military presence was also designed to serve broader strategic objectives. Given the Soviet Union's global role and her increased activity in the Indian Ocean and the Mediterranean, the establishment of military facilities in Egypt, as the only state, other than Israel, with coastal access to both of these fleet areas, became even more important. The significance of the Suez Canal was also greatly increased with the Soviet buildup.

However, most of these objectives—including the political and economic transformation of Egypt and the reopening of the Suez Canal—could not be achieved so long as the Arab–Israeli conflict remained unsettled. It was for these reasons that the Soviet Union became so involved in espousing the Arab cause against Israel. As long as the risk of another war remained, the Egyptian economy could not hope to recover, both because of the size of the defence budget and because of the burden on Cairo's overstretched resources of the refugees from the devastated cities along the Canal. Also, the desire to regain lost territory was the major preoccupation of the Egyptian government and people, preventing them from concentrating their efforts on economic and social reform. The closure of the Suez Canal would last so long as the Egyptians and Israelis faced each other on opposite banks. Not only would these objectives remain unfulfilled until a settlement was reached, but there was also a danger that if the Arabs lost another war, the Egyptian leadership's position and the Soviet Union's own prestige would be so undermined as to eliminate the possibility of ever achieving these objectives. As a result, the Soviets followed a two-pronged strategy; train and equip the Egyptian army to a level where one could reasonably expect that they might win a war, and then do everything possible to prevent them from using this capability. In particular, work with the other parties to bring about a political settlement, slow down the supply of arms and use the presence of experts to impede Egyptian preparations. It was Sadat's total disagreement with Soviet objectives and priorities which led to the expulsion of Soviet experts in 1972 and the reappraisal of Soviet policies.

1972–78

An article by Mohamed Heikal, which appeared immediately prior to the expulsion of Soviet experts, set out the points at which Soviet and Egyptian objectives had previously converged. The main Soviet objectives, according to Heikal, had always been the undoing of 'imperialist domination' in the Arab world. This objective had been 'the important point of agreement between the Soviet Union and the Arab revolutionary movement led by . . . Nasser'. A second Soviet objective had been 'to disseminate Marxism as a substitute for capitalism . . . Nasserism and Marxism succeeded in findings common ground for cooperation in the hostility against world imperialism and class exploitation and in the common ambition for social progress'. In giving aid and strengthening the cooperation with Egypt, Heikal wrote that

> the Soviet Union wanted all its gains from that cooperation to become additional assets strengthening its international ideological and economic positions facing the imperialist system which is led by the United States. Moreover, the Soviet Union wants the Arab region to be its passage to other regions in Asia and Africa.[13]

However, almost immediately upon coming to power, Sadat made it clear that if Nasser had agreed with these objectives, he did not. In the first place, as discussed elsewhere, Sadat was much more favourably inclined toward the West than Nasser had been. And having experienced many years of Soviet influence in Egypt, Sadat was not willing to rule out the possibility that 'imperialist domination' might be a feature of Soviet as well as of Western policy. Sadat certainly did not share Nasser's views about the point of possible coincidence between Marxism and Egyptian socialism.

In particular, he did not support the growing role that former communists and other left-wing elements were playing within the Arab Socialist Union. His dismissal of the Ali Sabri group in 1971 ended Soviet hopes of establishing a vanguard core within the ASU. It was this event which prompted Soviet leaders to enter into the Soviet–Egyptian Treaty of Friendship and although it secured Egypt's formal adherence to a socialist path, the treaty did little more than postpone the final break. Sadat also made it clear at a very early stage that the Soviets could not always rely on Egypt either as an unquestioning ally in Soviet calculations of the 'correlation of forces' between East and West or as an open door for spreading communist influence in Afro-Asia. This last point was clearly made when Sadat helped Sudan's President Numeiri defeat an attempted communist coup in 1971. Rather, Sadat's overriding objective was the recovery of lands lost to Israel in the 1967 War. And when the Soviets prevaricated in their support of this aim, Sadat expelled all the Soviet advisers.

Although relations between the Soviet Union and Egypt have not been universally bad since 1972, nevertheless Sadat's own ambivalence toward the Soviet Union and his policy of *infitah* toward the West have forced the Soviets to pursue more short-term and reactive objectives. Their main objective in the pre-1973 period was clearly to use whatever means were available to maintain their influence in Egypt. To this end they supplied Egypt with almost all the advanced weaponry requested by Sadat. Following the war, however, when Sadat encouraged Kissinger to reach a settlement between Egypt and Israel which would effectively exclude the Soviet Union, even this objective became unrealistic. And although the Soviets did not seek a break in relations, after 1975, when Brezhnev cancelled his planned trip to Cairo, they did not try to avert it. Arms and aid were virtually cut off and although trading links were not entirely severed, nevertheless relations between the Soviet and Egyptian governments were at their lowest ebb since 1972.

This does not, however, imply that Soviet policy as a whole ceased to exist or that the Soviet leaders had no objectives toward Egypt after 1975. Rather it would seem that they were first of all seeking to isolate Egypt from the rest of the Arab world, by establishing much closer relations with Syria, Iraq and Libya. Secondly, by refusing to reschedule the Egyptian debt and by stopping the supply of weapons, the Soviet leaders hoped to put pressure on Egypt's fragile economy and to limit Egypt's military capability. Finally with the improvement in Egypt's relations with the West, Soviet leaders had to evaluate the role of the Communist Party within Egypt. As long as Nasser was alive, the 'anti-imperialist' and 'anti-Western' values of the Soviet Union were pursued through the Egyptian regime itself. It was for this reason that Soviet–Egyptian leaders welcomed the voluntary disbandment of the Egyptian Communist Party in 1965 and encouraged its members to work within the ASU. However, with Sadat's *infitah* to the West, these values clearly could no longer be achieved via the Egyptian regime—a situation which led to the decision to reconstitute the Egyptian Communist Party early in 1976. If Soviet objectives are the outcome of the interaction between values and capabilities, then the extent to which the Soviet Union can pursue its maximum value of the transition to socialism inside Egypt has had to be downgraded due to the loss of its influence within that country. However, the break with Egypt has not forced it to 'retreat' to the pursuit of minimal and defensive values either. The diffusion of Soviet influence throughout the Middle East, the reopening of the Suez Canal in 1976, and the general strengthening of the Soviet Union's military forces have led both to an enhancement of Soviet capabilities and to a corresponding decline in Soviet dependence upon Egypt as the linchpin of its Middle Eastern policy. However, while the achievement of the Soviet Union's global political and strategic objectives has become less centred on Egypt, a rather different pattern emerges when one examines Soviet economic objectives.

ECONOMIC OBJECTIVES

For some time after Stalin's death Soviet commentators largely overlooked the unique features and particular problems facing individual countries in the Third World, preferring instead to advocate the uniform application of the Soviet model of development. The immediate tasks facing the developing countries were said to be the nationalisation of foreign holdings, the establishment of a strong state economic sector, the promulgation of agrarian reforms, and the pursuit of a Soviet-style programme of rapid industrialisation. It was thought that only by adopting these measures could the vestiges of colonialism and feudalism be eradicated, rapid economic development be achieved, and the economic basis for the transition to socialism be established.[14]

However, this rather uncritical advocacy of the Soviet model of development tended to underestimate the difficulties faced by those countries such as Egypt with scarce material resources, inadequately trained manpower, and one-crop economies. It was not until the 1960 meeting of Communist Workers' and Parties recognised the admissibility of various non-capitalist paths of development that a more flexible and critical approach to the economic problems of the developing world began to emerge and the broad outlines of a reorientation in Soviet economic objectives began to take shape.

Soviet long-term credits to Egypt and the other Arab states have always been concentrated in the state sector and have been designed to strengthen that sector against private enterprise. While Soviet economists continue to maintain that Soviet economic policy is 'chiefly aimed at developing the state sector of the Arab countries' national economy',[15] under Brezhnev and Kosygin the emphasis has definitely shifted away from advocating the rapid growth in the size of the state sector *per se* and towards greater concern with the economy's general performance and efficiency. R. A. Ul'yanovskiy, Ponomaryov's assistant in the International Department of the Central Committee, has stated, for example, that the 'revolutionary aspirations' of some of these progressive regimes has resulted in nationalisations which were both precipitate and 'economically unjustified'. He warns that unless nationalisation is sufficiently prepared, it should be postponed, even if it strengthens the 'broad front struggling for socialism', since it might result in a deterioration in the economic situation and a drop in the standards of living.[16] A certain disillusionment with the progress of the state sector in Egypt and throughout the developing world is evident from articles detailing cases of corruption, inefficiency, bureaucratisation and overextention in that sector. It is often proposed that under the present circumstances, governments in these countries might be better advised to allow the private sector to operate, particularly in the manufacturing and service industries, under central planning and control, until these initial problems are solved.[17] In an article on the role of private enterprise, one commentator even suggested that the dynamic force of the profit motive and the organisational benefits of those cost criteria determined by market forces might in some cases be utilised on a microeconomic level along with central planning as the most rational method of development in the Third World.[18] As such, the author readily conceded that the Soviet model of a command economy 'is not . . . once and for all definitive, independent of concrete conditions of place, time and the socioeconomic peculiarities of this or that country'.[19]

This de-emphasis of the universal applicability of the Soviet model does not, however, imply that Soviet economic credits were ever extended to strengthen private industry in Egypt. Rather, an increased proportion of Soviet credits have been allotted for the improvement of productivity, efficiency, and management skills rather than for the construction of new enterprises. Thus, the 1965 Soviet–Egyptian Credit Agreement was revised to allocate funds for raising the productivity of Soviet-built industrial plants. This followed Kosygin's 1968 visit to Cairo, where he was reportedly appalled by the inefficiency of existing Soviet-financed projects.[20]

While Soviet credits are increasingly directed at improving the efficiency rather than the size of the state sector, Soviet decision-makers have also become aware that an overemphasis on heavy industrialisation is ill-suited to the needs of many developing countries. Indeed, most commentators now stress the need for a more equitable balance between heavy and light industry and between industry and agriculture, since an imbalance 'creates blockages in the economy, causes excessive strain and in the long term, produces a deterioration in the general condition of economic growth'.[21] In this respect, Egypt was blamed in particular for 'overstepping in the direction of industrialisation'.[22]

If Soviet aid and trade were focused more on improving economic efficiency and productivity in Egypt, a further objective which emerged more clearly under Brezhnev and Kosygin was the Soviet Union's use of economic ties with the Arab states for its own economic advantage. Many Western observers maintain that economic considerations have always been foremost in the formulation of Soviet–Middle Eastern policy.[23] However, while economic objectives have played an important part in Soviet policy since the early 1970s, it would be an overstatement to say that this has always been the case. The Soviet Union has never been heavily trade dependent and beginning with the first five-year plan, the Soviet government has pursued a policy of economic autarchy. Up until the early 1960s Soviet leaders continued to stress that economic advantage was not an objective of their Middle Eastern policy, with Khrushchev himself stating in 1958:

While the Soviet Union and other socialist countries consider it their duty to help the underdeveloped countries, . . . we cannot say that our economic relations are based on mutual advantage. Generally speaking, from the commercial standpoint, our economic and technical assistance to underdeveloped countries is even unprofitable for us.[24]

However, beginning in 1961, the first signs of a reappraisal in the economic benefits which might accrue to the Soviet Union by an expanded and more carefully planned programme of aid and trade became evident when the Trade Minister, Anastas Mikoyan, speaking at the 22nd CPSU Congress, stated that 'it will be necessary to make wide use of foreign trade as a factor for economising in current production expenditures and in capital investment'.[25] While several articles in the Soviet press expanded on this theme, they were primarily concerned with the advantages of closer economic cooperation and coordination between socialist countries, and not between the Soviet Union and the developing world.[26]

However, following Khrushchev's fall, Prime Minister Kosygin signalled a major shift in Soviet policy when he announced at the 23rd CPSU Congress that economic relations with the developing world would henceforth enable the USSR to 'make better use of the international division of labour',[27] a policy which would encourage the importation of all those goods which could be produced at a cheaper cost abroad than at home. Since Kosygin's statement, mutual advantage and the international division of labour have replaced autarchy as the principles underlying Soviet economic policy. The Soviet journal *Vneshnyaya torgovlya* justified this shift in the following way:

It is not always possible or economically justifiable for each country to make the whole range of its own requirements. An excessive extention in the range of products may reduce the economic efficiency of social production. Consequently, it becomes increasingly important to make a balanced switch to a complex interaction between the national economies, a consistent development of international specialisation of economies and the development of foreign trade.[28]

In line with this shift, imports and exports were incorporated into

the five-year plans; long-term planning arrangements were concluded with many countries, including Egypt, Algeria and Mo-
rocco; and the Soviet Union constructed industries in Egypt and
throughout the Arab world 'whose output is of interest to the Soviet
national economy as well as to the economies of the Arab countries
themselves'.[29] Among these industries, Soviet commentators listed
the construction of ships in Egypt destined for the Soviet Union;
Egyptian aluminium exports to the Soviet Union from Soviet-
financed plants; and the shipment of raw materials, including
petroleum and gas, from Iraq, Iran and Syria in return for Soviet
assistance in geological exploration and development.[30]

Although Soviet economic relations with Egypt became more
firmly based on the principle of economic advantage in recent years,
it would not be true to say that in absolute terms these relations were
advantageous—in other words, that the Soviet Union derived more
economic benefit from them than Egypt. If Egypt had been a major
oil exporter or if she had been able to repay the economic and
military credits extended to her over the years by the Soviet Union,
then perhaps Moscow would have derived more benefit. But with
economic and military debts to the Soviet Union estimated by the
Egyptians themselves to be around $7000 million,[31] it would be
difficult to support the view that economic objectives had become
paramount in Soviet policy. Of all the economic objectives pursued
by the Soviet Union in Egypt, the most salient one was the
transformation of the Egyptian economy. And even this objective, it
could be argued, was subordinate to the Soviet Union's other
political and strategic goals.

9 The Instruments of Soviet Policy

Diplomacy, as perhaps the most traditional instrument of foreign policy, can be defined as the interaction between the official representatives of two or more states for the purpose of maintaining or modifying their relations. Diplomacy can be conducted by a variety of means. Prior to the First World War, diplomatic transactions were characterised by secret and bilateral negotiations between ambassadors. However, since that time there has been a growing tendency toward more open negotiations and more active involvement by prime ministers and heads of state. Furthermore, the trend toward regional, international and functional groupings has increased the frequency of multilateral negotiations and 'parliamentary diplomacy'.[1]

The highly centralised structure of both the Soviet and Egyptian political systems, coupled with the active involvement of the leaders of both states in foreign policy, has made personal diplomacy a particularly salient feature of Soviet–Egyptian relations. Unlike Stalin, his successors have made frequent trips abroad and have taken a personal interest in the formulation and conduct of Soviet policy towards Egypt. Soviet texts on foreign policy stress that in Soviet relations with the developing countries, 'a major role is played by personal contact between statesmen'.[2] Indeed Nasser had no less than ten summit meetings with either Khrushchev or Brezhnev, Kosygin and Podgornyy, while Sadat had five such meetings with the triumvirate including a large number of meetings with other Politburo members such as Grechko, Gromyko or Ponomaryov.

While personal diplomacy has been an important feature of Soviet–Egyptian relations, its impact on Soviet policy has not always been positive. In particular, Khrushchev's tendency to make brash and spontaneous statements, and his particular penchant for 'cocktail diplomacy' won him few friends either among his own colleagues or in Egypt. His characterisation of Nasser at a press conference as 'a young and rash' President,[3] and his assertion at a Kremlin reception for an Egyptian Parliamentary delegation in 1961 that 'Arab nationalism is not the zenith of happiness',[4] are only two instances of many such statements that were to constantly interrupt the progress of Soviet–Egyptian relations during Khrushchev's tenure.

However, the diplomatic support given by the Soviet Union to Egypt at the international level more than offset any of the temporary setbacks caused by 'personal diplomacy'. Of particular importance was the stand taken by the Soviet Union during the three major international crises which occurred during this period— the 1956 Suez Crisis, the 1967 Six-day War and the 1973 October war. In all three crises, Soviet diplomatic activity was aimed at publicising the Arab point of view and mobilising world public opinion against Western interference in the Middle East. Efforts on the diplomatic front included the despatch of numerous Soviet government statements on the crises; the representation of the Arab viewpoint in the UN Security Council and in international conferences such as the ones which met in London prior to the outbreak of the Suez Crisis and the Geneva Conference convened in December 1973; the issuance of thinly veiled threats of military retaliation if 'Western aggression' were not brought to a halt; and the enlistment of support from other socialist and non-aligned states. The major advantage for Egypt of Soviet international diplomacy was the Soviet representation of the Arab cause in the United Nations, where the Soviet delegate consistently voted on the Arab side, and vetoed many resolutions which were contrary to Arab interests.[5]

Outside the United Nations, however, the Soviet Union had few levers to back up her diplomatic activity. Constrained by her relative military weakness in the Mediterranean *vis-à-vis* the West (especially prior to 1967) and by the difficulties involved in exerting economic pressure to influence Egyptian policies, diplomacy proved to be of limited utility in the achievement of Soviet objectives. The effectiveness of Soviet diplomacy was greatest when Soviet and Egyptian policies and views on major issues converged. However, during other periods (and especially those which resulted in the 1972 expulsion of experts and the 1976 abrogation of the Treaty), diplomacy became secondary to other instruments, such as propaganda, cultural diplomacy, clandestine activities, and economic and military aid and trade.

ECONOMIC AID

A major feature of the basic realignment in Soviet foreign policy which occurred after Stalin's death was the increased reliance on economic methods of influencing countries of the 'Third World'. In July 1953, A. A. Arutiunian, the Soviet delegate to the United Nations Economic and Social Council, signalled this change by announcing that the Soviet government had decided to contribute one million dollars to the UN Expanded Programme of Technical Assistance for use in developing countries.[6] In the next three years, the Soviet Union signed economic trade and aid agreements with a number of countries, including India, Afghanistan, Syria, Egypt, Lebanon, Turkey and the Yemen. However, it was not until 1956 that the Soviet Union formalised its commitment to trade and aid as an active instrument of Soviet policy in the developing world. It was Khrushchev's speech to the 20th Party Congress that marked the shift:

> These countries [the developing countries] although they do not belong to the socialist world system, can draw on its achievements to build up an independent national economy and to raise the people's living standards. Today they need not go begging to their former oppressors for modern equipment. They can get it in the socialist countries free from any political obligations.[7]

Following the Congress, the Soviet bloc as a whole stepped up its economic activities in the Middle East, and by mid-1957, a total of 297 bilateral agreements between the countries of the Middle East and the Soviet bloc had been signed.[8]

Terms of Soviet Aid

The financial terms of Soviet credits to Egypt were generally uniform in nature. Credits were extended in roubles to be repaid with 2.5 to 3 per cent interest in equal annual instalments over a period of ten to twelve years, beginning one year after the completion of the project.[9] Although in fact repayments were usually made in Egyptian pounds to be used by the Soviet Union for commodity purchases in Egypt, credit agreements did sometimes contain a clause stating that payments 'may be freely converted into pounds sterling or any freely convertible currency which will be agreed upon between the two governments'.[10] However, the Soviet Union did not in fact ever insist that repayments be made in hard currency.

Under the terms of the credit agreements, the USSR undertook the costs of project surveys, machinery and equipment, the salaries of Soviet technicians and their travel expenses to and from the USSR. Egypt was obligated to cover all costs incurred by Soviet technicians while working within the host state, as well as local labour and materials indigenous to Egypt.[11] Within the terms of most of the credit agreements, the USSR also held the option to subcontract projects out to other East European countries. Thus, for example, in the case of the January 1958 Soviet–Egyptian agreement, of the 46 projects completed, the USSR subcontracted five projects to Czechoslovakia, two to Poland and one each to Bulgaria, East Germany and Hungary.[12]

Quantity and End Use of Soviet Aid

The programme of economic aid to Egypt has been impressive, with Egypt accounting for nearly 30 per cent of Soviet aid to all the countries of the Third World, a figure which rises to around 43 per cent if Soviet credits to South Asia are excluded. Table 9.1 gives a breakdown of the total bilateral commitments of capital by all the centrally planned Socialist countries to developing states, and shows

TABLE 9.1 Bilateral Commitments of Capital by Centrally Planned Economies to Developing Countries 1954–76 (in millions US dollars)

	1954–70	1971	1972	1973	1974	1975	1976
Total distributed	11,409	1,940	2,439	2,476	2,941	3,046	1,479
of which by USSR	6,174	1,016	957	1,230	1,260	1,642	875
Received by Egypt	1,844	313	511	130	218	125	0

Sources: UN, *Statistical Yearbook 1975* (New York: UN, 1976), p. 827; UN, *Statistical Yearbook 1976* (New York: UN, 1977), p. 821. US, CIA, *Communist Aid to the Less Developed Countries of the Free World 1976*, ER 77–10296 (August 1977), pp. 11–13.

both the amount distributed by the USSR and the amount received by Egypt.

When discussing the end-use of aid, it is usually classified into two categories—project and programme aid. The latter is for general and unspecified use by the recipient government and is primarily utilised to cover the import costs of machinery, commodities and spare parts, and to help combat economic difficulties, such as inflation and deficits in the balance of payments. Project aid, on the other hand, is granted to cover the costs of specific projects.

From the Soviet standpoint, the advantages of project over programme aid are three-fold. In the first place, it yields tangible results which have great public appeal in both the donor and recipient country. Secondly, it is much easier to account for funds allocated to specific projects as well as to plan for the technical expertise wich will be required of the donor country. Finally, unlike programme aid, project aid usually benefits and encourages the development of the state sector, one of the Soviet Union's primary economic objectives, as discussed in Chapter 8. As a leading official of the State Committee for Foreign Economic Relations wrote, only through the growth of the state sector can the 'economic basis for further progressive reforms' be established.[13] It is normally the case in developing countries, such as Egypt, that only the state sector has the capability necessary for the implementation of large-scale industrial projects. The inflow of Soviet credits, expertise and equipment to stimulate the expansion of that sector thus not only strengthens it *vis-à-vis* the private sector, but also results in the concentration of labour, the diversification of production, the passage of labour laws, and the introduction of long-term central planning, all of which are considered by Soviet leaders to be beneficial by-products of their aid programme.

A very large proportion of the Soviet credits to Egypt was used for the development of heavy industry and hydroelectric power— indeed nearly 80 per cent of the total, according to one source.[14] For example, the 1971 Soviet credit to Egypt of 380 million roubles included 230 million for industrial projects, 60 million for rural electrification and 70 million for land reclamation and the improvement of fishing on Lake Nasser.[15] Of all the Soviet projects, the Aswan Dam was by far the most important, both in terms of the size of the project and its political and economic impact.

It was more than two years after the American withdrawal of its offer to finance the Dam that Soviet leaders finally agreed to provide

$100 millions for the first stage only. The agreement for the final stages was signed in August 1960 only after Egypt had received a firm offer from West Germany for the remaining work. During construction, over 300 factories in the USSR participated in the manufacture of some 500,000 tonnes of equipment for the dam.[16] However, while the Soviet Union provided technical expertise and equipment, the Egyptians undertook the major responsibility for financing the project, with only 27.8 per cent of its final cost being borne by the Soviet Union, as indicated in Table 9.2. Since its completion in July 1970, the dam has helped to regulate irrigation in the Nile Valley and has led to the reclamation of 755,000 feddans of land. Moreover, Egyptian sources claim that as of 1974, the dam was supplying the country with 52.9 per cent of its electric power, thus saving the UAR £E82 million in fuel costs during the period when Israel occupied the Sinai oilfields. However, the dam was working at only 69.2 per cent of its total capacity in 1976 and was still causing Egyptian engineers certain problems, such as the loss of silt to fertilise agricultural land, the increase in the incidence of bilharzia from stagnating waters in Lake Nasser, and the decline in marine life in the Nile Delta.[17] Nevertheless these problems are gradually being solved and do not diminish the long-term benefits accruing to Egypt from the dam's construction.

TABLE 9.2 Soviet Financial Contribution to the Construction of the Aswan High Dam (in millions US dollars)

	Total cost	Soviet portion	Soviet percentage
First stage	614	100	16.2
Final stages	515	225	40.8
Total	1,165	325	27.8

Source: Marshall L. Goldman, *Soviet Foreign Aid* (New York: Praeger, 1967), p. 67.

In the sphere of heavy industry, Soviet exports of complete plants (classified in Soviet trade directories as Category 16 exports) to Egypt were a major feature of the Soviet aid programme in the late 1960s. While the supply of machinery remains an important part of Soviet assistance, nevertheless, as Table 9.3 shows, Category 16 exports drastically declined after 1970. This decrease can be attributed to three factors. The first is the realisation by Soviet decision-makers, as discussed in Chapter 8, that the Soviet model of

TABLE 9.3 Equipment and Materials Supplied for Works Being Built in Egypt through Soviet Assistance, 1955–76 (in millions US dollars)

	1955	1960	1965	1970	1975	1976
Total exports to Egypt	10.8	68.9	206.4	363.0	363.2	265.2
Total machinery	0.04	23.2	136.2	165.3	118.8	106.5
Total machinery financed by Soviet aid	na	na	na	na	63.2	na
Category 16	—	17.4	86.0	78.5	2.4	1.5

na not available   — negligible

Sources: *Vneshnyaya torgovlya SSSR za . . . god, statisticheskiy obzor*, Moscow (various years); UN, *Monthly Bulletin of Statistics*; UN, *Yearbook of International Trade Statistics* (various years).

rapid industrialisation was not ideally suited to the needs of all developing countries, and that Egypt in particular was in danger of 'overstepping in the direction of industrialisation'. Secondly, the ability of developing countries to absorb Soviet credits for large-scale industrial projects is strictly limited, primarily because the recipient state is held responsible for financing a large proportion of the projects undertaken by the USSR, as was the case with the Aswan Dam. Because of the difficulty of meeting the local costs, many projects outlined in the original credit agreements were never started, resulting in a large disparity between aid commitments and disbursements. US government sources state that of the $11,769 million extended by the USSR to less-developed countries between 1955 and 1976, only $6,560 million had actually been disbursed as of 1976.[18] However, Egypt, unlike many developing countries, does have the economic capacity to absorb large quantities of Soviet and East European credits. N. A. Ushakova states in her book that of the 750 projects financed by Soviet and East European credits in Egypt, over 600 were already in operation by 1974.[19] Furthermore of the 47 industrial projects included in Soviet–Egyptian agreements as of 1 January 1977, 31 had already been commissioned.[20] However, the drop in Category 16 exports from $78.5 million in 1970 to $1.5 million in 1976 would seem to indicate that work on even those projects which had been commissioned came to a standstill following the abrogation of the Treaty. The Egyptians alleged that work on Soviet-funded projects had slowed down not out of mutual consent, but because the Soviets were trying to put political pressure on Cairo by cutting off aid — an allegation which, if true, would imply that Soviet aid, like all other aid, is not given without political motives or without political strings.

Strings on Soviet Aid

The inevitable inequality of any donor–recipient relationship is bound to afford the donor a measure of political leverage over the activities of the recipient state. Even if the donor choses not to use aid to exert actual political influence, his potential ability to do so at any time is likely to affect the perceptions which both sets of decision-makers hold about the 'rules' governing the relationship between their two countries. Indeed, it is likely that Khrushchev had this implicit set of rules in mind when he wrote a letter to Nasser in April 1959, on the issue of the relationship between the Egyptian leader's anti-communist domestic policy and the continuation of Soviet aid. In this letter, Khrushchev allegedly posed the following question:

> Does not the present situation, when a campaign is going on in the United Arab Republic against the Soviet Union . . . give rise to complications for discharging our obligations under the agreement for the construction of the Aswan Dam? I hope you will understand that this is not a threat on our part but concern over the fact that a campaign against the Soviet Union is now going on in the UAR and that it will be very difficult for us to fulfil in these circumstances our obligation under the agreement that we signed with you.[21]

However, Khrushchev's 'threat' went unheeded, and anti-communist measures continued, as did Soviet work on the Aswan Dam, thus highlighting the difficulty of imposing political strings on aid after the original commitment has been made. In the highly competitive bipolar system of the 1950s, to impose political strings on aid to countries who had an alternative source of finance, as did the Arab states, would have been counterproductive to the achievement of Soviet objectives as a whole.

However, since the late 1960s with East–West *détente* and the American commitment to Israel, the Arab states could no longer so readily rely on non-bloc countries for alternative sources of economic aid. Under these circumstances, the utility to the Soviet Union of the economic instrument was enhanced. Soviet leaders repeatedly refused Egypt's requests to reschedule the massive debt despite Sadat's protestations that repayments represented a burden which could hinder future economic development. Not only did the Soviet Union refuse this request but it evidently slowed down the supply of Category 16 exports, spare parts and other industrial materials needed to maintain industrial capacity, not to mention industrial growth. Indeed, some reports claimed that 'twenty per cent of Egyptian industrial capacity has almost come to a halt through lack of spare parts and raw materials from the Russians, who want to settle the question of debts before resuming deliveries. . . .'[22]

Since Soviet leaders in the past acceded to Nasser's request to reschedule payments, lower commodity prices, and even cancel debts altogether, their attitude after the October War must be regarded as a major departure in the use of the economic instrument. While this departure is no doubt primarily a reaction to the openly anti-Soviet policy pursued by Sadat, purely economic motives cannot be discounted entirely. Given that the political returns on Soviet economic investments are presently at a minimum, it was perhaps to be expected that Soviet leaders would prefer to cut their losses rather than continue to invest their finances in an economy which was far from solvent.

TRADE

Unlike most Western countries where foreign trade is handled primarily by private enterprises, trade in the USSR is state-controlled and as such, constitutes an integral part of the Soviet Union's economic strategy. Beginning in 1955, Soviet leaders put increasing emphasis on the importance of establishing trade relations; and Marshal Bulganin, in a speech before the February 1955 session of the Supreme Soviet, signalled a shift away from economic autarchy when he declared that the Soviet Union 'stands for extensive trade with all countries irrespective of their state or social system.'[23]

Quantity

Commensurate with the general realignment in Soviet foreign policy following the 20th Party Congress, the volume of Soviet foreign trade has continued to witness a steady expansion. Soviet trade with the developing world, and particularly with those countries which are also recipients of Soviet aid, has grown more rapidly than Soviet trade with any other areas; and of the developing countries, the volume of Soviet trade has been the largest with South Asia and the Near East, with India and Egypt taking up the highest proportion. The quantity of Soviet trade with the developing world has expanded steadily over the last two decades; and in 1976, the developing market economies accounted for 19.3 per cent of the Soviet Union's total trade, with Egypt, India, Iran and Iraq alone constituting 4.8 per cent of the total trade figure in that year.[24] The countries of the Middle East themselves have never constituted more than about 7 per cent of the Soviet Union's total trade. Within this context, it would appear that for the Soviet Union, the economic impact of trade with the Middle East has been fairly minor, as indicated in Table 9.4.

TABLE 9.4 Foreign Trade of the USSR 1955–76 (in millions US dollars, f.o.b.)

Imports	1955	1960	1965	1970	1975	1976
Developed market economies	430	1,168	1,819	3,070	14,511	15,555
Centrally planned economies	2,298	3,817	5,074	6,862	16,280	16,825
Developing market economies	185	638	1,157	1,788	6,164	5,771
Egypt	15	121	163	311	621	439
World total	3,061	5,623	8,051	11,719	26,671	38,151
Exports						
Developed market economies	553	1,069	1,639	2,717	9,595	11,613
Centrally planned economies	2,723	4,078	5,031	7,389	17,549	18,803
Developing market economies	91	412	1,496	2,682	6,170	6,753
Egypt	11	70	209	363	363	265
World total	3,468*	5,558	8,166	12,787	33,316	26,573

* 1955 figures do not add up to World Totals.
Sources: UN, *Yearbook of International Trade Statistics*; UN, *Monthly Bulletin of Statistics*.

However, a different picture emerges when one considers the impact of Soviet trade on the Egyptian economy. Prior to the abrogation of the Treaty, Egypt was becoming increasingly dependent on the Soviet Union. Between 1970 and 1975, 37 per cent of Egyptian exports went to the Soviet Union. If one adds to this Egypt's trade with all centrally planned economies, the total rises to 60 per cent of Egypt's exports.[25] The major commodity exported to the Soviet Union has always been long-staple cotton. However, its proportion of the total has dropped from 66 per cent in 1965 to 23 per cent in 1976 as exports of other commodities such as oil and semi-manufactured goods have increased.[26] In August 1977, Sadat announced that Egypt had decided to suspend the export of cotton and cotton yarn to the Soviet Union because of its failure to deliver weapons which had been ordered.[27] The Soviets responded by decreasing the export of coking coal necessary for the Helwan iron and steel works,[28] forcing the Egyptians to seek an alternative source amongst hard currency markets and underlining some of the advantages and disadvantages of trading with the USSR.

Advantages

Perhaps the greatest advantage of trading with the Soviet Union stemmed from its ability to absorb surplus goods during slump periods, at least whenever it was politically expedient to do so. Such was the case with the massive Soviet and bloc imports of Egyptian cotton during the Suez crisis when the West (including the USA) imposed an economic boycott on Egypt. Soviet exports of wheat to the Middle East during periods when the Soviet Union was itself suffering from shortages provided a further illustration of the political motivation behind, and flexibility of, Soviet trade. Soviet writers frequently stress other advantages of trading with the USSR. It was often maintained, for example, that the Soviet Union did not export goods which would compete with local products; that countries could obtain sophisticated technology without depleting their own hard currency reserves; that long-term trade agreements with the Soviet Union ensured a steady flow of imports at stable prices; that the Soviet Union encouraged the economic development of the newly independent countries by importing their semi-manufactured goods; and that trading terms allowed payment for Soviet goods in instalments adjusted annually according to the ability of the recipient state to pay.[29]

Disadvantages

The criticism was often voiced that Soviet products fell short of quality standards, that deliveries were delayed, and that spare parts were always in short supply. A further allegation was that the Soviet Union re-exported merchandise purchased in Egypt. It was claimed on several occasions that not only was the Soviet Union re-exporting Egyptian cotton, but that these sales were at prices well below the norm, thus forcing down the price received by Egypt. In 1964, Nasser took measures to prevent Soviet re-exports, by deciding that the annual negotiations and contracts for the sale of cotton to bloc countries would be concluded only after contracts for sales to the West had been signed.[30]

Yet the main disadvantage of trading with the Soviet Union stems primarily from the bilateralism of Soviet trade patterns. Bilateralism tends to limit the general growth of a developing country's trading relations by narrowing and restricting that country's choice of partners, imports, and markets. This is particularly true of the weak one-commodity economies, such as Egypt, which are in danger of mortgaging their entire crop to the Soviet Union in order to gain short-term benefits, but are then left without any means of gaining hard currency with which to continue, or expand, trading in Western markets. Egypt was in this position for many years during the 1960s, with well over 50 per cent of its cotton crop being shipped annually to the Soviet Union and Eastern Europe.[31]

As with aid, overreliance on a single state both as a market for exports and as a source for vital imports breeds dependency. It also creates, however, a weak link in the economy which, if broken, can produce a wide-ranging crisis. Although the decision to suspend the trade of certain key items emanated from the Egyptian side, the Soviet Union showed itself prepared to withhold the shipment of goods vital for the economy and thus to push Egypt one step closer to the economic precipice. Egypt's expenditure was estimated at 50 per cent more than its production at the beginning of 1976,[32] and over $1,805 million of its 1977 budget was devoted solely to the repayment of foreign loans.[33] Although it is by no means certain that Egypt would have been able to avoid these problems had it continued to rely on the Soviet Union, nevertheless Sadat's policy since the October war has highlighted both the political disadvantages of dependency and the near futility for a country like Egypt of trying to survive without maintaining an economic umbilical cord to one of the Great Powers.

THE MILITARY INSTRUMENT

In the case of Soviet relations with Egypt, the military instrument has included arms transfers, the training of Egyptian military personnel, and both the direct and indirect use of Soviet armed forces. Like all the other instruments of foreign policy, the military instrument can be used not only to achieve military and strategic objectives, but also to advance political and economic aims as well. In the case of Soviet–Egyptian relations, while the buildup of the Soviet navy's presence in the Eastern Mediterranean has aided primarily in the achievement of the USSR's broader strategic objectives, other aspects of the military instrument, such as arms transfers, have been designed primarily to enhance the Soviet Union's prestige and influence in Egypt.

Arms Transfers

In the Middle East, over 93 per cent of all arms have been supplied by only four states—the USSR, the USA, Great Britain, and France, with the USSR alone supplying approximately 42 per cent of the total between 1950 and 1975.[34] Of the factors influencing the decision to deliver arms, two have been the most important. On the global level, due to the vital strategic and economic importance of the Middle East, arms supplies have been used to establish a hegemonic position in the area *vis-à-vis* the other Great Powers. Thus arms deliveries have served to reinforce the Egyptian governement, particularly when it was pursuing a policy sympathetic to Soviet interests. Secondly, the supply of military hardware has served as a means by which the USSR can support Egypt in various regional conflicts without actively involving its own forces in the dispute. The Arab–Israeli conflict is the most notable example, although the Yemeni civil war could perhaps also be cited as an illustration.

On the Egyptian side, a number of factors have influenced the demand for weapons. The most obvious is the purely military requirement: arms are needed when a state's objectives both domestically and externally can be accomplished only by force. In developing countries in general, and in the Middle East in particular, where state boundaries are often incongruent with ethnic and historical divisions, the incidence of conflict within and amongst states is unusually high, with the result that a steady supply of arms is perceived to be vital for defence against both external attack and internal distintegration. Secondly, the establishment of national armed forces, and the import of arms which this necessitates, serves as a symbol of independence and sovereignty, thus forging a new state's national identity as well as reinforcing the authority and legitimacy of the ruling elite. Thirdly, pressure for more advanced weaponry often emanates from within the army itself, which in the Middle East is never far from the centre of power, a fact fully appreciated by the Arab leaders, most of whom rose to power through the military. President Nasser himself stated in 1959 that 'the army is my Parliament. The army has not carried out the Revolution simply to make me a ruler and then to leave me and go'.[35]

Since 1955, the Soviet Union has concluded numerous arms agreements with many of the countries in the Middle East. The cost of the military hardware delivered is difficult to determine since estimates calculated in the West for the Soviet Union are often increased to compare favourably with the value of Western weaponry, even though the cost of producing weapons in the Soviet Union is thought to be considerably less than in Western defence industries.[36] However, it is estimated that during the period 1955–75 the value of Soviet military aid to the Middle East totalled well over $6,000 million, or nearly half of all Soviet military exports to the non-communist world, as shown in Table 9.5. Soviet exports to Egypt accounted for over half of all Soviet arms transferred to the Middle East prior to the October war and for almost one-quarter of all Soviet arms exports to non-bloc countries.[37] During and after the October War, the Soviet Union mounted a massive airlift to resupply the Arab armies. As a result, the Egyptian armed forces were returned to their prewar levels, as shown in Table 9.6.

With the deterioration of Soviet–Egyptian relations, however, arms supplies began to be curtailed. In 1974, Egyptian imports of weapons and military equipment from all sources fell to $118 million, from a high in the previous year of $655 million.[38] In particular, Egypt was unable to obtain either the spare parts for her existing stocks of Soviet armaments or the more advanced weaponry needed to keep pace with Israeli procurements. After 1974, Egypt made some progress towards diversifying her sources of supply. British and American firms began to overhaul Egypt's MiG-21 engines;[39] MiG-17 engines and spare parts were being supplied by China; and some Soviet weaponry including tanks and MiG-21

TABLE 9.5 Soviet and Egyptian Arms Trade 1955–1976 (in million US dollars, at constant 1968 prices)

	1955–59	1960–66	1967–73	1974	1975	1976
Total Soviet arms exports,						
excluding Warsaw Pact	777	3,115	7,130	1,232	1,000	na
of which to Middle East	546	987	2,958	849	738	155
of which to Egypt	223	536	1,769	–	281	0
Total Egyptian arms imports	3,185	556	1,833	–	369	73

na—data not available.
Middle East includes Egypt, Iran, Iraq, Lebanon, Syria and the two Yemeni Republics; Soviet arms exports to Egypt in 1974 amounted to $.4 million. Total Egyptian arms imports for 1974 amounted to $.5 million.

Sources: US Arms Control and Disarmament Agency, *World Military Expenditures and Arms Transfers 1966–1975* (Washington, DC, 1976), pp. 62, 78; SIPRI, *Arms Trade Registers* (Cambridge, Mass.: The MIT Press, 1975), pp. 154–5; SIPRI, *Worksheets for Soviet Arms Exports to the Middle East and for Egypt's Arms Imports, 1950–1976* (Stockholm: SIPRI, unpublished papers, 1977).

TABLE 9.6 Major Military Equipment Holdings by Egypt, 1973–76

	Strength on eve of October war	War losses	Strength in 1976
Combat aircraft	653	222	550
Tanks	2,450	1,000	2,500
Armoured personnel carriers	2,900	450	2,600
Artillery (guns)	2,200	300	2,200
Scud surface-to-surface missile launchers	9		24
SAM anti-aircraft missile batteries	146	44	155

Source: *Middle East Intelligence Survey* (15 March 1976), p. 197.

engines were received directly from the Soviet Union, as well as from North Korea, Czechoslovakia, Yugoslavia, Kuwait, Iraq, and Syria.[40] In addition, beginning in 1976, Egypt started to receive limited consignments of Western equipment, including Gazelle helicopters, C-130 transport aircraft and Mirage F-1 fighters, with the prospect of other more advanced weaponry, such as the American F-5E to follow.[41]

Soviet arms shipments to Egypt were disrupted following the October war both by the dispute over Egypt's inability to meet the repayments for previous weapons supplied and by Soviet disapproval of Sadat's reliance on American involvement to bring about a negotiated settlement. Egypt had made efforts in the past to repay the Soviet Union for military equipment. Prime Minister Mamdouh Salem, in a speech to the People's Assembly in January 1976, revealed that Egypt had settled all of its military debts to the Soviet Union for the 1955–60 period; 35 per cent for the 1960–67 period and 25 per cent for the 1967–73 period.[42] However, the enormity of the debt still remaining was disclosed by Dr Abdel Munim al-Qaisouni, Deputy Prime Minister for Finance and Economic Affairs, who stated in August 1977 that Egypt's military debt to the Soviet Union amounted to £E1,500 ($4000) million.[43] Although Egypt continued for some time following the October War to pay back part of the debt, by the autumn of 1977, relations had become so strained that Sadat saw little justification for exerting this further strain on the Egyptian economy. He announced that debt repayments for all military and economic credits extended by the USSR would cease as of January 1978 and would be repaid only after a ten-year grace period. Although Foreign Minister Fahmi reportedly had been told by Soviet leaders during his visit to Moscow in June 1977 that they would be willing to sell arms to Egypt for hard currency, they also made it clear that no sales would be considered at least until the beginning of 1978.[44] This Soviet intransigence reflects the extent to which weapons transfers were used to achieve political objectives, a point appreciated by Heikal in an article reprinted in *Pravda*:

We [the Egyptians] should have remembered that the decision of a Great Power to give weapons to another state is a political decision, and not simply a barter operation. It happened that we began to ask for Soviet weapons at the same time that it occurred to us that the solution of the Middle East conflict lay only with the Americans. And so in the political field, we addressed only the Americans, leaving for the Soviet Union the sole role of weapons supplier. This mistake arose out of the construction of the demarcation between weapons and diplomacy. We forgot that in fact they are two aspects of the same struggle.[45]

The Training of Egyptian Personnel

Following the 1967 Six-day War, considerable concern was expressed in both Moscow and Cairo about the level of military competence displayed by the Egyptian armed forces during the War. As a result, the Soviet army's Chief of Staff, Marshal Zakharov, was sent to Cairo to take charge of the restructuring and retraining of the entire Egyptian Army. Every brigade had a Soviet adviser attached to it and eventually there were more than 1500 such advisers in Egypt.[46] Equally, all the top Egyptian officers were sent to the Moscow War Academy for courses in Soviet weaponry and strategic doctrine.[47] The objectives behind these efforts were not only to improve the military standard of the Egyptian army, an objective which was undoubtedly achieved judging by Egypt's performance in the first days of the 1973 war, but also to enhance the Soviet Union's stature within Egypt and its control over Egypt's (and Israel's) ability to wage war. The achievement of the latter objectives can only be considered if one takes into account the other aspects of the Soviet Union's military involvement in Egypt.

The Establishment of Bases

This buildup in the Soviet Union's military presence in Egypt served two objectives. It gave the Soviet leadership far more direct influence over events in the region, since neither the Egyptians nor the Israelis could launch a major offensive without considering the increased possibility of Soviet involvement. It also, however, served broader Soviet strategic objectives by giving the Soviet Union forward bases for the pursuit of a more activist policy both in the Eastern Mediterranean and the Indian Ocean. Having lost its submarine port at Vlone Albania in 1961, the Soviets lacked the logistic ability to support forces deployed at sea until after the 1967 buildup in Egypt. From then until 1973, the annual number of Soviet ship/days in the Mediterranean increased dramatically, as indicated in Table 9.7. This increase was achieved both by sending more ships into the area (the number of surface combatants transiting the Turkish Straits increased from 39 in 1964 to 126 in 1973[48]) and by stationing them there for longer periods (the average surface combatant deployment from the Black Sea to the Mediterranean rose from 41 days in 1966 to 86 days in 1968[49]). The absence of aircraft carriers from the Soviet navy until July 1976 made it

TABLE 9.7 Soviet Naval Presence in the Mediterranean, 1964–76

	Annual ship days	Average daily strength
1964	1,500	5
1965	2,800	8
1966	4,400	12
1967	8,100	22
1968	11,000	30
1969	15,000	41
1970	16,500	45
1971	19,000	52
1972	18,000	49
1973	20,600	56
1974	20,200	55
1975	20,000	55
1976	18,600	50

Source: Robert G. Weinland, 'Land Support for Naval Forces: Egypt and the Soviet Escadra 1962–1976', *Survival*, Vol. 20, No. 2 (1978), p. 74.

dependent on land-based support. This was provided until 1972 by Soviet-piloted aircraft operating from seven Egyptain airfields. The increase in the average length in the duration of deployment also necessitated, and indeed was partly the result of, the provision of repair and resupply facilities at the Egyptian ports of Alexandria, Port Said, Mersa Matruh and Sollum. Access to these ports was not substantially affected by the 1972 expulsion of experts, although Egypt took control of all the Soviet military facilities in the country. In May 1975, however, Egypt curtailed Soviet naval facilities in Alexandria by stipulating that Soviet ships henceforth would have to give advance notice of arrival and departure. Then in May 1976, with the abrogation of the Treaty, Sadat gave the USSR one month to close down its remaining support facilities. Egyptian actions appear to have had a decisive impact on the Soviet naval presence in the Mediterranean, especially before the Soviets deployed the *Kiev* aircraft carrier and gained access to other Middle Eastern ports. Between 1973 and 1975, the number of Soviet surface combatants transiting the Straits declined by 40 per cent, from 126 in 1973 to 79 in 1975.[50] Moscow's continued failure to find facilities capable of replacing those in Egypt highlights that country's continued importance in Soviet strategic calculations.

Direct Military Involvement

In late January 1970 when Israel was conducting bombing raids
deep inside Egypt, Nasser sought urgent Soviet assistance to bolster
Egypt's air defences. In response, the Soviet leaders agreed to send
both pilots and missile crews to Egypt until such time as Egypt could
train enough men to meet her own needs. As a result, by the end of
1970, over 200 Soviet pilots were flying operationally over the
Canal, and between 12,000 and 15,000 Soviet personnel were
deployed at SAM-3 sites.[51] All of these personnel played an active
part in Egypt's air defence until they were expelled in July 1972.

Indirect Military Involvement

Although the Soviet Union's direct involvement in Egypt's defence
was confined to the period between 1970 and 1972, more indirect
methods, such as threats, manoeuvres, alerts and naval buildups,
have been a major feature of the use of the military instrument
throughout the period. In all the Middle Eastern crises, the Soviet
Union has used the threat of force as a means of supporting Egypt's
stand. Throughout the Suez crisis, Soviet government statements
upheld the Egyptian government's right to nationalise the Canal
and condemned the Tripartite aggression of Britain, France and
Israel, culminating at the end of the crisis in the threat to launch
rocket attacks against Britain and France and to send Soviet
'volunteers' to Egypt.[52] Similarly in the 1957 and 1958 Middle
Eastern crises, Soviet statements reminded Western leaders that the
Soviet Union possessed an arsenal of ICBM's and nuclear weapons
and that the USSR 'reserves the right to take the necessary measures
in any crisis which breaks out near its frontiers'.[53] In both the 1967
and 1973 wars, the Soviet leaders warned the United States that if
Israel did not cease hostilities the Soviet Union would take
unilateral military action.[54] In the cases of the threats issued in 1956
and 1967, Soviet leaders made these statements so close to the end of
hostilities that it is difficult to see how they could have been intended
as anything more than a political gesture of solidarity with the Arab
stand. The Soviet threat to intervene during the 1973 war had to be
taken more seriously, however. In the first place, far from the crisis
being over, the Egyptian Third Army was encircled on the west
bank of the Suez Canal when the threat was made. Secondly, unlike
1956 and 1967, the Soviet Union now actually possessed the

capability to intervene effectively on a limited scale to relieve the Third Army. These two factors, combined with the use of manoeuvres and a naval buildup in the Eastern Mediterranean made the threat of military force more plausible and thus more effective.

In all the major Middle Eastern crises, with the exception of the 1956 Suez War, the Soviet Union used limited 'shows of force' to back up threats of military action. Soviet manoeuvres were carried out on the areas bordering Turkey during the Syrian crisis of October 1957 as well as following the Western intervention in Lebanon and Jordan in July 1958. During the 1957 crisis, a Soviet naval squadron visited Latakia in a show of solidarity.[55] A similar visit was made to Alexandria and Port Said after the Six-day War.[56] In both 1967 and 1973, there was a massive buildup of Soviet warships in the Eastern Mediterranean; and in both crises Soviet airborne divisions were put on the alert. Only in 1956, when the Soviet Union was preoccupied in Hungary, was there no show of force. And only in 1973 was the Soviet show of force considered to be more than a rather transparent political gesture. It was taken more seriously because by 1973 the Soviet Union had obtained the regular use of Egyptian port and air-base facilities,[57] and also had developed its amphibious-landing and non-nuclear-fighting capability.[58] The fear that the Soviet Union might actually intervene in 1973 was certainly a major factor in the American decision both to impose a Stage 3 nuclear alert and to apply increasing pressure on Israel to obey the ceasefire. In the event, the siege of the Third Army was lifted, and the Soviet leaders once again achieved their objectives without actually having to use the military instrument.

While the threat or display of force was an effective means of supporting Egypt's stand in various regional crises, it proved rather more unwieldly when the Soviet leaders sought not to support Egypt's position but to change it. As had been shown, the Soviet Union on two occasions tried to use the military instrument to achieve its own objectives. The first instance was between 1971 and 1972 when according to the Egyptians, the Soviet Union tried to stabilise the Arab–Israeli conflict by slowing down the flow of arms and using its personnel in Egypt to impede Sadat's manoeuvrability. The attempt failed with the expulsion of Soviet experts, and a loss for the Soviet Union of its favourable position in that country. Similarly after 1974, when Soviet arms supplies were decreased, the Egyptians ultimately retaliated by abrogating the 1972 treaty.

Although both Egypt and the Soviet Union were adversely affected in different ways by the break in relations, the Soviet Union was not able to find any other Middle Eastern state able or willing to provide it with port and base facilities on the same scale as Egypt.[59] For these reasons the military instrument proved to be a double-edged sword, in more ways than one.

PROPAGANDA

Propaganda can be defined as 'the deliberate attempt by the government of one state to influence the values and opinions of the population of another state through the means of mass communications, so that the behaviour of those influenced will correspond to that desired by the communicating government'.[60] From this definition, the radio emerges as the most effective method of transmitting propaganda to the target population, primarily because it is also the method over which the recipient government has least control.

The Soviet Union has made wide use of the radio in disseminating its views abroad. Particularly in the developing countries of the Arab world where the rate of literacy was still very low and where the population was largely rural and spread over vast sparsely populated areas, the advent of the transistor radio in particular made it possible to reach an audience hitherto beyond the reach of both Soviet and Western propaganda. Although the USSR began Arabic-language broadcasts in 1943,[61] it was not until the late 1950s that Soviet radio began to expand its services to the Middle East. Thus, while Arabic-language broadcasts in 1953 only amounted to approximately ten hours,[62] from a total of over 700 hours per week of Soviet external broadcasts,[63] by 1959 this figure had risen to 42 hours per week and by 1976 to over 80 hours per week.[64] By 1975, however, Radio Moscow alone was broadcasting in 64 foreign languages for a total of 1250 hours per week, and Arabic-language services if anything had slightly declined as a proportion of the total.[65]

An analysis of Soviet propaganda to the Middle East reveals a number of recurring themes. By far the most salient were the expressions of Soviet solidarity with the Arab movements for liberation from Western imperialism. This basic theme took several forms, one of which was the tendency on the part of Soviet propagandists to divide the world not so much into the traditional Stalinist camps of socialism and capitalism, but rather into diametrically opposed forces, one characterised as being 'peace-loving' 'progressive', 'democratic', and 'patriotic', and the other identified as being 'reactionary', 'imperialist', 'militaristic', and 'aggressive'. The second group consisted not only of Western governments and oil companies but also of 'Zionists', pro-Western Arab rulers and also, beginning in the 1960s, the Chinese as well. Thus, a broadcast made in 1967, condemning the divisive activities of 'the Mao Tse-tung group' in advising Nasser to carry out a people's war against Israel, contained the following statement:

> This group tries to shout louder than anyone else, but not to expose the aims of imperialism and Zionist poisonous propaganda and its danger to the Arab peoples and to the forces of peace and progress in the world, but only to conceal the aims of this criminal campaign, coming out actually on the side of imperialism and Zionism.[66]

While 'anti-imperialism' was designed to manipulate and increase anti-Western and nationalist sentiments, the second recurring theme equally reflected a keen sensitivity on the part of the Soviet propagandist to the growing demands of people in all underdeveloped countries for rapid economic growth and the solution of outstanding social problems in these countries. Soviet broadcasts repeatedly asserted that the Soviet Union not only possessed both the expertise and the experience required to assist these countries in solving their immediate economic and social problems but also that the 'Soviet model' was the one most suited to the needs of the developing states. The economic prosperity of the Soviet republics of Central Asia relative to their counterparts in the Arab East was frequently cited as proof of the potential of the 'non-capitalist part'. One such broadcast asserted that

> the Soviet Eastern Republics have . . . shown the whole world that all the oppressed peoples . . . can throw off the imperialist yoke forever . . . The Soviet Eastern Republics, like a bright torch, are an example to those countries where the labour of the peoples and the wealth of the country are still being plundered and looted by the Western monopolists.[67]

While Soviet propaganda was able to dwell on the long history of economic backwardness in the Arab world, a situation attributed to Western colonial policy, the Soviet Union was itself at a serious disadvantage for its own record on the treatment of religious minorities. Charges from Western and anti-Soviet Arab propagandists that the Soviet Union was atheistic and an 'enemy of Islam' put the Soviet propaganda machine on the defensive and forced it to spend a disproportionate amount of time trying to convince the Arab world that religious freedom was one of the cornerstones of Soviet life. In this effort, speeches and testimonials by prominent Muslim leaders from the Soviet Union, the Arab world and other socialist states were used to 'verify' Soviet statements. One such testimonial was obtained from Amir Fahd al-Faysal, a Saudi prince, who made the following statement upon leaving the Soviet Union: 'We have offered prayers with thousands of Soviet Muslims in the mosques of Moscow, Leningrad and Baku. We are convinced that there is complete religious freedom in the Soviet Union. We shall talk to the sons of my homeland about all this'.[68]

A further theme which characterised Soviet broadcasts related to the USSR's role and status in the Middle East. In particular, the USSR was portrayed as a Great Power with a justifiable interest in the events of the area and with an ability to protect and advance both Soviet and Arab interests against Western and Israeli aggression. Further than this, the Soviets also repeatedly stressed the benefits which accrued to Egypt from Soviet military and economic aid. Thus for example in a broadcast typical of the Soviet propaganda effort prior to and since the abrogation of the Treaty, a Soviet commentator reminded his listeners:

. . . the Arab peoples know full well that the Soviet Union has been right from the very beginning and still is anxious to work assiduously and continually for a total and speedy settlement of the Middle East crisis. Not once has it abandoned its political, economic, moral and military support for the just struggle of the Arab peoples. Moreover, it is largely thanks to this support that Israel and its protectors were compelled to take increasingly into account the just demands of the Arabs. The Egyptian people saw this with particular clarity during the October war when the Arab armies used Soviet weapons and inflicted a telling defeat on Israel.[69]

Propaganda Techniques

In the transmission of these themes, Soviet propagandists used a variety of the techniques described by Holsti, including (a) Transfer, (b) Testimonial (c) Name-calling, (d) Bandwagon (e) Glittering Generality and (f) Scapegoat.[70] *Transfer* attempts to 'identify one idea, person, country or policy with another to make the target approve or disapprove it'.[71] One of the most effective methods of undermining the political opponents of Soviet policy is to identify them as 'agents of imperialism' or 'lackeys of the West'. For example, in the 1959 dispute between the Soviet Union and the United Arab Republic, Khrushchev himself accused Nasser of 'speaking with the tongue of the imperialists'.[72] By the same standard, these leaders or states sympathetic to Soviet policy were described as 'progressive', and 'freedom-loving'.

In the employment of *testimonial* as a technique the propagandist 'uses an esteemed person or institution to endorse or criticise an idea or political entity. [In other words], the target is asked to believe something simply because some 'authority' says it is true'.[73] The most common form of testimonial used by Soviet propagandists was elicited from prominent Soviet and foreign Muslim leaders to the effect that Soviet Muslims enjoyed complete religious freedom. An example of the use of the testimonial was given above.[74]

Name-calling is a popular technique which seeks to form an uncritical and subjective impression of a person or government in the minds of the target population. Given the radical anti-Israeli and anti-Western tendencies of the Egyptian people during most of the post-1955 period, the attachment of any label pertaining to an individual's or government's 'rightist' 'reactionary', 'Zionist', or 'imperialist' tendencies had the most derogatory effect. In the post-1973 period when Sadat began pursuing a more pro-Western policy, his government, the Egyptian press and the Egyptian bourgeoisie were repeatedly labelled as 'rightist', 'parasitic', 'reactionary', 'exploiting', and so forth.[75] In addition, individual labels were sometimes attached to particular leaders such as Moshe Dayan, who was dubbed 'the little Napoleon from Tel Aviv'.[76]

The *bandwagon* technique 'implies that the target is in a minority if he opposes the substance of the message—and should join the majority. Or, if the target is sympathetic to the propagandists, this technique will reinforce his attitudes by demonstrating that he is on the 'right side' along with everybody else'.[77] The bandwagon technique plays on people's desire to be on 'the winning side' or to be in accord with the majority. Thus, broadcasts carrying messages on Soviet policy or the activities of the West in the Middle East contained such phrases as 'it is widely known . . . ', 'everybody knows . . .', and 'all progressive mankind supports . . .'

A statement typical of the Soviet effort to convince the Egyptians that 'history was on their side' was one made in 1964 when the commentator alleged that 'colonialism is now facing not disunited people but the sweeping current of world socialism and the national liberation movement . . . No force on earth can check the advance of this sweeping current'.[78] Equally, once Soviet–Egyptian relations worsened, the Soviets used this technique to isolate the Egyptian stand, as in this broadcast denouncing Cairo's support for Somalia:

Only a few years ago, Egypt was virtually the major prop of the African national liberation movement. It often used to defend the victims of aggression, stand up to imperialist intrigues and protect developing countries. But today Egypt encourages aggression. This is a dangerous road which is leading it into international isolation from the forces of progress.[79]

The two remaining techniques are *glittering generality* and *scapegoat*. The first pertains to the tendency of propagandists to simplify complex ideas or relationships in order both to make the notion more 'digestible' and also to gloss over any undesirable aspects. 'Socialist solidarity', 'Arab unity', and 'the national-liberation movement' are examples of three commonly used terms which create an image of coherence and unity which in reality does not exist. The second technique, *scapegoat*, was frequently used by the Soviet Union in so far as the West, Israel, oil companies, NATO, the Baghdad Pact, and CENTO were all in their turn made responsible for all the problems faced by the Egyptians. Whether it was internal political strife, economic crisis or inter-Arab rivalries, 'imperialism' in one or another of its many disguises was made the scapegoat. The following excerpt from a 1967 broadcast provides a good example of the use of the various techniques and also illustrates the length the Soviets were prepared to go in seeking to make the West and in this case the oil companies a scapegoat for Arab setbacks.

At the outbreak of the June War, as the British *Sunday Telegraph* [*testimonial*] said at the time, the oil companies had little time for

hesitation . . . The private yacht of John Rockefeller arrived in the Mediterranean . . . Regular wireless contact was established between Tel Aviv and the private yacht of Rockefeller . . . On 7th June, a ham operator in Cyprus picked up a message sent in plain language which said:
Propose to the Syrians the formation of a new cabinet and acceptance of our terms which are: to refrain from establishing a national oil industry and to conduct talks on concluding agreements which correspond with our conditions. Then the attack on Damascus will stop. It is not known to whom this wireless message was sent but everything indicates that it was meant for . . . US imperialist representatives in Israel . . . [*transfer* and *glittering generality*].

The intrigues of the oil lords [*namecalling*] cannot but obstruct the development of a natural phenomenon, that is, the restoration of the oil riches taken by colonialism to their real owners, the Arabs. . . . This is the verdict of history, which nobody can change [*bandwagon*].[80]

THE CULTURAL INSTRUMENT

The cultural instrument can be defined as the selective presentation by a government of aspects of the social system within which it operates for transmission to a foreign population, with the official acquiescence of the recipient government, and for the purpose of creating a commonwealth of shared attitudes, images and goals between the two countries. Since cultural communication flows via the recipient government, that government is capable of blocking any attempt to inculcate values which are contrary to the prevalent belief system. However, the Soviet objective of minimising Western influence corresponded to Egyptian aspirations at least until the mid-1970s, with the result that the cultural instrument was always well-suited to the achievement of this common end.

The themes of cultural diplomacy were similar to those used in the propaganda effort and generally were chosen to reinforce existing attitudes and encourage nascent ones. The Soviets used the cultural instrument primarily to strengthen Egypt's awareness of its own cultural and political independence from the West. Intrinsic to the revival of Arab cultural diplomacy was the reassertion of Islamic fundamentalism in Egypt and elsewhere. However, the Soviet

Union made practically no attempt to dissuade the Egyptians from their belief in Islam. On the contrary, a consistent theme of cultural diplomacy, as with propaganda, was the projection of the Soviet Union as a state which both tolerates and respects the rights of the individual to hold and practice religious beliefs. Related to this was the emphasis put on the ethnic, geographical and aspirational affinities between the Soviet and Egyptian people, affinities which were said to be in sharp contrast to Western 'cultural imperialism' and 'decadence'. In the transmission of these themes, the Soviet Union utilised a wide range of activities, including the performing arts, exchange of delegations, tourism, printed media, films and education.

Performing Arts

In the field of the performing arts, Egypt was host to a tremendous number of Soviet troupes, orchestras and ensembles, including the Bolshoi ballet; the ballet companies of Leningrad, Novosibirsk and Tashkent; the folkdance troupes of Moldavia, Armenia, Uzbekistan, Azerbaidjan and Georgia; the State Folklore ensemble; the Moscow and Leningrad Orchestras; the State Puppet Theatre and the State Circus.[81] The Soviet Union also helped to establish in Egypt a national folklore ensemble and a State circus and to expand the Cairo Conservatory of Music.[82] But perhaps the most important Soviet contribution to the development of the performing arts in Egypt and in the Middle East as a whole was the establishment in Cairo in 1958 of the first ballet school in the whole of Africa and the Middle East; 77 Soviet ballet instructors and choreographers were involved in its work and several of the best graduates performed with the Bolshoi in Moscow.[83] Egyptian troupes and ensembles which performed in the Soviet Union included the ballet, the puppet theatre, the National folkdance troupe, the Ridha ensemble and the Cairo Symphony Orchestra, which on one occasion gave the premier performance of the 'Moscow' Symphony by the Egyptian composer Abu Bakr Khayrat.[84] These events were crowned in September 1970 by the visit to the Soviet Union of the premier Arabic singer Om Kalthum.[85]

Tourism

Tourism increased markedly following the 20th Party Congress, and by 1958 Intourist had concluded agreements with over 80 countries.[86] Although both the Soviet Union and Egypt placed certain restrictions on the free movement of foreign nationals within their countries, as well as on visits of their own nationals to other countries, limited arrangements for tourism were made between them beginning in May 1956, when the first tourist agreement was signed. Since then the number of Soviet tourists visiting Egypt has increased steadily, as indicated in Table 9.8.

TABLE 9.8 Tourists in Egypt, 1955–74

	1955	1959	1964	1969	1974
USSR	na	2687	na	12,838	20,027
UK	11,600	5694	41,491	17,379	18,673
USA	18,256	14,644	56,795	27,707	46,851

na: data not available

Source: UN, *Statistical Yearbook*, New York: UN (various years)

Printed Media and Films

In the realm of printed media and films, the Soviet agencies with primary responsibility for production and distribution in these spheres are the International Book agency (*Mezhdunarodnaya kniga*), *Novosti* and *Tass* for printed media, and Sovexport-film for films. These agencies have had ties with Egypt since 1955. Moreover, both the Soviet Writers' Union and the USSR Academy of Sciences have established direct links with their Egyptian counterparts, resulting in the exchange of books, manuscripts and newsletters and in the preparation of several joint projects and conferences.[87]

The scope of Soviet activities in these fields is illustrated in Table 9.9, which compares the quantity of imports of printed matter and films by Egypt from the Soviet Union, the United States and Great Britain. By examining this table, several points emerge. First, there has undoubtedly been a tremendous growth in Soviet exports to Egypt, and it is interesting that book exports did not decline after Sadat came to power. However, in seeking to analyse the causes for the increases it must be borne in mind that the cost of Soviet films and printed matter was between one-third and one-half of American and British imports, and also that Egypt was not obliged to pay

TABLE 9.9 Imports of Printed Matter and Films by Egypt, 1956–74

| | Printed matter[a] | | | Films[a] | | |
	USSR	UK	USA	USSR	UK	USA
1956	4	111	133	640	11,775	4,345
1959	5	62	89	2,831	8,341	735
1962	11	71	56	1,061	5,247	3,255
1966	na	122	44	na	13,000	5,000
1970	109	108	64	2,712	2,000	3,000
1974	268	126	35	425	1,825	225

a Books, magazines and newspapers in metric tonnes; films in kg.
na data not available
Sources: UAR, Department of Statistics, *Annual Statement of Foreign Trade*, Cairo (various years); UAR, Department of Statistics, *Monthly Bulletin of Foreign Trade*, Cairo (various years), UN, Statistical Papers, *Commodity Trade Statistics*, Series D, Vo. 24, No. 27 (New York: UN, 1975), p. 25; Federation of Egyptian Industries, *Yearbook 1975* (Cairo, 1975), p. 249.

for Soviet goods in hard currency. Consequently, although it was undoubtedly true that there was a genuine desire by the Egyptian leadership, at least under Nasser, to familiarise the population with Soviet life and culture, a direct comparison may yield misleading conclusions because of the very real economic advantages involved in obtaining these materials from the Soviet Union. A further observation which can be drawn from the table is the continuing high level of British and American imports throughout the period. Considering Egypt's anti-Western declaratory policies upto 1974, a gap between declaration and performance certainly seems to have existed. This situation suggests what was a continuing pro-Western cultural, if not political, orientation at least amongst the Egyptian elites, a subject discussed below.

Although the table indicates the scope of activity, it reveals little about the types of printed matter and films exported to Egypt. Comprehensive details of titles do not exist but a limited amount of information is available. The writings of Marx and Lenin were sold openly; Soviet scientific textbooks translated into Arabic were used in many universities; and the works of many Russian and Soviet authors were imported, particularly those of Tolstoi and Gorky.[88] Concerning the types of films exported to the Arab world by the Soviet Union, those films which were produced specifically for export reflect the themes dealt with earlier and dwelt particularly on the culture of the peoples of Soviet Central Asia and on the economic achievements of the Soviet Union.[89]

However, many films made for internal Soviet distribution were unacceptable abroad, particularly those showing or glorifying revolutionary political action at the expense of traditional religious values. The Russians learned this lesson at the 1957 Soviet film festival in Egypt when President Nasser ordered suspension of the film of Gorky's *Mother* in which a woman's rejection of religion in favour of Communism and atheism is praised. Ironically, the film was replaced by an American Western.[90]

Education

Perhaps the most important part of the Soviet cultural instrument was its assistance in the education of national cadres and in the development of technical training facilities in Egypt. In discussing the transformation of the developing countries it was the 23rd Congress of the CPSU which first declared that 'the creation of national cadres is no less an important task than the development of indigenous national industries'.[91] This view was reiterated by a recent Soviet publication which stressed the problems faced by developing countries in recruiting a corps of technical elites dedicated to national programmes and goals. The publication, in dealing with the 'brain drain' which it claimed was a 'serious impediment to the growth of the national intelligentsia',[92] cited the example of Egypt where, in 1967, 38 per cent of the Egyptian graduates of foreign universities did not return home.[93] The author concluded:

> A top-priority task today is to educate the African intelligentsia in the spirit of devotion to its people, to combat its bourgeois-colonial way of thinking, and to prepare it to go over to the positions of socialism. The character of social transformations in the African countries and the ways and forms of their further sociopolitical development largely depend on this.[94]

The construction of technical training centres had the most immediate effect on the educational system in Egypt. Between 1956 and 1975, the Soviet Union helped to build and equip 43 such centres from which over 85,000 Egyptians have graduated.[95] Emphasis in the centres has been on providing basic vocational skills but has also dealt with raising standards of literacy and with providing management skills. Official statistics on the number of

Soviet personnel working in Egypt are not available. Most of the
Soviet contingent were in any case stationed in Egypt in their
capacity as economic and military advisers. Although the presence
of these advisers could have been intended also to strengthen the
cultural ties between the two countries, nevertheless the number of
personnel (mainly academics) sent to Egypt under the cultural
agreements did not exceed 500 over the entire period. Of these the
majority were lecturers in science and in the Russian language.[96] In
September 1977, Egypt announced that it would no longer extend
financial support to Soviet and East European students and scholars
wishing to come to Egypt, thus bringing this aspect of the cultural
relationship to an end.[97]

A further area of activity in the field of education was in the
training of Egyptian students in the Soviet Union. The growth of
the Soviet programme is indicated in Table 9.10. In the period after
1973, the number of Egyptian students in the USSR continued to
decrease. In the 1975–76 academic year, there were only 364
Egyptian postgraduate students remaining in the Soviet Union.[98]
Then in 1977, Cairo announced that it was transferring all of its
students from the USSR and Eastern Europe to Western universities,[99] thereby ending what had been a well-established part of
the cultural programme between the two countries.

TABLE 9.10 Egyptian Students Abroad, 1959–73

	USSR	USA	UK	Students in home universities
1959	138	725	577	92,421
1961	240	923	344	107,789
1963	240	1,217	452	145,651
1965	248	1,059	426	177,123
1966	203	993	328	179,100
1969	450	1,015	178	197,055
1972	1,351	1,148	362	272,259
1973	631	1,163	488	315,352

Sources: UNESCO, *Statistical Yearbook* (various years); Samilovskiy, op. cit., p. 33; *al-
Jumhuriya* (12 February 1963); UNESCO, *Statistics of Students Abroad, 1962–1968* (Paris,
UNESCO, 1972), pp. 58–9; McLane, op. cit., p. 122; McLaurin, op. cit., p. 130; *al-Ahsaa al-
Senui al-Aam*, Cairo, 1965; République d'Egypt, Departement de la Statistique et de
Recensement, *Annuaire Statistique, 1960* (Cairo, 1962), pp. 132–3; Saddik Abdel Razik
Mohamed Saad, *Voprosy effektivnosti ekonomicheskovo sotrudnichestva mezhdu SSSR i ARE*,
Avtoreferat, dissertation for the degree of candidate of economics (Moscow, 1976), p. 24.

In analysing Table 9.10, several points need to be borne in mind. First, although the total figure of students abroad increased until 1973, their numbers relative to students registered for higher degrees at home universities drastically declined. Moreover, it must be noted that all the students in the Soviet Union received a scholarship either from the Egyptian or Soviet governments. On the other hand, very few of the Egyptian students in Western universities received scholarships. They were mostly either self-financed or on a government loan. Consequently, the fact that the larger proportion of students preferred to study in the West is a further indication of the continued pro-Western cultural orientation of the Egyptian elites. This contention was supported by R. H. Dekmejain's study of the Egyptian elite from 1952 to 1969, which revealed that of the Cabinet ministers holding BA degrees or higher 'not a single one of the 131 received a degree from a Soviet institution or even stayed there for prolonged specialised training'.[100] However, he admitted that this may be explained partially by the recent nature of the Soviet programme. Moreover, since 1955, Western institutions have maintained several schools and universities within Egypt such as the American University of Cairo and Alexandria College. These institutions, where the language of instruction is either English or French, have traditionally catered for the educated upper classes of the Arab world, and indeed Nasser's own daughter was a student at the American University of Cairo during the 1967 Arab–Israeli war. Consequently, it would seem that pro-Western cultural orientations were far more enduring than one might have expected judging from the declaratory statements of the elites and various measures taken on the political and economic plane such as the severance of diplomatic relations, the nationalisation of Western interests, and the promulgation of socialist measures.[101] With the closing of the Soviet cultural centres in Egypt at the end of 1977, cultural relations between the two countries more or less came to an end. Educational and artistic exchanges ceased, tourism was at a low ebb, and the import licence for three Soviet journals previously sold in Egypt was revoked,[102] thus underlining both the extent to which the use of the cultural instrument is determined by the willingness of the recipient government and the difficulties involved in achieving a fundamental reorientation of values amongst a target population in the short space of two decades.

CLANDESTINE ACTIVITIES

Clandestine activities can be defined as the unauthorised political and/or quasi-military penetration by one government into the affairs of foreign societies in order to achieve political objectives. The factor which most distinguishes clandestine activities from other instruments of foreign policy is its unauthorised nature, in as much as the government of State 'A' is undertaking activity in State 'B' without the prior consent and/or knowledge of the government of State 'B'. Cultural activity, economic aid and trade, and diplomacy are all activities undertaken with the prior consent of the recipient government. Of the other instruments discussed thus far, only propaganda is also unauthorised. Propaganda, however, can be distinguished from clandestine activities in two ways. Firstly, propaganda, as defined in this study, is limited to the transmission of messages via the channels of mass communication, while clandestine activities include the recruitment of agents, the manipulation and support of dissident groups within the recipient state, the bribing of officials, the creation of political scandals, and even assassination. Secondly, while propaganda seeks to bring about an attitudinal change in the target population with the result that the pressure of public opinion will force the recipient government to act in a way commensurate with the originating government's interests, clandestine activities rely on more direct action to influence governmental policy. Before dealing specifically with the nature and scope of Soviet activities in Egypt, one further point should be made. Whilst it is generally conceived that clandestine activities are directed at encouraging rebellion or popular disillusionment amongst disaffected groups within a society, they can equally be used to discourage or eliminate dissent. In this way, clandestine activities can also be aimed at preventing change, and are thus indirectly supportive of a government.

Because governments rarely admit to undertaking actions of a clandestine or subversive nature, the analyst is unable to ascertain with any degree of certainty the scope, nature or even utility of this method as an instrument for the achievement of a state's foreign policy. Information is generally limited to 'accusations' from target governments or 'confessions' from defectors—information which is often subjective and always difficult to verify. In the case of Soviet activities in Egypt, this problem is complicated further by the fact that no Soviet diplomat or adviser was ever implicated directly in any internal disorders, or declared *persona non grata*, although in December 1977, following Sadat's visit to Jerusalem, Soviet and East European consulates and cultural centres were closed because, according to the Egyptian Prime Minister, they had 'gone beyond rejection of the initiative . . . to what constitutes definite interference in the internal affairs of the Egyptian people'.[103] It is not known what activities Salem was referring to, although reports of unrest in the Egyptian army began to appear at about this time.[104] There is sufficient information, however, to suggest that two types of clandestine activities—the use of both the Egyptian Communist Party and various front organisations—were especially employed by the Soviet Union, and it is on these two that the section will concentrate.

Speaking at the 21st Party Congress, Khrushchev categorically dismissed the allegation that foreign communist parties were under the direct control of Moscow:

> The ideologists of imperialism . . . spread false allegations that the Communist movement is the work of Moscow's hands and that the Communist and Workers' Parties are dependent on the CPSU . . . It is absurd to think that it would be possible for anyone outside a country to organise in that country a political party of the working class . . .[105]

While the Soviet leader's sentiments were echoed by many communists, there were many Arab leaders, Western observers and disillusioned Arab communists who would argue with Khrushchev's claim of innocence. To be sure, the official Soviet attitude toward foreign communist parties underwent a striking change in the mid-1950s with the Soviet leadership and press refraining from issuing public orders to foreign communists, although their activities were still followed with the closest interest in Moscow. The shift in the Soviet attitude was due in part to the realisation of the objective weakness of the proletariat and the communist parties in most developing countries including the Arab East. Thus, for example, a 1962 article by R. Avakov and G. Mirskiy on the class structure in developing countries recognised that the choice of a socialist path of development in these countries was unlikely in the foreseeable future due to the peasant origins of the proletariat, their low level of concentration in urban centres, and the limited number of class-conscious workers (communists, for example) available to educate and organise the proletariat.[106] This view remained basically unchanged throughout the 1960s and early 1970s with R. A. Ul'yanovskiy writing in 1971 that in the Third World the 'conditions do not exist for ensuring the direct leadership of the working class'. Rather, it was a question of ensuring an all-round growth in the influence of the communist parties *'in the future'* (Ul'yanovskiy's emphasis).[107] Moreover, the question of the role of communist parties in developing countries was complicated by the emergence of popular, anti-Western nationalist leaders in these states who were capable of aiding in the achievement of the Soviet Union's immediate objectives of weakening Western influence and strengthening Soviet security. In line with these objectives the Soviet Union consistently urged the communists to join with the 'national bourgeoisie' in a broad anti-imperialist front.

Nowhere did the directives from Moscow put the Arab communists in a more untenable position than in Egypt. Throughout the period from 1955–70, the Soviet Union's Middle Eastern policy was very much dependent on Nasser's continued support. However, Nasser frequently emphasised that the main objective of his regime was the creation of an independent Egypt free of influence from 'East or West'. And even though he might 'lean to one side' in his foreign policy, in domestic affairs he made it clear that the communist party, as a group, had no role to play. As such, he wanted no part in any united front with the Egyptian communists, and he had no intention of either legalising their activities or discontinuing their suppression. Despite the treatment they received in their own country especially prior to 1965, because of the importance of Nasser's regime to the achievement of Soviet objectives, the Egyptian Communist Party felt constrained to support him. The following resolution published by the Egyptian Communist Party in 1957 (a time when practically the entire Egyptian Central Committee was in prison) highlights the untenability of their situation:

> We support the general orientation of President Nasser's policy: we are not in agreement with him, however, on certain issues of internal policy, such as his attitude to political parties in general and to the existence of a legal Communist Party in particular.[108]

However, in 1964–65 Nasser, under Soviet pressure, gradually released communists from prison and allowed them to join the Arab

Socialist Union, as individuals, on the condition that they dissolve their own party organisation. This they did, and between 1965 and 1971, 'Marxists', as they were now called, played an important role in the inner core of the ASU. Soviet sources readily admit that the Egyptian communists enjoyed their greatest influence during this period. In particular, emphasis is given to the part they played in making contributions to *al-Talia* and *al-Kateb*, the theoretical journals of the ASU; in establishing an institute for socialist studies; and in preparing the programmes for both the ASU and its associated youth movement.[109]

By Nasser's death, the Soviets had great hopes of using the inner core to ensure the continuation of Egypt's pro-Soviet, socialist orientation. The leader of this group was Ali Sabri, who although not a Communist, was amenable to the strengthening of Soviet influence in Egypt generally and of communist influence in the ASU specifically. After a visit he made to Moscow in December 1970, Moscow Radio felt able to make the following optimistic assessment of relations between the USSR and the UAR:

No longer are relations being developed and strengthened only between the two states; they are also being developed and strengthened in the party sphere. This is a logical development. The UAR, which has been following the progressive path in all fields of national life, is increasingly turning to the experience of the Soviet Communist Party, that rich experience acquired in building and developing the first socialist society in the world.[110]

However, Sadat did not share the Soviet view that this was 'a logical development'; and in 1971 he ousted Ali Sabri and other prominent left-wing leaders from the ASU. Prior to the October War, Sadat blamed 'leftist Marxist ideology' for fermenting student unrest, and he subsequently expelled 90 members from the ASU. It was at this point that reports first began to circulate that Egyptian communists might go underground to prepare for regrouping.[111] After the war, Sadat's denunciation of the left within Egypt and his *rapprochement* with the United States increased the calls for the reconstitution of the party. Sadat's disengagement agreement with Israel proved to be the last straw. On 4 August 1975, a manifesto signed by 'The Secretariat of the Communist Party of Egypt' was published in the Beirut newspaper *al-Safir*. The manifesto denounced Sadat for abandoning both the 'progressive policies of the

Nasserite regime' and the 'strategic alliance with the Soviet Union'. It did not advocate Sadat's overthrow, however, since to do so would be 'an adolescent stand that ignores the presence of nationalist elements and factions within the government'.[112] Whatever the power of these nationalist factions, the CPE did not in itself make any impact upon Sadat's policy in the two years after its re-establishment. All indications suggest that it is small, with a maximum of 500 members,[113] and that its support base is limited to the industrial centres of Cairo and Helwan. As such, its utility to the Soviet leaders is seriously limited. Indeed, it could be argued that it is of more value to Sadat who can use it as a scapegoat for explaining internal unrest, as he did during the food riots which erupted throughout Egypt in 1977.[114]

Front Organisations

Although front organisations are employed by many governments as instruments of foreign policy, it was the USSR and the Comintern which first developed their use. Front organisations were utilised in Soviet relations with Egypt primarily to mobilise support for the general line of Soviet foreign policy. As such, the predominant themes expounded by front organisations were wholly consistent with those conveyed by Soviet propaganda during the period, namely the necessity for disarmament and world peace, the applicability of the Soviet model of development, the inadvisability and disadvantageous effects of forming Western-sponsored military pacts and so on.

Front organisations have been formed for a wide spectrum of groups and interests and among the most active have been the World Peace Council, the World Federation of Trade Unions, the World Federation of Democratic Youth and the Soviet Committee for Solidarity with Asian and African Countries. The World Peace Council was established in Wroclaw, Poland in August 1948; and the first World Peace Conference was held in Paris in April the next year, at which time the 'Partisans for Peace' campaign was launched. The Peace Partisans were particularly important in publicising the Soviet commitment to disarmament and peaceful coexistence, especially following the 20th Party Congress. In the Middle East, the Peace Partisans were one of the most active of the Communist front organisations. The influential editor of *al-Masa*, Khalid Moheiddin, was the General Secretary of the UAR

National Peace Council,[115] which was legalised by Nasser in 1957. The Peace Partisans and the World Peace Council consistently publicised Soviet views on the resolution of the Middle East conflict, on the just rights of the Palestinians, and more recently on the necessity of reconvening the Geneva conference. In December 1977, Sadat announced that the Egyptian Peace Council had been banned 'since it is a communist council and since its chairman goes to Moscow to supply information and receive instructions'.[116]

The World Federation of Trade Unions was initially established by British trade unionists in 1943. However, they soon became disillusioned with the amount of control the Soviet Union was exerting within it, and they, along with some American and Dutch colleagues, established the rival International Confederation of Free Trade Unions.[117] Nevertheless, during the mid-1950s, the WFTU still claimed to represent over 106 million workers in 80 countries, although most of the membership resided in Communist countries.[118] In addition, the WFTU's international prestige has been considerably enhanced by the 'Category A' consultative status it holds with a number of UN organisations. Independent trade unions have never existed in Egypt, but in 1957 Nasser established a government-controlled Confederation of Labour which had a membership of 433,000.[119] Although the Confederation was not officially affiliated with the WFTU, Egyptian trade union delegations made many official visits to the USSR and participated in the establishment of several of its subsidiary bodies, such as the International Trade Union Committee of Solidarity with the Algerian Workers and People, founded in Cairo in September 1958.[120]

The World Federation of Democratic Youth was founded in 1945; and it has engaged in a number of activities including congresses, world youth festivals, and the publication of magazines and newsletters, in an effort to enlist support amongst young people in various countries for Soviet policies. The WFDY in conjunction with another front organisation, the International Union of Students, sponsored a scholarship scheme for study in the Soviet Union and East Europe. However, there is little evidence that Communist-controlled youth organisations made much headway in Egypt, where the regime was also trying to enlist support amongst the youth through the creation of mass organisations such as the Liberation Rally, the National Union and the Arab Socialist Union.

Indeed few of the Soviet-supported organisations met with any real success in Egypt. The only exception was the Afro-Asian Solidarity Council, which was established at the first Afro-Asian Solidarity Conference, held in Cairo in 1957. The conference set up a permanent council and an eleven-man secretariat which included a Chinese and a Russian delegate. Although the first conference was supportive of the overall orientation of Soviet foreign policy, with resolutions being passed calling for peace, disarmament, economic aid without strings, and denouncing colonialism and imperialism, the Soviet delegation soon lost control of the Council. By the third conference held in Tanganyika in February 1963, delegates were condemning imperialism from both the East and the West; and the Chinese had successfully exploited the racial issue to the disadvantage of the USSR.[121]

Despite their questionable success, all of the front organisations were designed to secure broader support for the general orientation of Soviet foreign policy. By popularising the appeals for peace, disarmament, and anti-imperialism, the Soviet Union hoped to increase public pressure on foreign governments to pursue policies acceptable to Soviet interests. Front organisations thus served not only to reinforce the other instruments of Soviet foreign policy by disseminating information and encouraging a favourable image of Soviet intentions, but they were also a vital source of information for Soviet leaders about conditions in these countries. However, the Soviet Union was able to maintain control over these organisations only as long as it maintained its hegemonial position in the Bloc. By 1961, Soviet leadership was no longer assured, with the Chinese making their own bid for support, not only in the front organisations but also among the communist parties. Thus, for example, at the fifth Congress of the WFTU the Chinese delegate supported a more militant line and defiantly declared that China's growing friendship with other developing countries 'is evergreen and indestructible by any force'.[122]

EFFECTS

It is practically impossible to determine precisely the effect which any particular instrument had on achieving a particular outcome, since in reality all the various instruments interacted with each other and with other factors both in the psychological environment of the decision-makers and in the external environment to produce a set of outcomes. In this interaction, instruments had various intended and unintended effects. For example, the Soviet Union supplied arms to Egypt primarily to bolster the latter's anti-Western foreign policy and thereby to enhance the Soviet Union's world position and decrease the threat to her security which emanated from Western manoeuvres near the Soviet southern perimeter. However, by improving Egypt's military capability, the Soviet Union also increased the likelihood of war in the region. During periods of conflict, the American presence in the Mediterranean was if anything increased, resulting in a renewed threat to Soviet security. Thus, it could be argued that the arms transfers produced effects wholly contrary to Soviet intentions. This was why, as has been discussed, the Soviet leaders continued to supply weapons but did everything in their power to prevent the outbreak of hostilities. Furthermore, the use of the military instrument helped to bolster Egypt's anti-Western foreign policy only as long as the Egyptian leaders themselves perceived the West to be the primary antagonist both in regional and international affairs. However, when this ceased to be the case, and when the Egyptian government sought to continue obtaining weapons from the Soviet Union while improving its relations with the United States, then arms transfers ceased to be effective for the achievement of Soviet objectives.

If it is difficult for decision-makers to control the effects an instrument will have on outcomes, it is equally difficult for the analyst to isolate the role which any particular instrument has played in producing that outcome. For example, if it can be said that a commonwealth of shared attitudes and goals (the main objective of propaganda and the cultural instrument) did exist between the Soviet Union and Egypt during the latter part of Nasser's rule, then one would be hard put to determine which was the most influential instrument in creating this unity of purpose. A convincing argument could be put forward to support the view that the delivery of even one MiG did far more to strengthen Soviet–Arab friendship that the thousands of tonnes of films and books imported from the Soviet Union each year. While it is difficult to draw any specific conclusion about the *effects* of particular instruments, nevertheless certain general observations can be made about the *effectiveness* of certain instruments. The potential impact of some instruments—particularly economic and military aid—is very much related to a state's capabilities. Thus so long as the Soviet

Union did not possess the military capability to intervene on a limited scale in the Middle East, her military manoeuvres and threats of force lacked credibility. Other instruments are however less related to capabilities in any concrete sense. In particular, diplomacy, propaganda, clandestine activities and the cultural instrument are not so clearly and directly related to a state's economic and military capabilities. The effectiveness of British diplomacy since the decline of her world role is due more to skill and continued prestige (admittedly both capabilities in one sense) than to economic and military power. In a similar vein, Nasser relied heavily on propaganda to compensate for Egypt's ineffectiveness in the military and economic sectors.[123] The effects and effectiveness of instruments are, therefore, only a part of a wider network of relationships between capabilities, constraints, objectives and instruments, and it is these factors which interact with decision-makers' images and perceptions as well as with events in the external environment to produce outcomes.

10 Outcomes and Consequences

By the spring of 1978, Soviet influence in Egypt was at its lowest point since 1955; and many observers were concluding that the Soviet Union's current position in Egypt marked the failure of its objectives and the bankruptcy of its policy towards both Egypt and other states of the Third World. It was in 1962 that one American analyst, writing on the similar failures of Western policies in the Middle East, stated that 'if history teaches anything, it is that a power or group of powers apparently on the decline can do nothing right, while an apparently or really rising power can do nothing wrong'.[1] Recent Soviet setbacks in the Middle East would seem to run counter to the conclusion that the Soviet Union 'can do nothing wrong'. Likewise, the improvement of Egypt's relations with the West and its recognition of the role which the United States could play in bringing about a settlement to the Arab–Israeli conflict underline the almost capricious nature of alignments in Middle Eastern politics and the resultant difficulties in determining the overall success or failure of Great Power policies.

In seeking to analyse the results of Soviet involvement in Egypt, as well as the reasons for these results, the criteria to be used in judging Soviet policy must first be established. The success of any policy clearly can only be determined by comparing outcomes with objectives. Soviet involvement during the height of the Nasser era and Soviet exclusion after the takeover by Sadat can be deemed a success or failure only to the extent that they lived up to, or fell short of, stated Soviet objectives. Moreover, the analysis must take into consideration the long-term results of Soviet policy throughout the period of its involvement since 1955 and not just the setbacks it has suffered in recent years. Finally, given that Soviet relations with Egypt were only part of a much, broader strategy pursued by Moscow, consideration must also be given to the extent to which those relations were instrumental in producing changes in the balance of power in other area.

The objectives pursued by the Soviet Union in Egypt since 1955, as discussed in Chapter 8, were found to be clustered around several key issue-areas. In the early period from 1955–58, strategic-military considerations dominated Moscow's policy, with the USSR establishing relations with Egypt and other countries of the Middle East in order to reduce the perceived threat to Soviet security emanating from Western attempts to establish a collective security system on the Soviet Union's southern perimeter. This objective was upgraded in the 1958–67 period, when Soviet leaders sought to use Nasser's pre-eminent position throughout the Middle East and the Third World for the formation of a broad progressive front both to decrease Western influence in the Arab world and to support the Soviet stand on issues—such as Vietnam, Czechoslovakia, Berlin, and disarmament—which were fairly peripheral to the Egyptian leadership. During the same period, Soviet interests in encouraging domestic reforms inside Egypt also took shape, although it was not until Soviet influence reached its zenith in 1967–72 that Moscow sought the radical retransformation of Egyptian society, and the establishment in Egypt of port and base facilities for the pursuit of broader Soviet strategic goals in the eastern Mediterranean and the Indian Ocean. With the downfall of the Ali Sabri group in 1971 and the expulsion of experts in 1972, Soviet objectives were downgraded to include the maintenance of whatever influence was possible with the Sadat regime and, failing that, the isolation of Egypt from the rest of the Arab world.

In the achievement of these objectives, the Soviet Union certainly met with some success. The elimination of the immediate threat to Soviet security was largely achieved following the 1958 Iraqi revolution which brought to power a government committed to an anti-Western stand. After that year, Western hopes of obtaining Arab participation in a collective security pact were ended. Indeed with the adherence by other Arab regimes to Nasser's rather pro-Soviet brand of non-alignment, the Soviet influence on, and benefits from, the foreign policy stances of these regimes increased tremendously over the pre-1955 level. Moscow benefited from the reorientation in Egypt's foreign policy both directly and indirectly. The West could no longer rely on Egypt to provide naval facilities or military support in a war which would threaten vital shipping routes through the Suez Canal. Nor could it depend upon enlisting Nasser's considerable prestige in upholding Western interests in either the Middle East or the Third World. Indeed, from the time of

Suez until after the October war, Egypt almost without exception
(Sadat's support of Numeiri's counter-coup against the Sudanese
communists in 1971 was one such exception) actively worked to
undermine Western economic and political interests both domestically, through the nationalisation of banks and the restrictions on
foreign capital and externally, by supporting anti-Western and
anti-colonial movements in such countries as the Yemen, Aden,
Algeria, the Congo and Nigeria. Moreover, Nasser's status in the
Middle East was such that many of the regimes which came to
power during the period (such as in Syria between 1956–58, Iraq
between 1963–68, Yemen between 1962–70, post-1969 Libya and
Sudan, as well as in Egypt for several years after Nasser's own death)
adhered to 'Nasserism' and its implicit anti-Western orientation. In
this way, the Soviet Union also benefited indirectly from the spread
of Egypt's influence. Having then established their own presence in
these other countries, the Soviet leaders in many cases were able to
build up a relationship with these regimes which was independent of
Cairo's attitude towards Moscow, and which accordingly was able
to survive the Soviet–Egyptian rift following Sadat's assumption of
power. This has been one success for Soviet policy which, thus far,
has not been eroded by the deterioration of relations between
Moscow and Cairo.

A second objective which was pursued with perhaps more
temporary and partial success was the attempt to align Egypt's
foreign policy in such a way that it would completely coincide with
Soviet interests. Certainly, Egypt did support the Soviet stand on
most international issues at least up until 1974, when this unity of
purpose soon faded with Sadat's condemnation of Soviet activities
in Africa and elsewhere. During the height of its influence in Egypt
from 1967 to 1972, the Egyptian willingness to allow the Soviets
access to base and port facilities contributed to the change in the
Soviet perception of its role in the Middle East and Africa and a
resultant expansion of its military presence in these areas. Although
Egypt retook control of the airfields used by the USSR in 1972 and
denied the Soviet navy access to Egyptian ports in 1976, nevertheless there seems no indication that these events have produced a
diminution of the Soviet perception of its role in the area. Rather,
the Soviets have attempted, as far as possible, to find other countries
capable and willing to supply the facilities they formerly enjoyed in
Egypt. Thus while the exclusion of Soviet military influence cannot
be termed a success for the Soviet Union, nevertheless the

upgrading of its presence in the area as a whole, which remains relatively undisturbed, was certainly a legacy of its past relationship with Cairo.

If the Soviet leaders were able to enlist Egypt's support for the general line of Soviet foreign policy, as well as for the expansion of the USSR's strategic role, they were also able to exert not inconsiderable leverage over Egypt's own policy, especially towards Israel. The Soviet Union successfully exercised influence on both decisions and outcomes in that issue-area in a number of ways. Consultation between the Soviet and Egyptian governments over their joint approach to the Arab–Israeli problem has been a regular feature of their relations ever since 1955.[2] Although their views did not always converge, nevertheless the Soviet attitude to the conflict was an important input into the Egyptian decision-making process both directly, through negotiations, letters and the intervention of the Soviet ambassador in Cairo, and indirectly, through the Egyptian perception of possible Soviet reaction to any particular course of action which the Egyptians might take. Thus, while the Soviets were not party to many of those Egyptian decisions which led to the 1967 and 1973 wars, nevertheless Egyptian calculations of Soviet responses were vital components of the decision-making process and were important determinants of the Egyptian decisions not to launch a pre-emptive strike in 1967 and not to attack Israel within its pre-1967 borders in 1973.[3] Even when the Soviets were not able to influence Egyptian decisions directly, they were in a strong position to influence outcomes. For example, the Soviet military commitment to the defence of Egyptian airspace during the War of Attrition led to the cessation of Israel's bombing of targets deep inside Egypt. The Soviet reluctance to supply Cairo with all the weapons on the Egyptian shopping list was given by Sadat as the reason for not launching a war against Israel in 1971 during his 'year of decision'. Soviet recalcitrance to supply arms after 1974 has also influenced outcomes since the military option effectively is no longer open to the Egyptian leaders. During the 1973 war, the combination of Soviet diplomatic pressure and its threat of military intervention, along with American activities, saved Egypt's Third Army.[4] Finally, the level of Soviet arms supplies to Egypt has decisively influenced outcomes in so far as Soviet leaders have withheld those weapons which would allow the destruction of the state of Israel while supplying those arms which would prevent total Egyptian defeat (if one accepts the argument that the 1967 defeat was due not to the lack of Soviet arms, but to Israel's superior performance and the failure of the Egyptians to master the use of Soviet arms). In all of these ways, the Soviet Union was able to exert a high degree of control over both Egyptian decisions, and the outcomes of those decisions. Soviet inability to exercise total control, however, has contributed to the continuing instability of the region and as such constitutes a failure for Soviet policy, as will be discussed below.

A final objective which met with some success was the radical transformation of the Egyptian economy. Prior to Soviet involvement Egypt had virtually a one-crop economy, with the state sector accounting for only fifteen per cent of the Gross Domestic Product (GDP) in 1953.[5] The influx of Soviet credits and technical assistance helped Egypt to industrialise, and reduce her dependence upon the import of many vital commodities. It also led to a marked increase in the size of the state sector, which in 1975 produced over 55 per cent of the total Egyptian GDP, and 80 per cent of the total industrial output.[6] Sadat's expressed intention to reduce the size of this sector has proved difficult, with the 1978–82 five-year plan earmarking for the public sector £E10,000 million out of the total £E14,000 million allocated for investment.[7] Moreover, the Soviets were successful to a certain extent in reorienting Egyptian trade away from the West, with the Soviet Union still receiving more Egyptian exports in 1977 than any other country, a position which partially reflects Egypt's use of trade to repay its debt to the USSR. The provision of vast quantities of Egyptian long-staple cotton certainly has helped to meet the growing demand for consumer goods in the Soviet Union and has offset some of the economic disadvantages the Soviets have incurred in their relations with Cairo.

Examining the balance-sheet of Soviet involvement in Egypt, on the credit side one would have to include a number of political, strategic and economic gains. But it is a moot point whether, given the losses incurred by the Soviet Union in Egypt after 1972, the debits to the Soviet Union of that relationship up to 1978 did not outnumber the credits. In the first place, while Soviet activity in the Middle East in the mid-1950s contributed to the Western failure to elicit Arab membership in a regional defence system, the threat to Soviet security was minimised only as long as the West was dependent upon land bases contiguous to Soviet frontiers as a means of undermining Soviet security. With the development of the ICBM, the Polaris submarine, inflight refuelling techniques and aircraft carriers, the West no longer absolutely required such bases. This is not to say that NATO and CENTO bases in Greece, Turkey, Pakistan, and Iran were no longer important in Soviet strategic calculations. Rather, the closedown of these bases would no longer eliminate the perception of Western threat to Soviet security emanating from the Middle East. Instead, this threat now resided primarily in the possibility that a war between Israel and the Arab states could result in a confrontation between the Great Powers. In this way, the Soviets found themselves in a dilemma. They established influence in the Middle East largely through their ability to supply arms which the Arabs then turned against Israel. While the Soviets regarded Israel as an 'outpost of imperialism' and supported Arab efforts to recapture lost territory, at the same time they feared both a total Arab victory (which they calculated the Americans would prevent, thus possibly forcing them also to intervene) and a total Arab defeat (which they would likewise have to prevent at the risk of losing all credibility in the area). Soviet diplomatic and military activity was gauged, therefore, to prevent either eventuality. Nevertheless, as long as the Soviets felt compelled to provide arms as a means of establishing and maintaining influence, and as long as they were unable to completely control the use to which these armaments were put by the Arab states, the possibility of Great Power confrontation existed, and the threat to Soviet security remained—and will remain until the conflict is resolved.

Soviet security thus was undermined by the continuing instability in the area. Its influence also was threatened by Soviet behaviour in the various Middle East crises and by the performance of its weapons in the hands of the Arabs. The Soviets came under criticism in 1956, 1967 and 1973 for their extreme cautiousness. The Egyptian belief that Moscow basically gave 'too little, too late' and that Israel received far more from the United States than the Arabs received from the Soviet Union led to the widely held view that the Soviets were unreliable allies whose priorities overwhelmingly lay with preventing a superpower confrontation. Additionally, the successive Arab defeats exposed the Soviets to criticism both of their weapons and of their military doctrine, with its concentration on massive firepower and static lines of defence. While Soviet objectives were not served by the conflict in the Middle East, this did not necessarily mean that the Soviet Union had an interest in supporting the settlement of that conflict at any cost. Soviet behaviour throughout the period showed that it was concerned only with a settlement which would conform with Soviet interests—in other words, the recognition of the USSR as a Great Power with a legitimate role in the area. Soviet denunciation of the Rogers' plan, Kissinger's step-by-step approach, and the Sadat initiative, and its concomitant support of the Geneva conference, in which it was co-chairman, were consistent with the view that the Soviet Union would rather not have a settlement than to have one which excluded Soviet participation. This attitude was not contrary to the Soviet belief, shared by many Arab leaders, that its own partici-pation was also the best guarantee of a settlement which conformed with Arab demands. Because of the past coincidence of Soviet–Arab views on a settlement, it remains to be seen whether the Soviets would support a settlement which met Arab demands, while at the same time excluding Soviet interests.

The final area in which Soviet objectives did not meet with complete success was in the establishment of a pro-Soviet socialist regime in Egypt. Their support of Nasser's policies and their commitment of vast quantities of economic and technical aid were based on the view that although Nasser himself was not a communist, conditions could be created which would eventually result in the socialist reorientation of the Egyptian social and economic system. Aid to the state sector and the encouragement of industrialisation was given out of the ideological belief that the transformation of the economic base would eventually produce conditions forcing a corresponding change in the political super-structure. The reforms undertaken by Nasser, and in particular the increased role of leftist elements in the Arab Socialist Union, were thought to be the first fruits of Soviet policy. The growth in the number of industrial workers, particularly in large enterprises with a high concentration of labour, was also thought to have long-term consequences for the eventual reorientation of Egyptian society. Thus, as late as 1976, Soviet commentators maintained that these fundamental changes in Egypt's economic system

enable the working class to act more and more successfully against the policy of the national bourgeoisie whenever it clashes with national interests, against any strengthening of foreign capital, in defence of its economic rights and trade union freedoms, and for the ruling circles' socioeconomic policy to be changed in favour of a socialist reorientation.[8]

However, Sadat's economic policy of encouraging the private sector and foreign investment clearly repudiated the Soviet view that the process begun under Nasser was 'irreversible'. Soviet analysts thus warned that 'the reactionary forces . . . have not abandoned their fight against socialist orientation. The actions of the reactionary forces in the Arab Republic of Egypt against the public economic sector and socialist orientation is, on the whole, a striking example of this'.[9] The failure of the Soviet Union to maintain Egypt's momentum towards socialism exposed the Soviet leadership to criticism from within the communist movement that there was no substitute for proletarian hegemony, and that the years spent by the Egyptian Communist Party 'wandering in the wilderness' had been wasted. Soviet leaders, in reply, pointed to the failure of Sadat's economic policy to attract the required foreign investment and to the January 1977 food riots in Cairo as proof that Sadat ultimately would have to take cognisance of the fundamental and lasting changes which occurred in Egypt under Nasser. The re-emergence of Islamic fundamentalism and the reconstitution of the Wafd Party, banned sinced 1953, would seem to indicate, however, either that the Soviets have overestimated the durability of these changes or that Sadat intended to proceed despite them.

Obviously, therefore, the Soviet leaders miscalculated the extent to which the adherence by Egypt to an anti-Western foreign policy would lead inexorably to the establishment of the political and economic foundations for a pro-Soviet and quasi-socialist regime. The explanation for this miscalculation lies to a large degree in the fact that by increasing Egypt's ability to resist Western influence, the Soviet Union in a number of ways helped to produce a situation incompatible with the realisation of their long-term goal. By supporting the espousal of anti-Western sentiment, by encouraging nationalist fervour when it was directed against Western influence, by failing to condemn the revival of Islamic fundamentalism when it served as a unifying agent against the 'cosmopolitanism' of Western culture, the Soviet Union paradoxically also strengthened the legitimacy of leaders and the intransigence of values and attitudes antithetic to communism and to the Soviet political and social system. Thus, far from contributing to the establishment and permanency of Soviet influence in Egypt, the strategy adopted for expelling Western influence, if anything, actually undermined the possibility of strengthening the Soviet position.

The problems faced by the Soviet leaders in formulating and

implementing a successful policy towards Egypt highlight the anarchical nature of the international system and the difficulty, for policy-makers and analysts alike, of assessing and forecasting the relationship between objectives and outcomes. Because the psychological and operational environments are incongruent; because the role of personality is important yet indeterminate; because changes in leadership are disruptive, yet often decisive; and because influences from the domestic and external environments are largely outside the control of decision-makers—for all these reasons, outcomes very rarely coincide with objectives. Some Soviet analysts have recognised the difficulties involved in formulating a clear and coherent policy in the Middle East, and many of them accept that in the politically unstable developing countries, it is almost impossible to assume that the achievement of one goal will lead to the fulfilment of another or that any political trend is irreversible. Thus, as stated by K. Ivanov in a 1962 article which has continued relevance today:

> The picture of the historical process as a straight and continuous ascent from the lower to the higher stages belongs to the realms of fantasy . . . Zigzags, sudden twists and turns, outbursts of contradictions, occasional advances and retreats, steps forward and steps back are all interwoven into the live fabric of every people's history. This is especially manifest in the national liberation movement of countries where the working class is only emerging . . . Here nothing is automatically certain in advance, every step forward has to be won in battle, and progress is often attained at the price of bitter disappointments, mistakes and searches.[10]

Few quotations would better summarise the volatile nature of Soviet–Egyptian relations since 1955 and underline the folly of predicting future trends. Thus, just as analysts in 1971 thought it inconceivable that Soviet experts would be expelled from Egypt a year later, so it would be equally precipitant to assume that the present impasse caused by the abrogation of the treaty is of a permament nature.

Notes and References

NOTES TO CHAPTER I

1. J. Stalin, *Pravda* (November 1918), as quoted in Stanley W. Page, *Lenin and World Revolution* (New York: McGraw-Hill Book Company, 1972), p. 142.
2. The various debates at the Second Congress can be found in Seymour Becker, *Russian Protectorates in Central Asia. Bukhara and Khiva, 1865–1924* (Cambridge, Mass.: Harvard University Press, 1968), pp. 240–57; and Helene Carrere d'Encausse and Stuart R. Schram, *Marxism and Asia* (London: Allen Lane, The Penguin Press, 1969), pp. 149–68.
3. J. Stalin, as quoted in E. H. Carr, *Socialism in One Country, 1924–1926*, Vol. 3 (London: Macmillan and Co., 1964), p. 650.
4. Quoted in Jane Degras, ed., *The Communist International 1919–1943*, Vol. 3 (London: Oxford University Press, 1956), p. 78.
5. Ibid., p. 347.
6. Maurice Thorez, Report to the Ninth Congress of the French Communist Party (December 1937), from Carrere d'Encausse and Schram, op. cit., p. 249.
7. Ye. Zhukov, 'Obostrennyy krizis kolonial'noy sistemy', *Bol'shevik*, No. 23 (15 December 1947), pp. 51–64.
8. Ye. Zhukov, 'Voprosy natsional'no-kolonialnoy bor'by posle vtoroy mirovoy voyny', *Voprosy ekonomiki*, No. 9 (1949), p. 58.
9. Ibid.
10. L. Vatolina, 'Yegipet i krizis Britanskoy kolonial'noy politiki', *Imperialisticheskaya bor'ba za Afriku i osvoboditel'noye dvizheniye narodov* (Moscow, 1953), p. 127. A similar view is expressed in L. Vatolina, 'Bor'ba Yegipetskovo naroda za mir i nezavisimost', *Voprosy ekonomiki*, No. 2 (1952), pp. 61–73; and L. Gordonov, *Yegipet* (Moscow, 1953).
11. D. S. Carlisle, 'The Changing Soviet Perception of the Development Process in the Afro-Asian World', *Midwest Journal of Political Science*, Vol. 8, No. 4 (1964), p. 388.
12. Stephen Page, *The USSR and Arabia* (London: Central Asian Research Centre, 1971), p. 19.
13. David J. Dallin, *Soviet Foreign Policy After Stalin* (London: Methuen and Co., 1960), pp. 15–17; and Isaac Deutscher, *Stalin* (London: Penguin, 1966), p. 602.
14. The influence of these factors will be analysed in greater detail in Chapter 5 below.

NOTES TO CHAPTER 2

1. Stockholm International Peace Research Institute, *The Arms Trade with the Third World* (London: Paul Elek Ltd., 1971), p. 555.
2. Mohamed Heikal, *Nasser: The Cairo Documents* (London: New English Library, 1972), p. 52; Erskine Childers, *The Road to Suez* (London: MacGibbon and Kee, 1962), pp. 120–21. A similar view was expressed by Nasser in his interview with Richard Crossman in *The Hindu* (2 February, 1954).
3. Robert Stephens, *Nasser* (London: Allen Lane, The Penguin Press, 1971), p. 149.
4. British Broadcasting Corporation, *Summary of World Broadcasts, Part IV: The Arab World, Israel, Greece, Turkey, Iran* (henceforth referred to as *SWB IV* (24 April 1955), pp. 26–7.
5. *Izvestiya* (17 April 1955).
6. Views on the date of the conclusion vary. Those sources putting the date of the agreement in October 1955 include Miles Copeland, *The Game of Nations* (London: Weidenfeld and Nicolson, 1969), pp. 130–36; Heikal, op. cit., pp. 56–60; L. Dvorzak, *Mirovaya sistema sotzialisma i razvivayushchikhsiye strany* (Moscow, 1965), p. 102; an editorial by Heikal in *al-Ahram* (25 December 1958); and Prague radio which claimed the agreement had been signed on 8 September 1955, in *SWB IV* (20 September 1955), p. 9. Those sources which claim that the deal was concluded before Egyptian negotiations with the United States had broken down in May 1955 include K. Ivanov, 'National Liberation Movement and Non-Capitalist Path of Development', *International Affairs*, No. 5 (Moscow, 1965), p. 61; and Uri Ra'anan, *The USSR Arms the Third World* (Cambridge, Mass.: MIT Press, 1969). For an interesting and full, if controversial, account of events surrounding Nasser's decision to accept Soviet arms, see Humphrey Trevelyan, *The Middle East in Revolution* (London: Macmillan, 1970).
7. Heikal, op. cit., p. 58.
8. Heikal in *al-Ahram* (25 December 1958); *Pravda* (20 February 1956); Ra'anan, op. cit., pp. 86–130; D. Dallin, op. cit., p. 399. This claim is discussed in greater detail in Chapter 6 below.
9. See G. Akopyan, 'O natsional'no-osvoboditel'nom dvizhenii narodov Blizhnevo i Srednevo Vostoka', *Voprosy ekonomiki*, No. 1 (1953), pp. 58–75; L. Sh. Gordonov, op. cit.; L. N. Vatolina, 'Yegipet i krizis Britanskoy kolonial'noy politiki', op. cit., pp. 92–127.
10. *SWB IV* (6 July 1956), p. 13; *SWB IV* (22 May 1956), p. 18. For the possible motives behind the recognition of the CPR see Trevelyan, op. cit., p. 34; and Heikal, op. cit., p. 65.
11. *Al-Akhbar* (10 August 1955), quoted in Walter Laqueur, *The Soviet Union and the Middle East* (London: Routledge and Kegan Paul, 1959), p. 219.
12. I. Bochkarev, 'The New Spirit in Egypt', *New Times*, No. 3 (1957), p. 8.
13. See, for example, the accounts of Khrushchev's interview with *al-Ahram* and Shepilov's refusal to publicly back the Arabs against Israel during his visit to Damascus in the *New York Times* (24 June 1956); *The Observer* (1 July 1956); *The Scotsman* (5 July 1956).
14. *Izvestiya* (18 April 1956).

15. The conditions were reported by various sources to include:

(1) Supervision of Egyptian Government accounts.
(2) the restriction of Egypt's right to conclude payments agreements with foreign countries and the subjection of these agreements to World Bank approval.
(3) World Bank authority to fix a limit to Egypt's foreign indebtedness.
(4) one-third of Egypt's internal revenue was to be diverted to the High Dam for the next ten years.
(5) the imposition of statutory controls to curb the growth of inflation; and
(6) construction contract tenders for various aspects of the Dam were not to be awarded to any Communist-bloc country.

SWB IV (27 October 1958), p. 1; Anthony Nutting, *Nasser* (London: Constable, 1972), p. 132; and Trevelyan, op. cit., p. 132.

16. Details of British and American objections to the Dam can be found in *New York Times* (18 June 1956); *New York Times* (20 June 1956); *The Times* (11 October 1955); and Stephens, op. cit., pp. 189–90.
17. N. Frankland and V. Kine, eds., *Documents on International Affairs, 1956* (London: Oxford University Press, 1959), pp. 69–70.
18. British Broadcasting Corporation, *Summary of World Broadcasts, Part I: The Soviet Union* (hereafter referred to as *SWB I*) (3 August 1956), p. 55.
19. For the texts of Soviet statements during the Suez Crisis, see *Suez, The Soviet View* (London: Soviet News, Booklet No. 21, 1956); *Suez and the Middle East: Documents* (London: Soviet News, Booklet No. 25, nd); and D. T. Shepilov, *Suetskiy Vopros* (Moscow, 1956).
20. Heikal, op. cit., p. 111; and *SWB IV* (6 November 1956), p. 3.
21. *Izvestiya* (5 November 1956).
22. Heikal, op. cit., p. 122.
23. Quoted in D. Dallin, op. cit., p. 418.
24. *New York Times* (6 January 1956).
25. *Izvestiya* (13 January 1957). Also *Izvestiya* (8 January 1957); and I. M. Lemin, '"Doktrina Eizenkhyara"—programma kolonial'novo zakabaleniya Blizhnevo Vostoka', *Sovetskoye vostokovedeniye*, No. 1 (1957), pp. 3–21.
26. *Izvestiya* (13 February 1957); 'SSSR i Arabskiy Vostok', *Sovremennyy vostok*, No. 3 (1957), pp. 1–3; and *SWB IV* (15 February 1957), p. 1.
27. Patrick Seale, *The Struggle for Syria: A Study of Post-War Arab Politics, 1945–1958* (London: Oxford University Press, 1965), p. 284.
28. The actual strength of communist influence in Syria and the objectives pursued by the Soviet Union there remain a source of some controversy amongst analysts. David Dallin makes the forthright statement that 'exact information in the possession of Western foreign offices left no doubt that Moscow really expected to acquire Syria as a satellite' (Dallin, op. cit., p. 469). However, he does not substantiate his views, which are largely at odds both with the conclusions drawn by other observers of Arab affairs and with Soviet policy towards the Arab communist parties during this period. Soviet policy was aimed at supporting those groups most capable of furthering the achievement of the Soviet objective of meeting the challenge to Soviet security posed by the Baghdad Pact and the Eisenhower Doctrine. The

Arab communist parties were encouraged to ally with other groups in a broadly based national front to achieve this objective, with communist hegemony in the front not even specified. Indeed in the 1957 Syrian byelections, the Soviet embassy is reported to have intervened to secure the withdrawal of a communist candidate in both Damascus and Homs in favour of a more generally acceptable left-wing representative (H. A. R. (Kim) Philby, *Observer Foreign News Service*, No. 12238, 30 April 1957). Moreover, extensive coverage and encouragement was given not so much to the Syrian Communist Party's General Secretary, Khalid Bagdash, as to Khalid al-Azm and other pro-Soviet but anti-communist leaders. These factors lend weight to the views held by Walter Laqueur, Patrick Seale, M. S. Agwani and others that for the Soviet Union, the anti-Western foreign policy of a state was 'all that mattered' (Laqueur, op. cit., p. 254), and that 'Moscow evidently was not in a mood to disturb its good relations with the dominant elements in Syria for the sake of local Communist gains of dubious value' (M. S. Agwani, *Communism in the Arab East* (London: Asia Publishing House, 1969), p. 95. Also see Stephens, op. cit., p. 265; and Seale, op. cit., p. 287).

29. For example, Radio Amman, in a broadcast typical of the steady stream of propaganda kept up by the anti-unity forces throughout the troubled months claimed that 'nothing grieves us more than this ill-fortune of . . . Syria where communists are now staging the greatest tragedy ever suffered by Arab states'. The broadcaster went on to blame 'the Communist-administered Syrian Deuxième Bureau' for creating an 'atmosphere of anarchy and chaos inside Jordan' (*SWB IV*, 26 September 1957, pp. 6–7). In fact, the Deuxième Bureau (Syria's military intelligence) under Colonel Abd al-Hamid Saraj was one of the groups which later pressed Nasser to form the UAR precisely because of its own fears about the growth of communist influence. Moreover it was the Deuxième Bureau which participated most actively in the 1959 suppression of the Syrian Communist Party.

30. *SWB IV* (4 September 1957), p. 7.

31. *SWB I* (27 September 1957), p. 11.

32. Dwight D. Eisenhower, *The White House Years, Vol II, Waging Peace* (New York: Doubleday, 1965), p. 197.

33. See Gromyko's press interview in *Pravda* (11 September 1957); also *Izvestiya* (24 August 1957); *SWB I* (6 September 1957), pp. 7–8.

34. *Soviet News* (16 September 1957).

35. D. Dallin, op. cit., p. 471. Also see Chapter 6 for an account of Marshal Zhukov's involvement in the crisis and his subsequent removal.

36. *SWB IV* (5 October 1957), pp. 9–10.

37. *Pravda* (15 February 1958). For the earliest Soviet coverage of the creation of the UAR, see *Pravda* (2 February 1958) and the articles by S. Kondrashov in *Izvestiya* (4 February 1958 and 7 February 1958).

38. K. Ivanov, 'A New Arab State', *International Affairs*, Moscow, No. 3 (1958), p. 57.

39. *Al-Akhbar* (16 May 1958).

40. Tom Little, *Modern Egypt* (London: Ernest Benn Ltd., 1967), p. 190.

41. Heikal, op cit., pp. 131–32.

42. *SWB IV* (17 December 1958), pp. 8–9; and the *Mizan Newsletter* (London: The Central Asian Research Centre), Vol. I, No. 8 (1959), pp. 10–11.

43. *SWB IV* (29 December 1958), p. 9.
44. See *The Times* (18 April 1959).
45. *SWB I* (2 February 1959), p. 12.
46. *Izvestiya* (16 March 1959), quoted in the *Mizan Newsletter*, Vol. I, No. 4 (1959), Appendix I.
47. Nasser's Damascus speeches can be found in UAR, Department of Information, *President Gamal Abd al-Nasser's Speeches and Press Interviews, 1959* (Cairo), pp. 130–84.
48. *Pravda* (30 March 1959).
49. Quoted in John Ericson, 'The Dislocation of an Alliance: Sino–Soviet Relations, 1960–1961', in D. C. Watt, ed., *Survey of International Affairs, 1961* (London: Oxford University Press, 1965), p. 185.
50. Nikita Khrushchev, 'Za novuyu pobedu mirovovo Kommunisticheskovo dvizheniya', *Kommunist*, No. 1 (1961), pp. 3–37.
51. Boris Ponomaryov, 'O gosudarstve natsional'noy demokratii', *Kommunist*, No. 8 (1961), p. 41.
52. *SWB IV* (10 June 1961), ME/661/A/4–8 and Heikal, op. cit., p. 146.
53. 'Observer', *Pravda* (25 May 1961).
54. *SWB IV* (16 June 1961), ME/662/A/1.
55. *SWB IV* (10 June 1961), ME/661/A/7–8.
56. Quoted in the *Mizan Newsletter*, Vol. 3, No. 8 (1961), p. 8.
57. Robert M. Slusser, *The Berlin Crisis of 1961: Soviet–American Relations and the Struggle for Power in the Kremlin, June–November 1961* (Baltimore, Md.: Johns Hopkins University Press, 1973), pp. 157–70.
58. *SWB I* (19 September 1961), SU/746/A/4.
59. *SWB I* (27 October 1961), SU/779/C/47.
60. *Pravda* (13 October 1961).
61. For the different phases in Egypt's foreign policy, see A. I. Dawisha, *Egypt in the Arab World: The Elements of Foreign Policy* (London: Macmillan, 1976).
62. For articles basically hostile to the reforms, see V. Mayevskiy's *Pravda* article of 17 July 1962; Belyaev in *Pravda* (26 November 1963); *Bakinskiy Rabochiy* (23 June 1962), quoted in *Mizan Newsletter*, (July–August 1962), pp. 8–9; R. Avakov and G. Mirskiy, 'O klassovoy strukture v slaborazvitykh stranakh', *Mirovaya ekonomika i mezhdunarodnyye otnoshenii* (henceforth referred to as *MEIMO*) No. 4 (1962), pp. 68–82. For articles which stressed the reforms' more positive features, see G. Mirskiy, 'The UAR Reforms', *New Times*, No. 4 (1962), pp. 12–15; Y. Rozaliyev, 'State Capitalism in Asia and Africa', *International Affairs*, Moscow, No. 2 (1963), p. 36; Primakov's *Pravda* article (9 September 1963); and Demchenko in *Pravda* (10 March 1964).
63. 'Save Our Lives' (appeal by imprisoned Egyptian Communists), *World Marxist Review*, Vol. 6, No. 6 (1963) pp. 93–5; V. V. Lezin, 'K voprosu o gegemonii rabochevo klassa v natsional'no-osvoboditel'noi revolyutsii', in *Akademiya Obshchestvennykh Nauk Pri Ts. K. KPSS, Voprosy mezhdunarodnovo rabochevo i natsional'no-osvoboditel'novo dvizheniya na sovremennom etape* (Moscow: Sbornik Statei, 1963); R. Avakov and L. Stepanov, 'Sotsialyye problemy natsional'no-osvoboditel'noi revolyutsii', *MEIMO*, No. 5 (1963), pp. 46–54; V. Kiselev, 'Rabochiy klass i natsional'no-osvoboditel'nyye revolyutsii', *MEIMO*, No. 10 (1963); pp. 93–8; and Ponomaryov's *Pravda* article of 18 November 1962.

64. *SWB IV* (2 October 1962), ME/1062/A/12.

65. *Pravda* (16 August 1963).

66. Togliatti, the Italian Communist leader had said, in a letter written only weeks before his death, that Khrushchev's visit to Egypt had been a major Soviet victory over the Chinese—*New York Times* (5 September 1964); Walter Laqueur, *The Struggle for the Middle East: The Soviet Union and the Middle East, 1958-1968* (London: Routledge and Kegan Paul, 1969), p. 71.

67. *Pravda* (17 October 1964).

68. Laqueur, *The Struggle for the Middle East*, p. 69; Yaacov Ro'i, *From Encroachment to Involvement: A Documentary Study of Soviet Policy in the Middle East, 1945-1973* (New York: John Wiley and Sons, 1974), p. 385.

69. *Mizan Newsletter*, Vol. 6, No. 5 (1964), p. 61.

70. The Praesidium of the Supreme Soviet is vested by Article 49 of the Constitution with the exclusive right to award all titles of honour. The *Sunday Times* (25 October 1964) reported that Suslov in particular condemned Khrushchev for exceeding his constitutional authority.

71. *Radio Cairo* (20 May 1964) as quoted in Ro'i, op. cit., p. 385.

72. *Mizan Newsletter*, Vol. 6, No. 5 (1964), p. 65.

73. Ibid.

NOTES TO CHAPTER 3

1. *Al-Jumhuriya*, as quoted in *Pravda* (21 October 1964).

2. *Al-Ahram* (23 October 1964).

3. *Arab World* (6 September 1965), as quoted in Laqueur, *The Struggle for the Middle East*, p. 73.

4. I. I. Garshin, quoted in Ye. M. Zhukov, *Sovremennyye teorii sotsializma 'natsional'novo tipa'* (Moscow, 1967), p. 148.

5. UAR, *Majmu'at Khutab wa Tasrihat wa Bayanat al-Rais Gamal Abd al-Nasser*, Vol. 5 (Cairo: Maslahat al-Insti'lamat, nd), p. 488.

6. This subject will be dealt with in greater depth in Chapter 9.

7. Quoted in Jon D. Glassman, *Arms for the Arabs* (Baltimore, Md; The Johns Hopkins University Press, 1975), p. 38.

8. Ibid. p. 39.

9. Nasser's speech of 23 July 1967, quoted in Stephens, op. cit., p. 468.

10. Quoted in Laqueur, *The Road to War 1967* (London: Weidenfeld and Nicolson), 1968, p. 75.

11. Quoted in Stephens, op. cit., p. 469.

12. *Krasnaya zvezda* (18 May 1967). Also see *Izvestiya* (17 May 1967); and *SWB I* SU/2469/A4/1-2.

13. Arthur Lall, *The UN and the Middle East Crisis, 1967* (New York: Columbia University Press, 1968), p. 30; Theodore Draper, *Israel and World Politics* (New York: The Viking Press, 1968), pp. 80-1.

14. Soviet Government Statement of 24 May 1967, in *SWB I*, SU/2474/A4/2.

15. Heikal, *Nasser: The Cairo Documents*, pp. 218-19.

16. Stephens, op. cit., p. 484.

17. Heikal, *Nasser: The Cairo Documents*, p. 220.

18. Stephens, op. cit., p. 503.

19. Soviet Government Statement of 7 June 1967, in *SWB I*, SU/2484/A4/1.
20. Michael Bar-Zohar, *Embassies in Crisis* (Englewood Cliffs, N.J.: Prentice-Hall, 1970), p. 228.
21. *Pravda* (11 June 1967).
22. *Pravda* (10 June 1967).
23. Lyndon B. Johnson, *The Vantage Point: Perspectives on the Presidency* (New York: Holt, Rinehart and Winston, 1971), p. 302.
24. Norman Polmar, *Soviet Naval Power: Challenge for the 1970s* (New York: National Strategy Information Center, 1972), p. 46.
25. See Kosygin's speech to the UN General Assembly on 19 June 1967, contained in *Pravda* (20 June 1967); also see *SWB I*, SU/2583/A4/1.
26. *Za Rubezhom* article released by *Tass* on 29 June 1967, *SWB I*, SU/2505/A4/2 (6 September 1967); *Izvestiya* (14 July 1967).
27. See for an example George Mirskiy's article in *Literaturnaya Gazeta* (9 August 1967).
28. *Pravda* (6 December 1967).
29. George Lenczowski, *Soviet Advances in the Middle East* (Washington DC: American Enterprise Institute for Public Policy Research, 1972), p. 150; Heikal in *SWB IV* ME/3189/A/6–10 (29 September 1969).
30. Quoted in Mohamed Heikal, *The Road to Ramadan* (London: Fontana, 1976), p. 49.
31. *The Times* (11 July 1969).
32. *Krasnaya zvezda* (12 November 1968).
33. Heikal, *The Road to Ramadan*, p. 45; Sadat's statement is contained in Glassman, op. cit., p. 67.
34. Heikal, *The Road to Ramadan*, pp. 81–8.
35. Ibid., p. 88; and William B. Quandt, 'Soviet Policy in the October Middle East War—I', *International Affairs*, Vol. 53, No. 3 (July 1977), p. 378.
36. *Pravda* (3 January 1968).
37. *Pravda* (27 August 1969).
38. *Pravda* (7 May 1969).
39. Stephens, op. cit., p. 538.
40. Ibid., p. 531.
41. Nasser's interview with *Le Monde* (21 February 1970), in *SWB IV* ME/3311/A/3.
42. *Keesing's Contemporary Archives*, Vol. 16 (29 July – 5 August 1967), p. 22180.
43. Ibid (23–30 September 1967), p. 22276.
44. Heikal's account of the meeting appeared in *al-Ahram* (10 July 1968).
45. *Pravda* (6 June 1969).
46. *The Strategic Survey, 1970* (London: Institute for Strategic Studies, 1971), p. 47.
47. *Keesing's Contemporary Archives*, Vol. 17 (1–8 August 1970) p. 24118.
48. *Pravda* (30 July 1970).
49. *Pravda* (29 August 1970).
50. *Keesing's Contemporary Archives*, Vol. 17 (10–17 October 1970), p. 24230.
51. *Pravda* (4 October 1970).
52. Heikal in *SWB IV*, ME/3774/A/3 (31 August 1971).
53. Nasser in *SWB IV*, ME/3391/A/7 (30 May 1970).

NOTES TO CHAPTER 4

1. See Chapter 2 above for a fuller account of this incident.
2. Heikal, *The Road to Ramadan*, p. 117.
3. Ibid., pp. 115–16. Also see Glassman, op. cit., p. 87; *Strategic Survey 1971* (London: International Institute of Strategic Studies, 1972), pp. 35–6; and Yair Evron, *The Middle East: Nations, Super-powers and Wars* (London: Paul Elek Ltd., 1973), pp. 208–12.
4. *Pravda* (28 February 1971).
5. See Sadat's speech in *SWB IV*, ME/3629/A/4 (9 March 1971). Also Heikal, *The Road to Ramadan*, p. 117; and Glassman, op. cit., p. 87.
6. 'The Soviet Attitude to the Palestine Problem: From the Records of the Syrian Communist Party, 1971–72', *Journal of Palestine Studies*, Vol. 2, No. 1 (1972), p. 201.
7. Ibid, pp. 200–1.
8. *New York Times* (17 September 1971).
9. 'The Soviet Attitude . . .', op. cit., p. 199.
10. Quoted in Jaan Pennar, *The USSR and the Arabs. The Ideological Dimension*, (London: C. Hurst and Company, 1973), p. 85. Also *Pravda* (12 December 1970).
11. *Moscow Radio* (28 December 1970), quoted in *USSR and the Third World*, (London: Central Asian Research Centre, 1971), Vol. I, No. 1, p. 24.
12. Boris Ponomaryov, 'Under the Banner of Marxism–Leninism and Proletarian Internationalism: The 24th Congress of the CPSU', *World Marxist Review*, Vol. 14, No. 6 (1971), p. 3.
13. A full and interesting account of this episode is contained in Heikal, *The Road to Ramadan*, pp. 121–38.
14. A. Mikhailov, 'Kto oslozhnyaet sovetsko–egipetskiye otnosheniya', *Agitator*, Journal of the Central Committee of the CPSU, No. 9, (1976), p. 24; D. Vol'skiy and A. Usvatov, 'Kair-Moskva, fakty i tol'ko fakty', *Novoye vremya*, No. 14 (1976), p. 18.
15. Robert Stephens, 'The Egyptian–Soviet Quarrel in 1972: Russia, the Arabs and Africa', in Colin Legum, ed., *Africa Contemporary Record: Annual Survey and Documents, 1972–1973*, Vol. 5, (London: Rex Collings, 1973), p. A25.
16. 'Treaty of Friendship and Cooperation Between the Union of Soviet Socialist Republics and the United Arab Republic', *Pravda* (28 May 1971).
17. *Cairo Radio* (3 June 1971), quoted in *USSR and the Third World*, Vol. 1, No. 6 (1971), p. 317.
18. See Ye. Primakov, *Pravda* (5 June 1971); V. Kudryavtsev, 'Indestructible Friendship', *New Times*, No. 23 (1971), p. 10; *Pravda* (13 June 1971); *Izvestiya* (15 June 1971); and E. Dmitriev, 'Soviet–Arab Friendship: A New Stage', *International Affairs*, Moscow, No. 8 (1971), pp. 66–8. For the reaction of the military press, see Chapter 7.
19. *Pravda* (31 July 1971).
20. Sadat's ASU speech, *SWB IV*, ME/4050/A/1–17 (26 July 1972); Sadat's interviews in *al-Hawadith* (19 March 1975) and *al-Anwar* (27 June 1975).
21. Heikal, quoted in *SWB IV*, ME/4072/A/3 (21 August 1972).
22. Sadat in his memoirs claims 15,000 were expelled (*Observer*, 19 March 1978).

Also see Heikal, *The Road to Ramadan*, pp. 171–75; and Glassman, op. cit., p. 96.

23. *Pravda* (20 July 1972).
24. *Pravda* (19 August 1972).
25. Heikal, *The Road to Ramadan*, p. 176. Also *al-Ahram* (7 August 1972), and Sadat's speech to the People's Assembly on 17 August in *Arab Report and Record*, No. 16 (16–31 August 1972), p. 394.
26. *USSR and the Third World*, Vol. 2, No. 9 (1972), p. 514.
27. Sadat interview with Arnaud de Borchgrave, *Newsweek* (9 April 1973). For an account of the period from October 1972 to July 1973, see Alvin Z. Rubinstein, *Red Star on the Nile, The Soviet–Egyptian Influence Relationship Since the June War* (Princeton, N. J.: Princeton University Press, 1977), pp. 209–47; and Galia Golan, *Yom Kippur and After, The Soviet Union and the Middle East Crisis* (Cambridge: Cambridge University Press, 1977), pp. 36–42.
28. Quoted in Quandt, 'Soviet Policy . . . I', op. cit., p. 382.
29. Sadat's 16 July speech, cited in Robert O. Freedman, *Soviet Policy Towards the Middle East Since 1970* (New York: Praeger Publishers, 1975), p. 115.
30. *SWB IV*, ME/4355/A/9 (25 July 1973).
31. Cited in G. Golan, op. cit., p. 53.
32. Glassman, op. cit., p. 100.
33. Heikal, *The Road to Ramadan*, p. 22; also Sadat's interviews with *al-Nahar* (1 March 1974); *al-Anwar* (28 March 1974); and the *Observer* (19 March 1978).
34. Heikal, *The Road to Ramadan*, pp. 207–8. This account coincides both with Vinogradov's own reply to the Egyptians, which appeared in the Beirut daily *al-Safir* on 17 April 1974, and with the author's interviews with Syrian embassy officials in Moscow on 6 May 1977.
35. *Pravda* (8 October 1973).
36. *New York Times* (9 October 1973); *Tass* (7 October 1973).
37. The question of whether the USSR and the USA started the resupply first is still a controversial and unresolved point. Varying interpretations are offered by Heikal, *The Road to Ramadan*, pp. 215–18; Glassman, op. cit., pp. 130–1; Freedman, op. cit., p. 129; G. Golan, op. cit., pp. 84–90; Rubinstein, op. cit., pp. 267–8; Peter Mangold, *Superpower Intervention in the Middle East* (London: Croom Helm, 1978, pp. 127–8); and William Quandt, 'Soviet Policy in the October Middle East War—II', *International Affairs*, Vol. 53, No. 4 (1977), pp. 590–3.
38. Matti Golan, *The Secret Conversations of Henry Kissinger* (New York: Bantam Books, 1976), pp. 74–6.
39. *Pravda* (26 October 1973).
40. *New York Times* (10 April 1974).
41. Quandt, 'Soviet Policy . . . II', op. cit., pp. 590, 598.
42. *L'Orient Le Jour* (16 March 1977); Golan, op. cit., p. 123; E. Zumwalt, *On Watch, A Memoir* (New York: Quadrangle, 1976), pp. 443–8; Marvin Kalb and Bernard Kalb, *Kissinger* (Boston: Little, Brown and Co., 1974), pp. 493–4; F. Kohler, L. Goure, M. L. Harvey, *The Soviet Union and the October 1973 Middle East War: The Implications for Détente* (Miami: Center for Advanced International Studies, 1974), p. 65; and Nixon's interview with David Frost (12 May 1977).

43. G. Golan, op. cit., p. 123; Quandt, 'Soviet Policy . . . II', op. cit., p. 598; Heikal, *The Road to Ramadan*, pp. 251–3; and Brezhnev's own admission that they had sent 'representatives' into the area, following Sadat's request for a joint force, *Pravda* (27 October 1973).

44. Quandt, ibid., p. 596n.

45. Ibid., p. 598.

46. *Pravda* (27 October 1973).

47. *Pravda* (28 October 1973).

48. G. Mirskiy, 'The Middle East—New Factors', *New Times*, No. 48 (1973), pp. 18–20. These arguments were reiterated in a later article by Hannes Adomeit, 'Soviet Foreign Policy—Some Contradictory Trends', in Peter Jones, ed., *The International Yearbook of Foreign Policy Analysis*, Vol. 1 (London: Croom Helm, 1976). Another Soviet analyst of Middle Eastern affairs listed further advantages which had accrued to the Arabs, and to the USSR, as a result of the war: Israel had been isolated following the war when 24 African states broke off diplomatic relations, a rift in the NATO alliance had been produced by American actions, and the Palestinians had gained international recognition of their cause, especially in the UN (Ye. Primakov, '"Sbalansirovannyy Kurs" na Blizhnem Vostoke ili staraya politika inymi sredstvami?', *MEIMO*, No. 12 (1976), pp. 46–50.

49. M. Golan, op. cit., p. 158.

50. *Pravda* (25 January 1974).

51. Brezhnev's note to Sadat in January 1974 (cited in G. Golan, op. cit., pp. 174–5) and his speech in Moldavia the following October (cited in Rubinstein, op. cit., p. 305) both referred to the short-term benefits derived from the disengagement agreements. Also see Dmitry Volsky, 'Middle East: Time Presses', *New Times*, No. 42 (1974), p. 9; and Ye. Primakov, '"Sbalansirovanyy Kurs" na Blizhnem Vostoke ili staraya politika inymi sred-stvami?', *MEIMO*, No. 1 (1977), pp. 51–3.

52. *Pravda* (14 April 1974).

53. *New York Times* (7 June 1974).

54. *Pravda* (16 June 1974).

55. *New Times*, No. 28 (1974), p. 23.

56. *Izvestiya* (25 July 1974).

57. *Soviet News* (22 October 1974).

58. Quoted in *USSR and the Third World*, Vol. 5, No. 1 (1975), p. 16.

59. *Pravda* (28 December 1974).

60. Sadat's speech was quoted in the *New York Times* (9 January 1975).

61. Syrian–Soviet joint communiqué in *Pravda* (4 February 1975); Egyptian–Soviet joint communiqué, *Pravda* (6 February 1975).

62. *Pravda* (20 April 1975).

63. This is discussed in greater detail in Chapter 9 below.

64. *New York Times* (5 September 1975).

65. *Pravda* (25 October 1975).

66. 'Arab Republic of Egypt', *Africa Contemporary Record*, Vol. 6, (1973–74), p. C208.

67. *Keesing's Contemporary Archives* (2 July 1976), p. 27810.

68. Ibid (9 April 1976), p. 27666.

69. *Al-Jumhuriya* (9 February 1976).

70. *Egyptian Gazette* (15 March 1976).
71. *New York Times* (5 April 1976).
72. *The Times* London (17 March 1976).
73. *Tass* article, quoted in *Soviet News* (23 March 1976).
74. Text in *Soviet News* (2 March 1976).
75. *Krasnaya zvezda*, quoted in *Soviet News* (13 April 1976). Also see *Pravda* and *Izvestiya* (3 April 1976).
76. *Arab Report and Record*, No. 3 (1–14 February 1976), p. 69, and No. 8 (16–30 April 1976), p. 248.
77. The author's interviews with Syrian embassy officials in Moscow on 6 May 1977; and Dr A. I. Dawisha's interview with Ahmed Iskander, the Syrian Minister of Information, in Damascus on 13 January 1978.
78. The Brezhnev letter of 11 July 1976, which according to Assad was leaked by the Soviets themselves, is contained in *Events*, London, No. 1 (1 October 1976), p. 23. Assad's allegation, plus the report of the Kosygin–Assad talks can be found in his interview in the same issue of *Events*.
79. *Cairo Radio* (13 September 1976), as reported in *Arab Report and Record*, No. 17 (1–15 September 1976), p. 535.
80. *Pravda* (30 August 1976), praised Qadhafi's 'political line' and condemned those 'imperialists and reactionaries' seeking to depose him. On 2 September 1976, Fahmy summoned the Soviet *chargé d'affaires* to complain of recent *Pravda* articles reporting Egyptian troop concentrations on the Libyan border.
81. The text of Brezhnev's speech is contained in *Soviet News* (2 November 1976), p. 384.
82. Author's interview in Moscow (16 May 1977).
83. Fahmy's speech to the People's Assembly (22 March 1977), contained in *Arab Report and Record*, No. 6 (16–31 March 1977), p. 192; and *The Middle East*, No. 26 (London, 1976), p. 73.
84. *Arab Report and Record*, No. 24 (16–31 December 1976), p. 750.
85. See *al-Akhbar* (24 January 1977), for allegations of communist involvement; *Pravda* (22 January 1977), for Soviet view of riots; and *al-Ahram* (28 January 1977), for the postponement of the trade protocol.
86. Author's interview in Moscow (21 May 1977).
87. *Pravda* (22 March 1977).
88. Gromyko's press conference, *Pravda* (1 April 1977).
89. *Arab Report and Record*, No. 19/20 (1–31 October 1977), p. 880.
90. *Washington Post* (28 April 1977).
91. *Arab Report and Record*, No. 11 (1–15 June 1977), p. 433.
92. Cairo charged that the Soviet squadron stationed off Egyptian territorial waters was jamming Egyptian radio communications. *New York Times* (25 July 1977); *al-Ahram* (26 July 1977); and Sadat's televised interview on ABC as reported in *Arab Report and Record*, No. 14 (16–31 July 1977), p. 585.
93. *Al-Jumhuriya* (17 August 1977); and *al-Ahram* (17 August 1977).
94. *Al-Anbaa*, Kuwait (13 September 1977).
95. *SWB I*, SU/5680/A4/4 (30 November 1977).
96. *SWB I*, SU/5759/A4/1 (7 March 1978).
97. *SWB I*, SU/5725/A4/1 (28 January 1978).

NOTES TO CHAPTER 5

1. David Easton, 'An Approach to the Analysis of Political Systems', *World Politics*, Vol. 9 (April, 1957), pp. 383–400.
2. Erik P. Hoffmann and Frederic J. Fleron, eds., *The Conduct of Soviet Foreign Policy* (London: Butterworths, 1971); Jan F. Triska and David Finley, *Soviet Foreign Policy* (New York: Macmillan, 1968); Frederic C. Barghoorn, *Politics in the USSR* (Boston: Little, Brown and Co., 1966).
3. George F. Kennan, *Russia and the West under Lenin and Stalin* (Boston: Little, Brown and Co., 1961); W. W. Kulski, *Peaceful Coexistence, An Analysis of Soviet Foreign Policy* (Chicago: Henry Regnery, 1959); Adam B. Ulam, *Expansion and Coexistence, Soviet Foreign Policy, 1917–1973*, 2nd ed. (New York: Praeger, 1974); Richard Pipes, 'Operational Principles of Soviet Foreign Policy', *Survey*, Vol. 19, No. 2 (1973), pp. 41–62.
4. Robert C. Tucker, 'The Dictator and Totalitarianism', *World Politics*, Vol. 17, No. 4 (1965), pp. 555–84; Robert C. Tucker, *The Soviet Political Mind* (London: Allen and Unwin, 1971).
5. Raymond A. Bauer, Alex Inkeles and Clyde Kluckhohn, *How the Soviet System Works* (Cambridge, Mass.: Harvard University Press, 1956).
6. Hannah Arendt, *The Origins of Totalitarianism* (London: Allen and Unwin, 1966).
7. Carl Friedrich and Zbigniew Brzezinski, *Totalitarian Dictatorship and Autocracy* (New York: Praeger, 1965).
8. Graham T. Allison, *Essence of Decision: Explaining the Cuban Missile Crisis* (Boston: Little, Brown and Co., 1971), pp. 10–39.
9. Graham T. Allison and Morton H. Halperin, 'Bureaucratic Politics: A Paradigm and Some Policy Implications', in Raymond Tanter and Richard H. Ullman, eds., *Theory and Policy in International Relations* (Princeton, N. J.: Princeton University Press, 1972), pp. 40–80.
10. Allison, op. cit., p. 182.
11. Michael Brecher, Blema Steinberg and Janice Stein, 'A Framework for Research on Foreign Policy Behaviour', *The Journal of Conflict Resolution*, Vol. 13, No. 1, 1969, pp. 75–101; and Michael Brecher, *The Foreign Policy System of Israel* (London: Oxford University Press, 1972).
12. For a further discussion of the difference between the psychological and operational environments, see Harold and Margaret Sprout, *The Foundations of International Politics* (London: Van Nostrand Co., Inc., 1962), pp. 46–53; and Joseph H. de Rivera, *The Psychological Dimension of Foreign Policy* (Columbus, Ohio: Charles E. Merrill Publishing Co., 1968). However, the distinction between the psychological and operational environments is far from being universally accepted. One study which considers the operational environment to be irrelevant in the policy process is Richard C. Snyder, H. W. Bruck and Burton Sapin, *Foreign Policy Decision-Making: An Approach to the Study of International Politics* (New York: Free Press, 1962).
13. Brecher, Steinberg, and Stein, op. cit., p. 81. Also see Jonathan Wilkenfeld, ed., *Conflict Behaviour and Linkage Politics* (New York: David McKay Co., 1973); and Kenneth Boulding, 'National Images and International Systems', *The Journal of Conflict Resolution*, Vol. 3, No. 2 (1959), pp. 120–31.

14. See William Zimmerman, *Soviet Perspectives on International Relations, 1956–1967* (Princeton N.J.: Princeton University Press, 1969).

NOTES TO CHAPTER 6

1. R. D. McLaurin, *The Middle East in Soviet Policy* (Lexington, Mass: Lexington Books, 1975), p. 15.
2. 'Islam', *Bol'shaya Sovetskaya Entsiklopediya*, Vol. 18 (1953 edition), p. 516. Also see L. I. Klimovitch, *Islam, yevo proiskhozhdeniye i sotsial'naya sushchnost'* (Moscow, 1956).
3. USSR, Central Statistical Board, *Narodnoye khozyaistvo SSSR v 1970 godu* (Moscow: Statistika Publishers, 1971), pp. 15–17.
4. E. Borcierkiw, 'Religion in the USSR after Khrushchev', in John W. Strong, ed., *The Soviet Union under Brezhnev and Kosygin* (New York: Van Nostrand Reinhold Co., 1971), p. 136.
5. *Voprosy filosofii*, No. 12 (1966), as quoted in Geoffrey Wheeler, 'National and Religious Consciousness in Soviet Islam', *Survey*, No. 66 (1968), p. 68.
6. 'Soviet Muslims in Mecca', *News*, Moscow, No. 22 (1954), p. 28; and David Lane, *Politics and Society in the USSR* (London: Weidenfeld and Nicolson, 1970), p. 444.
7. 'Islam', *Bol'shaya Sovetskaya Entsiklopediya*, 3rd ed. Vol. 10, (Moscow, 1972), pp. 484–6.
8. A recent example is provided by R. Tuzmuhamedov, *How the National Question was Solved in Soviet Central Asia* (Moscow: Progress Publishers, 1973).
9. Helene Carrere d'Encausse, 'The Collapse of Ideology', unpublished paper presented at the London School of Economics (3 March 1978).
10. K. Vermishev, 'Ob urobne ekonomicheskovo razvitiya soyuznoy respubliki', *Voprosy ekonomiki*, No. 4 (1970), p. 128.
11. I. Potekhin, *Afrika smotrit v budushcheye* (Moscow, 1960), pp. 28–9.
12. This was the conclusion reached by Zev Katz using such indicators as income, savings, trade turnover, education, literacy, urban–rural division, and professional attainment. Zev Katz, ed., *Handbook of Major Soviet Nationalities* (New York: Free Press, 1975), pp. 462–3.
13. US, Central Intelligence Agency, *Soviet Economic Plans for 1976–80: A First Look*, ER 76-10471 (August 1976), p. 3.
14. Morton Schwartz, *The Foreign Policy of the USSR: Domestic Factors* (Encino, Cal.: Dickenson Publishing Co., 1975), p. 27.
15. Werner Gumpel, 'Soviet Oil and Soviet Middle East Policy', *Aussen Politik*, English ed., Vol. 23, No. 1 (1972), p. 106.
16. Ibid.
17. Ibid., p. 109.
18. US, Congress, Joint Economic Committee, *Soviet Economic Prospects for the Seventies* (Washington DC: US Government Printing Office, 1973), p. 773.
19. L. Tomashpol'skiy, 'Mirovoi energeticheskiy balans: problemy poslednei treti veka', *MEIMO*, No. 2 (1967), pp. 28–9.
20. US, Central Intelligence Agency, *Prospects for Soviet Oil Production*, ER 77-10270 (April 1977), p. 9.
21. T. Honta, 'Some Problems in the Development of the Oil and Gas Industry in

the Ukraine', *Kommunist Ukrainy* (Kiev, January 1967), pp. 9–11, trans. in *Digest of Soviet Ukrainian Press*, PROLOG (April 1967), pp. 10–11.

22. US, *Prospects for Soviet Oil Production*, p. 9.

23. Ibid.

24. G. Starko, 'How to Solve the Oil Problem', *New Times*, No. 35, (1958), pp. 13–15; R. A. Andreasyan and A. Ya. El'yanov, *Blizhniy Vostok: neft' i nezavisimost'* (Moscow, 1961); N. N. Polyakov, 'Arabskiye strany na puti k ekonomicheskoy nezavisimosti', *Vneshnyaya torgovlya*, No. 9 (1956), pp. 4–7; Y. Vasilyev, 'Oil Politics Takes a New Turn', *New Times*, No. 39 (1957), pp. 9–11.

25. Arthur Jay Klinghoffer, *The Soviet Union and International Oil Politics* (New York: Columbia University Press, 1977), p. 141.

26. P. A. Reynolds, *An Introduction to International Relations* (London: Longman Group Ltd., 1971), p. 71.

27. Marshall I. Goldman, 'Red Black Gold', *Foreign Policy*, No. 8 (1972), pp. 144–5; and Klinghoffer, op. cit., p. 296.

28. *The Times* (21 October 1976).

29. L. Brezhnev, 'Speech to the International Conference of Communist and Workers' Parties, 7 June 1969', contained in Myron Rush, ed., *The International Situation and Soviet Foreign Policy* (Columbus, Ohio: Charles E. Merrill Publishing Co., 1970), p. 355.

30. J. Frankel, *The Making of Foreign Policy* (London: Oxford University Press, 1963), p. 99.

31. Karen Dawisha, 'The Roles of Ideology in the Decision-Making of the Soviet Union', *International Relations*, Vol. 4 No. 2 (1972), pp. 156–8.

32. I. D. Ovsyany *et al.*, *A Study of Soviet Foreign Policy* (Moscow: Progress Publishers, 1975), p. 12.

33. D. Tomashevsky, 'Some Questions of International Relations Research in the Light of Lenin's Teachings', *International Affairs*, Moscow, No. 6 (1970), p. 75, as quoted in Schwartz, op. cit., p. 101.

34. Ovsyany, op. cit., pp. 14–15.

35. V. I. Lenin, 'Report to the VIII Party Congress, 18 March 1919', in Rush, ed., op. cit., p. 12.

36. J. Stalin, 'Report to the XV Party Congress, 3 December 1927' in ibid., p. 61.

37. G. Arbatov, 'O Sovetsko–Amerikanskikh otnosheniyakh', *Kommunist*, No. 3 (1973), p. 108.

38. G. Shakhnazarov in *Pravda* (27 December 1975).

39. Ibid.

40. L. Brezhnev, in *Pravda* (7 September 1973).

41. Ovsyany, op. cit., p. 16.

42. Ibid., pp. 16–17.

43. *SWB IV* (10 June 1961), ME/661/A/7–8.

44. Nasser's introduction to a book entitled *The Truth About Communism* quoted in *al-Ahram* (5 January 1955).

45. Reynolds, op. cit., p. 172.

46. Frankel, op. cit., p. 99.

47. Laqueur, *The Soviet Union and the Middle East*, p. ix.

48. As reported by Robert Stephens in the *Scotsman* (5 July 1956).

49. Seale, op. cit., p. 231.

50. Ibid., and Nasser's interview in *The Hindu* (2 February 1955).
51. Heikal, *The Road to Ramadan*, p. 88.
52. 'The Soviet Attitude to the Palestine Problem . . .', p. 188.
53. Quoted in *SWB IV* (29 August 1967), ME/2554/A/8.
54. Sadat's interview with the Cairo weekly, *October* (11 December 1977).
55. H. Gordon Skilling, *Czechoslovakia's Interrupted Revolution* (Princeton, N.J.: Princeton University Press, 1976), p. 633.
56. Heikal's article in *al-Ahram* on the Czech Arms Deal, *SWB IV* (30 December 1958), p. 5.
57. Ye. Zhukov, 'The Impact of the Chinese Revolution on the National Liberation Struggle', *World Marxist Review*, Vol. 1, No. 3 (1958), p. 17.
58. It was initially thought in the Communist world that the overthrow of the Iraqi monarchy was the signal for a general left-wing takeover throughout the Middle East. However, the American and British landings in the Lebanon and Jordan not only precluded the possibility of indigenous Communist parties gaining the ascendancy in these countries, but also limited the range of possible Soviet responses. Apparently unwilling to resort to the use of force, Soviet leaders agreed to hold a Great Power summit conference on the Middle East in the United Nations Security Council, where Communist China was still not represented. Peking's reaction was sufficiently violent to force Khrushchev to withdraw his proposal and make an unscheduled visit to Peking. Talks were evidently held on both the Middle Eastern and the Taiwan Straits crises, and a Joint communiqué issued on 3 August stated that relations between the two countries were being developed successfully and becoming more firmly established. However, Chinese criticism of Soviet policy was to continue. An editorial in the Chinese *People's Daily*, which appeared while Khrushchev was still in Peking, asserted:

    Some soft-hearted advocates of peace naively believe that in order to relax tension at all costs, the enemy must not be provoked . . . Some groundlessly concluded that peace can be gained only when there is no armed resistance against the attacks of the imperialists and colonialists.

    For an excellent account of this episode see Donald S. Zagoria, *The Sino-Soviet Conflict, 1956–1961* (Princeton, N.J.: Princeton University Press, 1962), p. 30.
59. Ibid., pp. 245–77.
60. Ibid., p. 261; also see *The Times* (1 October 1959); *SWB IV*, (12 November 1959), ME/W30/A/1; and Khalid Bagdash, 'Two Trends in the Arab National Movements', *World Marxist Review*, Vol. 2, No. 11 (1959), pp. 26–32.
61. *Al-Jumhuriyah* (9 September 1959), as quoted in *SWB IV* (1 October 1959), ME/144/A/3–4.
62. Hsun Fu, 'The National Liberation Movement and the Defence of Peace', *International Affairs*, Moscow, No. 3 (1959), p. 84.
63. Ibid.
64. 'Statement of the Meeting of Representatives of Communist and Workers' Parties, Moscow, November 1960', *World Marxist Review*, Vol. 3, No. 12 (1960), p. 16.

65. Ibid., p. 17.
66. Ibid.
67. See for example *SWB I* (29 August 1963), SU/1338/A4/7.
68. Ye. Zhukov's speech at the Baku Conference on the October Revolution and the National Liberation Movement, quoted in *SWB I* (3 October 1967), SU/2584/C/1.
69. Heikal, *Nasser: The Cairo Documents*, pp. 282–3.
70. *Izvestiya* (30 December 1971).
71. Ibid.
72. *New China News Agency Report* (27 September 1976).
73. *Pravda* (15 July 1975).
74. See for example, *Pravda* (28 December 1974), and Brezhnev's speech in *Pravda* (2 February 1975).

NOTES TO CHAPTER 7

1. Michael Brecher, *The Foreign Policy System of Israel* (London: Oxford University Press, 1972), pp. 8–9, 117–34; James N. Rosenau, ed., *Domestic Sources of Foreign Policy* (New York: Free Press, 1967); David O. Wilkinson, *Comparative Foreign Relations: Framework and Methods* (Belmont, Cal.: Dickenson Publishing Co. Inc., 1969), pp. 101–36; Frankel, op. cit.; K. J. Holsti, *International Politics, A Framework for Analysis* (Englewood Cliffs, NJ: Prentice-Hall Inc., 1972), pp. 353–401.
2. V. V. Aspaturian, 'The Formulation of Soviet Foreign Policy', in V. V. Aspaturian, ed., *Process and Power in Soviet Foreign Policy* (Boston, Mass.: Little Brown and Co., 1971), p. 555.
3. *Sunday Times* (25 October 1964).
4. This was the case during Brezhnev's June 1973 visit to Washington when he was authorised to sign on behalf of the Soviet state—see the *New York Times* (26 June 1973).
5. D. Richard Little, 'Soviet Parliamentary Committees After Khrushchev: Obstacles and Opportunities', *Soviet Studies*, Vol. 24, No. 1 (1972), p. 57.
6. *Soviet News* (2 March 1976).
7. *Pravda* (1 and 3 December 1973).
8. V. M. Chkhikvadze, *The Soviet Form of Popular Government* (Moscow: Progress Publishers, 1972), p. 120.
9. O. E. Kutafin, 'Vzaimootnosheniya postoyannykh komissiy palat Verkhovnovo Soveta SSSR s Prezidiumom Verkhovnovo Soveta SSSR i s Sovetom Ministrov SSSR', *Sovetskoye gosudarstvo i pravo*, No. 4 (1966), pp. 37–8.
10. *Pravda* (4 June 1977).
11. *Pravda* (20 February 1956). Although the top party organ was called the Praesidium from 1952–66, the term 'Politburo' will be used here to distinguish it from the Praesidiums of the Council of Ministers and the Supreme Soviet.
12. *Pravda* (4 April 1971).
13. Heikal, *The Road to Ramadan*, p. 80.
14. Bohdan Harasymiw, 'Nomenklatura: The Soviet Communist Party's

Leadership Recruitment System', *Canadian Journal of Political Science*, Vol. 2, No. 4 (1969), p. 498.

15. See Vladimir Petrov, 'Formation of Soviet Foreign Policy', *Orbis*, Vol. 17, No. 3 (1973), pp. 819–51.

16. Valerian A. Zorin, *Osnova diplomaticheskoi sluzhby* (Moscow, 1964), p. 116.

17. *Soviet News* (2 March 1976).

18. N. Petrov, op. cit., p. 827; and V. V. Aspaturian, 'The Formulation of Soviet Foreign Policy', in V. V. Aspaturian, op. cit., p. 563.

19. *Soviet News* (2 March 1976).

20. Heikal, *Nasser: The Cairo Documents*, p. 132.

21. Heikal, *The Road to Ramadan*, p. 110.

22. Ibid., p. 86.

23. Ibid., pp. 92–3.

24. I. D. Ovsyany, op. cit., p. 365.

25. The report of one such meeting is contained in 'V Politburo TsK KPSS, Prezidiume Verkhovnovo Soveta SSSR, Sovete Ministrov SSSR. Ob itogakh vizita General'novo sekretarya TsK KPSS, Predsedatelya Prezidium Verkhovnovo Soveta SSSR L. I. Brezhneva vo Frantsiyu', *Kommunist*, No. 10, 1977, pp. 3–5.

26. *SWB I*, SU/5681/A4/1 (1 December 1977).

27. *SWB I*, SU/5741/A4/1 (15 February 1978); *SWB I*, SU/5761/A4/2 (11 March 1978).

28. Sadat's interview with the Cairo weekly, *October* (26 February 1978).

29. See Chapter 5 above.

30. H. Gordon Skilling and Franklyn Griffiths, eds., *Interest Groups in Soviet Politics* (Princeton, N.J.: Princeton University Press, 1971); Milton C. Lodge, *Soviet Elite Attitudes Since Stalin* (Columbus, Ohio: Charles E. Merrill Publishing Co., 1969); Andrew C. Janos, 'Group Politics in Communist Society: A Second Look at the Pluralist Model', in S. P. Huntington and C. H. Moore, eds., *Authoritarian Politics in Modern Society* (New York: Basic Books, 1970), pp. 437–50; and William E. Odom, 'A Dissenting View on the Group Approach to Soviet Politics', *World Politics*, Vol. 28, No. 4 (1976), pp. 542–67.

31. Mohamed Heikal, 'Search for an End', Cairo Radio, *SWB IV* (25 December 1958), p. 5. Heikal claimed that 'there were conflicting views and trends at the Soviet Foreign Ministry regarding the new Sphinx [Nasser] in Egypt and his policy'.

32. *Pravda* (20 February 1956).

33. *Soviet News* (2 March 1976).

34. The author spent the spring of 1977 in Moscow and Leningrad under the auspices of the British Council and conducted interviews with academics at the Institute of Orientology, the Institute of Africa, the Institute for the Study of the USA and Canada, the Institute of World Economy and International Relations, the Institute of Asia and Africa (attached to Moscow State University), and with officials of both the Soviet Ministry of Foreign Affairs and the Egyptian, Iraqi, Syrian, Lebanese, Tunisian, British and American embassies in Moscow.

35. See Chapter 2 above.

36. Thomas W. Wolfe, *Soviet Power and Europe, 1945–1970* (Baltimore, Md.: Johns Hopkins University Press, 1970), p. 339, fn. 117. The Soviet account of the

resolutions taken at that June plenum are contained in *Spravochnik Partiinovo rabotnika*, Vol. 7 (Moscow: Izdatel'stvo politicheskoy literatury, 1967), pp. 114–7.

37. Ilana Dimant-Kass, '*Pravda* and *Trud*, Divergent Attitudes Towards the Middle East', Hebrew University of Jerusalem, Soviet and East European Research Center, Research Paper No. 3 (June 1972), pp. 60–9.

38. Confirmed by interviews with both research workers and embassy personnel.

39. J. M. Mackintosh, *Strategy and Tactics of Soviet Foreign Policy* (London: Oxford University Press, 1962), p. 229.

40. The existence of this agreement was revealed by Sadat in a speech to the Egyptian Students Union at Alexandria University on 3 April 1974, and was reported in FBIS, *Daily Report: The Middle East and North Africa*, Vol. 66 (4 April 1974), p. D7.

41. Matthew P. Gallagher and Karl F. Spielmann, Jr., *Soviet Decision-making for Defense* (New York: Praeger, 1972), pp. 29–30; Douglas F. Garthoff, 'The Soviet Military and Arms Control', *Survival*, Vol. 19, No. 6 (1977), pp. 245–6; and Leonard Schapiro, 'The Role of the Military in the Making of Soviet Foreign Policy', unpublished paper presented at the London School of Economics (21 February 1978).

42. These observations were drawn primarily from Heikal, *The Road to Ramadan*, and Sadat's speeches and press interviews, particularly those with the Cairo weekly *October*.

43. Ilana Dimant-Kass, 'The Soviet Military and Soviet Policy in the Middle East 1970–73', *Soviet Studies*, Vol. 26, No. 4 (1974), pp. 502–21.

44. *Pravda* (12 March 1970, 23 May, 5 June 1971), quoted in ibid., p. 507.

45. *Soviet Military Review* (1971), No. 12, p. 51. See also *Krasnaya zvezda* (25 April 1971, 28 March 1972); *Morskoi sbornik*, No. 7 (1971), pp. 3–5; *Kommunist vooruzhennykh sil*, No. 12 (1971), p. 39, and ibid., p. 508.

46. *Krasnaya zvezda* (30 May 1971). See also *Krasnaya zvezda* 4 (19 June 1971), as referred to in Dimant-Kass, ibid., p. 516.

47. *Pravda* (13 and 18 June 1971).

48. *Krasnaya zvezda* (16 October 1973).

49. See Allison, op. cit.; and Allison and Halperin, op. cit.

NOTES TO CHAPTER 8

1. See Ye. Zhukov, 'Raspad kolonialnoy sistemy imperialisma', *Partiynaya zhizn'*, No. 16 (1956), p. 42; and L. A. Gordon and L. A. Fridman, 'Osobennosti sostava i struktury rabochevo klassa v ekonomicheski slaborazvitykh Azii i Afriki: na primere Indii i OAR', *Narody Azii i Afriki*, No. 2 (1963), pp. 3–22.

2. Discussed in Chapter 6 above.

3. See *Izvestiya* (18 April 1956); and for the Arab reaction, *New York Times* (24 June 1956).

4. N. S. Khrushchev's interview with James Reston in the *New York Times* (10 October 1957).

5. The development of the ICBMs by the Soviet Union reduced the strategic imbalance between the two Superpowers, while the perfection of the Polaris

234   *Notes and References to pp. 155–64*

submarine and inflight refuelling techniques drastically reduced the American requirement for forward strategic air bases. See A. S. Becker and A. L. Horelick, *Soviet Policy in the Middle East* (The Rand Corporation, R-504-FF, 1970); and C. J. Jacobsen, *Soviet Strategy—Soviet Foreign Policy* (Glasgow: R. Maclehose and Co. Ltd., 1972).

6. *Pravda* (19 October 1961).

7. *Pravda* (31 May 1961).

8. This point is developed by K. J. Holsti, op. cit., p. 132.

9. *SWB I* (6 March 1964), SU/1497/A4/2.

10. *SWB I* (17 November 1964), SU/1711/A4/1 (my italics).

11. This view is especially evident in the excellent book by I. P. Belyaev and Ye. M. Primakov, *Egipet: vremya prezidenta Nasera* (Moscow, 1974), Chapter 7.

12. Ibid., pp. 281–3, p. 313.

13. *SWB IV* (3 July 1972), ME/4030/A/1–7.

14. See for example, AN, SSSR, *Mezhdunarodnyye otnosheniya posle vtoroi mirovoi voiny* (Moscow, 1962); P. Demchenko, *Siriyskaya Respublika na strazhe svoey nezavisimosti* (Moscow, 1957); A. F. Fedchenko, *Araby v bor'be za nezavisimost'* (Moscow, 1957); G. Mirskiy, *Bagdadskiy Pakt: orudiye kolonializma* (Moscow, 1956).

15. V. Smirnov and I. Matyukhin, 'USSR and the Arab East: Economic Contacts', *International Affairs*, No. 9, (Moscow, 1972), p. 87.

16. R. A. Ul'yanovskiy, 'Nauchnyy sotsializm i osvobodivshiyesya strany', *Kommunist*, No. 4 (1968), p. 104.

17. N. A. Ushakova, *Arabskaya Respublika Egipet: sotrudnichestvo so stranami sotsializma i ekonomicheskoye razvitiye (1952–1972 gg)* (Moscow, 1974), pp. 44–53; R. A. Andriasyan and A. Ya. El'yanov, 'Razvivayushchiyesya strany: diversifikatsiya ekonomiki i strategiya promyshlennovo razvitiya', *MEIMO*, No. 1 (1968), p. 39; V. M. Kollantai, *Puti preodoleniya ekonomicheskoi otstalosti* Moscow, 1967), p. 206; N. Schmelyov, 'Stoimostnyye kriterii ikh rol' v ekonomike razvivayushchikhsya stran', *MEIMO*, No. 6 (1968), pp. 50–1.

18. Schmelyov, ibid., p. 50.

19. Ibid., p. 51.

20. *The Hindu Weekly Review* (25 March 1968), p. 10, in Elizabeth Kridl Valkenier, 'New Trends in Soviet Economic Relations with the Third World', *World Politics* Vol. 22, No. 3 (1970), p. 427; and Charles McLane, *Soviet–Middle East Relations* (London: Central Asian Research Centre, 1973), p. 120.

21. Andriasyan and El'yanov, op. cit., p. 30.

22. Ibid., p. 31.

23. Robert L. Allen, 'Economic Motives in Soviet Foreign Trade Policy', *Southern Economic Journal*, Vol. 25, No. 2 (1958), pp. 189–201; Stanley J. Zyzniewski, 'The Soviet Bloc and the Underdeveloped Countries', *World Politics*, Vol. 2, No. 3 (1959), pp. 378–99; Glen A. Smith, *Soviet Foreign Trade* (New York: Praeger, 1973), pp. 224–55.

24. *Pravda* (7 July 1958).

25. *Pravda* (22 October 1961), cited in Valkenier, op. cit., p. 415.

26. V. Alkhimov and V. Mordvinov, *Foreign Trade of the USSR* (London: Soviet Booklets, 1958), p. 16; M. Zakhmatov, 'S.Sh.A. i "Obshchiy rynok"', *Vneshnyaya Torgovlya*, No. 7 (1964), p. 29; V. Sergeev, 'K voprosu kategorii

vsemirnyi rynok', *Vneshnyaya torgovlya*, No. 4 (1963), pp. 17–24.
27. *Pravda* (6 April 1966).
28. Yu. Konstantinov, 'Investitsionnyy bank sotsialisticheskikh stran', *Vneshnyaya torgovlya*, No. 8 (1971), p. 12.
29. Smirnov and Matyukhin, op. cit., p. 87.
30. Ibid.
31. Finance Minister Ahmad Abu-Ismail announced that half of Egypt's total debts were to the Soviet Union (*Arab Report and Record*, 1975, No. 24 (16–31 December 1975), p. 685). *Al-Ahram* (2 January 1976) then put Egypt's total foreign indebtedness at £E5517 million ($14,101 million).

NOTES TO CHAPTER 9

1. See Fred C. Ikle, *How Nations Negotiate* (New York: Harper and Row, 1964); Sir Harold George Nicolson, *Diplomacy*, 2nd ed. (London: Oxford University Press, 1952); Sir Harold George Nicolson, 'Diplomacy Then and Now', *Foreign Affairs*, Vol. 40, No. 1 (1961), pp. 39–49; Dean Rusk, 'Parliamentary Diplomacy: Debate versus Negotiations', *World Affairs Interpreter*, Vol. 26 (1955), pp. 121–38.
2. Ovsyany, op. cit., p. 100.
3. *SWB I* (23 March 1959), p. 8 For Nasser's reaction, see *SWB IV* (24 March 1959), p. 3.
4. Heikal, *Nasser: The Cairo Documents*, p. 146; and *The Mizan Newsletter*, Vol. 3, No. 12 (1961), pp. 2–4. The Egyptian reply to Khrushchev can be found in *al-Ahram* (9 June 1961).
5. See Sydney D. Bailey, *Voting in the Security Council* (London: Indiana University Press, 1969), pp. 41, 228–31.
6. Robert S. Walters, *American and Soviet Aid: A Comparative Analysis* (Pittsburgh, Pa: University of Pittsburgh Press, 1970), p. 30.
7. *SWB I*, Supplement No. 1, Proceedings of the 20th Congress of the CPSU, 16 February 1956, p. 13.
8. Laqueur, *The Soviet Union and the Middle East*, p. 265.
9. Ushakova, op. cit., p. 83; James Richard Carter, *The Net Cost of Soviet Foreign Aid* (New York: Praeger, 1969), p. 16.
10. From the text of the Soviet–Egyptian agreement on the Aswan Dam, in Marshall I. Goldman, *Soviet Foreign Aid* (New York: Praeger, 1967), p. 225. This same agreement, however, states that hard currency would only be demanded 'in exceptional circumstances' if Soviet importers were not offered the same terms as their hard currency competitors or if orders were delayed.
11. Leo Tansky, *US and USSR Aid to Developing Countries: A Comparative Study of India, Turkey and the UAR* (New York: Praeger, 1967), p. 153; R. Petrov, 'The Soviet Union and the Arab Countries', *International Affairs*, Moscow, No. 11 (1972), p. 26; and Carter, op. cit., p. 16.
12. Tansky, *US and USSR*, p. 154.
13. I. Kapranov, 'Economic and Technical Cooperation Between the Soviet Union and Foreign Countries', *Foreign Trade*, No. 6 (1977), p. 13.
14. Ushakova, op. cit., p. 84.

15. Interview with Nabil Ali Sadek, Minister Plenipotentiary (Commercial), Egyptian Embassy, Moscow (18 May 1977).

16. ARE, Ministry of Culture and Information, State Information Service, *The High Dam*, Cairo (July 1972), pp. 45–6.

17. *The Economist* (22–28 March 1975), p. 59; *al-Ahram* (19 May 1976).

18. US, CIA,.*Communist Aid to the Less Developed Countries of the Free World 1976*, ER 77–10296 (August 1977), p. 7.

19. Ushakova, op. cit., p. 84.

20. Kapranov, op. cit., p. 13.

21. Heikal, *Nasser: The Cairo Documents*, p. 141.

22. *The Middle East*, No. 10 (London 1975), p. 23.

23. *SWB I* (14 February 1955), p. 6.

24. USSR, Ministry of Foreign Trade, *Vneshnyaya torgovlya SSSR za 1976 god, statisticheskiy obzor* (Moscow, 1977).

25. UN, Department of Economic and Social Affairs, *Yearbook of International Trade Statistics 1975*, Vol. 1 (New York: United Nations, 1976), p. 334.

26. *Vneshnyaya torgovlya SSSR za 1975 god*, p. 244; *za 1976 god*, p. 271.

27. *Al-Jumhuriya* (17 August 1977).

28. *Akhbar al-Yom* (24 September 1977).

29. V. Spandaryan, 'Nasha torgovlya so stranami Yugo-Vostochnoy Azii i Blizhnevo Vostoka', *Vneshnyaya torgovlya*, No. 11 (1957), pp. 61–9; M. F. Gataullin and M. V. Malyukovskiy, 'Yegipetskaya respublika po puti k ekonomicheskoy nezavisimosti', *Sovetskoye vostokovedeniye*, No. 3 (1956), pp. 119–29; and V. Rimalov, *Economic Cooperation Between the USSR and Underdeveloped Countries* (Moscow, n.d.), pp. 70–82.

30. *The Egyptian Gazette*, Cairo (1 September 1964).

31. UAR, Central Agency for Public Mobilisation and Statistics, *Foreign Trade of the UAR*, Cairo (annually).

32. *L'Orient Le Jour* (25 December 1975).

33. *Middle East News Agency* (24 August 1977).

34. SIPRI, *The Arms Trade with the Third World* (London: Penguin, 1975), p. 202; US, Arms Control and Disarmament Agency, *World Military Expenditures and Arms Transfers 1966–1975* (Washington DC, 1976), p. 78.

35. *Al-Ahram* (22 July 1959). Unconfirmed reports also suggest that there was unrest in the Egyptian army over Sadat's failure to obtain Western weapons, culminating in the reported arrest of 168 officers, including the Chief of Staff, Lieutenant-General Mohamed Ali Fahmi. They had evidently signed a letter to Sadat prior to his visit to Jerusalem demanding a reinforcement of the eastern front. *al-Nida*, Beirut (18 December 1977); *SWB I*, SU/5685/A4/4 (6 December 1977).

36. On the cost to the USSR of military aid, see Gur Ofer, 'The Economic Burden of Soviet Involvement in the Middle East', *Soviet Studies*, Vol. 24, No. 3 (1973), pp. 329–48.

37. As shown in Table 9.5. Also see R. D. McLaurin, *The Middle East in Soviet Policy* (London: Lexington Books, 1975), p. 105.

38. US Arms Control and Disarmament Agency, op. cit., p. 62.

39. *Sunday Telegraph* (11 September 1977); *Arab Report and Record*, No. 17 (1–15 September 1977), p. 718.

40. *New York Times* (3 February 1977);*Middle East Reporter*, Beirut (3 June 1977); and Sadat's interview in *October* (19 February 1978).

41. *The Military Balance, 1977–1978*, p. 35.

42. *Al-Ahram* (30 January 1976).

43. *Al-Ahram* (29 August 1977).

44. For Sadat's 26 October speech announcing cessation of debt repayments, see *Arab Report and Record*, No. 19/20 (1–31 October 1977), p. 825. For the account of Fahmi's Moscow visit given by Sadat in his 14 August speech, see *Arab Report and Record*, No. 15 (1–15 August 1977), p. 630.

45. *Pravda* (8 May 1977).

46. Heikal, *The Road to Ramadan*, p. 49.

47. Ibid., p. 177; and US, CIA, ER 77–10296, op. cit., p. 6.

48. Robert G. Weinland, 'Land Support for Naval Forces: Egypt and the Soviet Escadra 1962–1976', *Survival*, Vol. 20, No. 2 (1978), p. 74.

49. Ibid.

50. Ibid.

51. *Strategic Survey 1970*, p. 47.

52. Soviet government statements on Suez can be found in *Izvestiya* (16 September 1956, 1 November 1956, 3 November 1956; 6 November 1956—rocket threats; 11 November 1956—volunteers). Also see *SWB IV* (1 November 1956), pp. i–ii; and *Pravda* (9 December 1956) on Soviet volunteers.

53. *Izvestiya* (17 July 1958). Also *SWB I* (13 September 1957), pp. 16–17; and Mackintosh, op. cit., p. 227.

54. Lyndon B. Johnson, *The Vantage Point: Perspectives on the Presidency* (New York: Holt, Rinehart and Winston, 1971), p. 302; *New York Times* (21 November 1973).

55. *SWB I* (23 September 1957), p. 9.

56. George S. Dragnich, 'The Soviet Union's Quest for Access to Naval Facilities in Egypt prior to the June War of 1967', in Michael MccGwire *et al.*, eds., *Soviet Naval Policy* (New York: Praeger, 1975), p. 267.

57. Ibid., p. 269; *Strategic Survey 1971*, pp. 30–4.

58. Compare in this respect the growth in the size of the Soviet navy generally and the naval air force and naval infantry (marines) in particular between 1957 and 1973, as contained in *The Military Balance* for those two years.

59. *Aviation Weekly* (5 July 1976).

60. A. I. Dawisha, op. cit., pp. 162–3. For a further discussion of the definition and uses of propaganda as an instrument of foreign policy, see K. J. Holsti, op. cit., Chapter 9; Raymond Aron, *Peace and War* (London: Weidenfeld and Nicolson, 1962); Lindsay Fraser, *Propaganda* (London: Oxford University Press, 1957); Robert T. Holt and Robert W. van de Velde, *Strategic Psychological Operations and American Foreign Policy* (Chicago: University of Chicago Press, 1960); Terence Qualter, *Propaganda and Psychological Warfare* (New York: Random House, 1965); and Andrew M. Scott, *Revolution in Statecraft* (New York: Random House, 1967).

61. Ivar Spector, *The Soviet Union and the Muslim World 1917–1958* (Seattle: University of Washington Press, 1959), p. 252. Also see John C. Clews, *Communist Propaganda Techniques* (London: Methuen and Co. Ltd., 1964).

62. *SWB I* (25 November 1955), p. 3.

238   *Notes and References to pp. 186–93*

63. Frederick C. Barghoorn, *Soviet Foreign Propaganda* (Princeton, NJ: Princeton University Press, 1964), p. 279.

64. *SWB IV*, ME/W11/7 (2 July 1959); BBC, *USSR (External Services) Moscow Chronological Schedule, Autumn/Winter, 1976* (Reading: BBC, 1976); BBC, *USSR (External Services) Regional Radio Centres, Chronological Schedule Winter 1976* (Reading: BBC, 1976).

65. UNESCO, *World Communications*, 5th ed. (Paris: UNESCO, 1975), p. 511.

66. *SWB I*, SU/2596/A4/1 (17 October 1967).

67. *SWB I*, SU/1074/A4/4 (16 October 1962). Also see *SWB I* (27 May 1955), p. 23; *SWB I* (20 September 1957), p. 30; and *SWB I* (10 November 1958), p. 10.

68. *SWB I*, SU/1054/A4/1 (2 September 1962). Also see *SWB I* (31 March 1957), p. 23; and *SWB I*, SU/2655/A4/7 (29 December 1967).

69. Moscow Radio in Arabic (26 August 1975), as quoted in *USSR and the Third World*, Vol. 5 No. 6–8 (1976), p. 349.

70. The techniques are described in greater detail in K. J. Holsti, op. cit., Chapter 9.

71. Ibid., p. 259.

72. *Izvestiya* (16 March 1959).

73. Holsti, op. cit., p. 259.

74. See footnote 68 above.

75. Moscow Radio in Arabic (15 July 1975 and 24 July 1975); Radio Peace and Progress (17 July 1975, 14 August 1975 and 28 November 1975), as quoted in *USSR and the Third World*, Vol. 5, No. 6–8 (1976), pp. 354–7.

76. *SWB I*, SU/2509/A4/3 (6 July 1967).

77. Holsti, op. cit., p. 259.

78. *SWB I*, SU/1590/A4/2 (27 June 1964).

79. *SWB I*, SU/5744/A4/4 (20 February 1978).

80. *SWB I*, SU/2595/A4/1 (16 October 1967).

81. I. V. Samilovskiy, *Nauchnyye i kul'turnyye svyazi SSSR so stranami Azii i Afriki* (Moscow, 1963), pp. 47–53; and O. M. Gorbatov and L. Ya. Cherkasskiy, *Sotrudnichestvo SSSR so stranami Arabskovo Vostoka i Afriki*, (Moscow, 1973), pp. 300–6.

82. Gorbatov and Cherkasskiy, ibid., p. 303.

83. Interview with Abd al-Munim Tahawi, Director-General of the Ministry of Foreign Cultural Relations, Cairo (14 January 1974).

84. G. A. Mozhayev, *Mezhdunarodnyye kul'turnyye svyazi SSSR* (Moscow, 1959), p. 33; and Gorbatov and Cherkasskiy, op. cit., pp. 300–6.

85. *Om Kalthum fi al-Ittihad al-Soveti*, Cairo, 1970. For further details of these exchanges, see K. A. Guseinov, *Internatsional'nyye svyazi profoyuzov SSSR s prosoyuzami stran Azii i Afriki* (Moscow, 1965); McLane, op. cit.; US Department of State, Bureau of Intelligence and Research, Research Memorandum, *Educational and Cultural Exchanges Between Communist and Non-Communist Countries*, RSB–46 (1963); RSB–85 (1964); RSB–49 (1965); RSB–10 (1966); RSB–40 (1967); RSB–65 (1968); RSB–25 (1969); RSB–35 (1970); no code (1972). Hereafter referred to as Educational and Cultural Exchanges.

86. *SWB I* (16 January 1959), p. 62.

87. See S. G. Korneev, *Nauchnyye svyazi Akademii Nauk SSSR so stranami Azii i*

Afriki (Moscow, 1969); and N. A. Kuznetsova and L. M. Kulagina, *Iz istorii Sovetskovo vostokovedeniya* (Moscow, 1970), Chapter 4.

88. *Educational and Cultural Exchanges*, RSB–40, p. 45; and from personal observations made while in Cairo in 1973–4.

89. Samilovskiy, op. cit., pp. 47–52; *SSSR i strany vostoka—ekonomicheskoye i kul'turnoye sotrudnichestvo* (Moscow, 1961), p. 89; and from a personal observation in Cairo.

90. Spector, op. cit., p. 261.

91. *Materialy XXIII s"ezda KPSS* (Moscow, 1966), p. 169.

92. *Opyt istorii i sotsial'nyy progress v Afrike* (Moscow, 1972), p. 123.

93. Ibid.

94. Ibid., p.124.

95. *Pravda* (9 January 1975).

96. Compiled from Gorbatov and Cherkasskiy, op. cit., pp. 297, 302; *SSSR i strany vostoka* . . ., p. 118; Samilovskiy, op. cit., p. 30; and *Educational and Cultural Exchanges* (various years).

97. *Al-Anbaa*, Kuwait (13 September 1977).

98. Saddik Abdel Razik Mohamed Saad, *Voprosy effektivnosti ekonomicheskovo sotrudnichestva mezhdu SSSR i ARE*, Avtoreferat, dissertation for the degree of candidate of economics (Moscow, 1976), p. 24.

99. *Al-Anbaa*, Kuwait (13 September 1977).

100. R. Hrair Dekmejain, *Egypt under Nasir*, (London: University of London Press, 1971), p. 187.

101. For a more detailed discussion of the Soviet cultural effort, see Karen Dawisha, 'Soviet Cultural Relations with Iraq, Syria and Egypt, 1955–1970', *Soviet Studies*, Vol. 27, No. 3 (1975), pp. 418–40.

102. *Al-Jumhuriyah* (12 January 1978).

103. *Arab Report and Record*, No 23/24 (1–31 December 1977), p. 966.

104. See note 35 above.

105. *The Mizan Newsletter*, No. 8, (London, 1959), p. 1.

106. Avakov and Mirskiy, op. cit., p. 73.

107. R. A. Ul'yanovskiy, 'Sovremenniy etap natsional'no-osvoboditel'novo dvizheniya i krest'yanstvo', *MEIMO*, No. 5 (1971), p. 100.

108. *World News* (23 November 1957), as quoted in Laqueur, *Soviet Union and the Middle East*, p. 298.

109. Belyaev and Primakov, op. cit., pp. 282–3.

110. Moscow Radio (28 December 1970), as quoted in *USSR and the Third World*, Vol. 1, No. 1 (1971), p. 24.

111. *Arab World Weekly*, Beirut (10 February 1973).

112. *Al-Safir*, Beirut (4 August 1975), quoted in Richard F. Staar, ed., *Yearbook on International Communist Affairs, 1976*, (Stanford, Cal.: Hoover Institution Press, 1976), pp. 540–1.

113. Ibid., p. xvii.

114. *Al-Akhbar* (24 January 1977), claimed that Colonel Qadhafi, 'the madman of Libya', had assembled 'a gang of expatriate Egyptian communists' and put on a show 'to win the favour of his atheist comrades in Moscow'. *Pravda* on 22 January denied any communist involvement, claiming that the Egyptian leaders were trying to 'distract attention from the real reasons for the outbursts of public indignation'.

115. Iain Phelps-Fetherston, *Soviet International Front Organisations*, (New York: Praeger, 1965), p. 13.
116. Sadat interview in *October* (11 December 1977).
117. Phelps-Fatherston, op. cit., p. 36.
118. *News Times*, No. 40 (1957), pp. 14–15.
119. Charles Issawi, *Egypt in Revolution* (London: Oxford University Press, 1963), p. 196.
120. Phelps-Fatherston, op. cit., p. 55.
121. *African Digest*, Vol. 10, No. 5, (London, 1963), pp. 173–4.
122. *SWB I*, SU/821/C/2–4 (15 December 1961).
123. A. I. Dawisha, op. cit., pp. 162–73..

NOTES TO CHAPTER 10

1. G. Liska, 'The Politics of "Cultural Diplomacy" ', *World Politics*, Vol. 14, No. 3 (1962), p. 541.
2. Rubinstein (op. cit., pp. 355–66) in a detailed thematic analysis of the communiqués issued following each high-level negotiation between Soviet and Egyptian leaders during the 1968–75 period, indicates that the Middle East conflict was discussed in 23 out of the 25 bilateral meetings.
3. See Chapters 3 and 4 above.
4. The decisive influence of the Soviet threat to intervene on Israel's decision to allow non-military supplies through to the Egyptian Third Army is discussed by Michael Brecher and Benjamin Geist in their forthcoming book on Israel's behaviour during the 1967 and 1973 crises, to be published by University of California Press in 1979.
5. Patrick O'Brien, *The Revolution in Egypt's Economic System* (London: Oxford University Press, 1966), p. 154.
6. Derived from figures given in Central Bank of Egypt, *Annual Report 1976* (Cairo, June 1977), p. 15; and US, Department of Commerce, Overseas Business Reports, *Market Profiles for the Near East and North Africa*, OBR 77–51 (Washington: USGPO, October 1977), p. 5.
7. *Arab Report and Record*, No. 16 (16–31 August 1977), p. 675.
8. B. Solodovnikov, M. Braginsky, 'The Working Class in the African Countries' Social Structure', *International Affairs*, Moscow, No. 10 (1976), p. 47.
9. Ibid., p. 49.
10. K. Ivanov, 'The National Liberation Movement and the Non-Capitalist Path of Development', *International Affairs*, Moscow, No. 2 (1966), p. 12.

Bibliography

BOOKS, DOCUMENTS AND ARTICLES

Adie, W. A. C. 'China, Russia and the Third World', *China Quarterly*, Vol. 11(1962), pp. 200–13.

Adomeit, Hannes 'Soviet Foreign Policy: Some Contradictory Trends', in Peter Jones, ed., *The International Yearbook of Foreign Policy Analysis*, Vol. 1 (London: Croom Helm, 1974), pp. 30–57.

——, 'Soviet Risk-Taking and Crisis Behaviour: From Confrontation to Coexistence?', *Adelphi Papers*, No. 101, London: International Institute for Strategic Studies (1973).

Agwani, M. S. *Communism in the Arab East* (London: Asia Publishing House, 1969).

Akademiya Nauk SSSR, Institut Mirovoy Ekonomiki i Mezhdunaradnykh Otnosheniy, *Mezhdunarodnyye otnosheniya posle vtoroi mirovoi voiny* (Moscow, 1962).

Akopyan, G. 'O natsional'no-osvoboditel'nom dvizhenii narodov Blizhnevo i Srednevo Vostoka', *Voprosy ekonomiki*, No. 1 (1953), pp. 58–75.

Aleksandrov, V. S. ed., *Politicheskaya strategiya i taktika Kommunisticheskykh Partii* (Moscow, 1971).

Alkhimov, V. and V. Mordvinov, *Foreign Trade of the USSR* (London: Soviet Booklets, 1958).

Allen, Robert L. 'Economic Motives in Soviet Foreign Trade Policy', *Southern Economic Journal*, Vol. 25, No. 2 (1958), pp. 189–201.

Allison, Graham T. 'Conceptual Models and the Cuban Missile Crisis', *American Political Science Review*, Vol. 63, No. 3 (1969), pp. 689–718.

——, *Essence of Decision: Explaining the Cuban Missile Crisis* (Boston Mass.: Little, Brown and Co., 1971).

Andriasyan, R. A. and A. Ya, El'yanov, *Blizhniy Vostok: neft' i nezavisimost'* (Moscow, 1961).

241

——, 'Razvivayushchiyesya strany: diversifikatsiya ekonomiki i strategiya promyshlennovo razvitiya', *Mirovaya ekonomika i mezhdunarodnyye otnsoheniya*, No. 1 (1968), pp. 29–41 (hereafter referred to as *MEIMO*).

ARE, Ministry of Culture and Information, State Information Service, *The High Dam*, Cairo (July 1972).

Arbatov, G. 'O Sovetsko–Amerikanskikh otnosheniyakh', *Kommunist*, No. 3 (1973), as translated in *Survival*, Vol. 15, No. 3 (1973), pp. 124–31.

——, *Soviet-American Relations, Progress and Problems* (Moscow: Novosti Press Agency, 1976).

Arendt, Hannah *The Origins of Totalitarianism*, (London: Allen and Unwin, 1966).

Aspaturian, Vernon V. 'Dialectics and Duplicity in Soviet Diplomacy', *Journal of International Affairs*, Vol. 17, No. 1 (1963), pp. 42–60.

Aspaturian, Vernon V. ed. *Process and Power in Soviet Foreign Policy* (Boston, Mass.: Little Brown and Co., 1971).

——, 'The Soviet Military–Industrial Complex—Does it Exist?' *Journal of International Affairs*, Vol. 26, No. 1 (1972), pp. 1–29.

Avakov, R. and G. Mirskiy 'O klassovoy strukture v slaborazvitykh stranakh', *MEIMO*, No. 4 (1962), pp. 68–82.

Avakov, R. and L. Stepanov, 'Sotsialyye problemy natsional'no-osvoboditel'noi revoliutsii', *MEIMO*, No. 5 (1963), pp. 46–54.

Bagdash, Khalid 'The Crisis and the Problems of the Middle East', *World Marxist Review*, Vol. 1, No. 1 (1958), pp. 68–70.

——, 'Two Trends in the Arab National Movements', *World Marxist Review*, Vol. 2, No. 11 (1959), pp. 26–32.

Bailey, Sydney D. *Voting in the Security Council* (London: Indiana University Press, 1969).

Balabushevich, V. V. 'O nekotorykh osobennostyakh rabochevo dvizheniya v stranakh Vostoka na sovremennom etape', *Problemy vostokovedeniya*, No. 2 (1959), pp. 49–61.

Barghoorn, Frederick C. *The Soviet Cultural Offensive* (Princeton NJ: Princeton University Press, 1960).

——, *Soviet Foreign Propaganda* (Princeton NJ: Princeton University Press, 1964).

Bar-Zohar, Michael *Embassies in Crisis* (Englewood Cliffs, NJ: Prentice-Hall, 1970).

Baskin, V. *et al.*, eds., *Ekonomicheskoye Sotrudnichestvo SSSR so stranami Afriki* (Moscow, 1968).

Bibliography

243

Becker, Seymour *Russian Protectorates in Central Asia. Bukhara and Khiva, 1865–1924* (Cambridge, Mass.: Harvard University Press, 1968).

Becker, A. S. and Horelick, A. L. *Soviet Policy in the Middle East*, The Rand Corporation, R–504–FF (1970).

Be'eri, E. *Army Officers in Arab Politics and Society* (Jerusalem: Israel University Press, 1969).

Bell, Coral 'The October Middle East War: A Case Study in Crisis Management During *Détente*', *International Affairs*, Vol. 50, No. 4 (1974), pp. 531–43.

Belyaev, I. P. and Ye. M. Primakov, *Egipet: vremiya presidenta Nasera* (Moscow, 1974).

Berry, John A. 'Oil and Soviet Policy in the Middle East', *The Middle East Journal*, Vol. 26, No. 2 (1972), pp. 149–61.

Binder, Leonard *The Ideological Revolution in the Middle East*, New York: John Wiley & Sons, Inc., 1964.

——, 'The Middle East as a Subordinate International System', *World Politics*, Vol. 10, No. 3 (1958), pp. 408–29.

Bochkarev I. 'The New Spirit in Egypt', *New Times*, No. 3 (1957), pp. 6–9.

Bol'shaya Sovetskaya Entsiklopediya, 2nd and 3rd eds. (Moscow).

Borcierkiw, E. 'Religion in the USSR after Khrushchev', in John W. Strong, ed., *The Soviet Union Under Brezhnev and Kosygin* (New York: Van Nostrand Reinhold Co., 1971), pp. 135–56.

Boulding, Kenneth 'National Images and International Systems', *The Journal of Conflict Resolution*, Vol. 3, No. 2 (1959), pp. 120–31.

Bralina, E. 'Planirovaniye—metod razvitiya natsional'noi ekonomiki', *Kommunist*, No. 13 (1962), pp. 99–101.

Brecher, Michael Blema Steinberg and Janice Stein 'A Framework for Research on Foreign Policy Behaviour', *The Journal of Conflict Resolution*, Vol. 13, No. 1 (1969), pp. 75–101.

Brecher, Michael *The Foreign Policy System of Israel* (London: Oxford University Press, 1972).

British Broadcasting Corporation, *Summary of World Broadcasts, Part I: The Soviet Union*, London: BBC (daily).

——, *Summary of World Broadcasts, Part IV: The Arab World, Israel, Greece, Turkey, Iran*, London: BBC (daily).

——, *USSR (External Services) Moscow, Chronological Schedule, Autumn/Winter 1976* (Reading: BBC, 1976).

——, *USSR (External Services) Regional Radio Centres, Chronological Schedule, Winter 1976* (Reading: BBC, 1976).

Bromke, Adam 'Ideology and National Interest in Soviet Foreign Policy', *International Journal*, Vol. 22, No. 4 (1967), pp. 547–62.

Brzezinski, Z. 'Communist Ideology and International Affairs', *Journal of Conflict Resolution*, Vol. 4, No. 3 (1960), pp. 266–91.

Brzezinski, Z. and S. Huntington, *Political Powers, USA/USSR* (New York: The Viking Press, 1964).

Burton, John *Systems, States, Diplomacy and Rules* (London: Cambridge University Press, 1968).

Buss, Robin 'Wary Partners: The Soviet Union and Arab Socialism', *Adelphi Papers*, No. 73 (London: Institute for Strategic Studies, December, 1970).

Byely, Colonel B. *et al.*, *Marxism–Leninism on War and Army* (Moscow, 1972).

Calvocoressi, Peter. *World Politics Since 1945* (London: Longmans, 1968).

Cantori, Louis J. and Stephen Spiegel, ed., *The International Politics of The Regions: A Comparative Approach* (Englewood Cliffs, NJ: Prentice-Hill, Inc., 1970).

Carlisle, Donald S. 'The Changing Soviet Perception of the Developmental Process in the Afro-Asian World', *Midwest Journal of Political Science*, Vol. 8, No. 4 (1964), pp. 385–407.

——, 'Stalin's Post-War Foreign Policy and the National Liberation Movement', *Review of Politics*, Vol. 27, No. 3 (1965), pp. 352–4.

Carr, E. H. *Socialism in One Country 1924–1926*, Vol. 3 (London: Macmillan and Co. Ltd., 1964).

Carrere d'Encausse, Helene and Stuart Schram, *Marxism and Asia* (London: Allen Lane, The Penguin Press, 1969).

Carter, James Richard *The Net Cost of Soviet Foreign Aid* (New York: Praeger, 1969).

Chernov, L. N. 'Kommunisty stran Azii i Afriki v avangarde bor'be za svobodu i natsional'nuyu nezavisimost', *Narody Azii i Afriki*, No. 5 (1961), pp. 15–32.

Childers, Erskine *The Road to Suez* (London: MacGibbon and Kee, 1962).

Chkhikvadze, V. M. *The Soviet Form of Popular Government* (Moscow: Progress Publishers, 1972).

Clews, John C. *Communist Propaganda Techniques* (London: Methuen and Co. Ltd., 1964).

Cohn, Stanley H. 'The Economic Burden of Soviet Defence Outlays', in US Congress, Joint Economic Committee, *Economic*

Performance in the Soviet Economy (Washington DC: US Government Printing Office, 1970), pp. 166–89.

——, 'General Growth Performance of the Soviet Economy', in US, Congress, Joint Economic Committee, *Economic Performance and the Military Burden in the Soviet Union* (Washington DC: US Government Printing Office, 1970), pp. 9–18.

Confino, M. and S. Shamir, eds., *The USSR and The Middle East* (New York: John Wiley and Sons, 1973).

Conquest, Robert *Power and Policy in the USSR* (London: Macmillan, 1962).

Copeland, Miles *The Game of Nations* (London: Weidenfeld and Nicolson, 1969).

Cottrell, Alvin J. 'Soviet–Egyptian Relations', *Military Review*, Vol. 49, No. 12 (1969), pp. 69–77.

Crankshaw, Edward ed., *Khrushechev Remembers* (London: Sphere Books Ltd., 1971).

Cremeans, Charles K. *The Arabs and the World* (New York: Praeger, 1963).

Current Soviet Leaders (Oakville, Ont.: Mosaic Press, 1976).

Curtis, Michael 'Soviet–American Relations and the Middle East Crisis', *Orbis*, Vol. 15, No. 1 (1971), pp. 403–28.

Dallin, Alexander *Soviet Union at the UN*, London: Methuen and Co., 1962.

——, 'A Soviet View of the UN', *International Organization*, Vol. 16 (1962), pp. 20–36.

Dallin, David *Soviet Foreign Policy After Stalin* (London: Methuen and Co., 1960).

Dann, Uriel *Iraq Under Qassem: A Political History 1958–1963* (New York: Praeger, 1969).

Dawisha, A. I. *Egypt in the Arab World: The Elements of Foreign Policy* (London: Macmillan, 1976).

——, 'The Principle Decision-Maker in Foreign Policy: The Case of Nasser of Egypt', *International Relations*, Vol. 4, No. 4 (1973), pp. 400–9.

——, 'The Transnational Party in Regional Politics: The Arab Baath Party', *Asian Affairs*, Vol. 61, No. 1 (1974), pp. 23–31.

Dawisha, Karen 'The Roles of Ideology in the Decision-Making of the Soviet Union', *International Relations*, Vol. 4, No. 2 (1972), pp. 156–72.

——, 'Soviet Cultural Relations with Iraq, Syria and Egypt, 1955–1970', *Soviet Studies*, Vol. 27, No. 3 (1975), pp. 418–40.

——, 'Soviet Policy in the Middle East: Present Dilemmas and Future Trends', *Millennium,* Journal of International Studies of the London School of Economics, Vol. 6, No. 2 (1977), pp. 182–90.

Degras, Jane ed., *The Communist International, 1919–1943,* 3 vols. (London: Oxford University Press, 1956).

Dekmejian, R. Hrair *Egypt Under Nasir* (London: University of London Press, Ltd., 1971).

Demchenko, P. *Siriyskaya Respublika na strazhe svoey nezevisimosti* (Moscow, 1957).

Deutscher, Isaac *Ironies of History* (London: Oxford University Press, 1966).

——, *Stalin* (London: Penguin, 1966).

Dimant-Kass, Ilana *'Pravda* and *Trud,* Divergent Attitudes Towards the Middle East', Hebrew University of Jerusalem, Soviet and East European Research Centre, Research Paper No. 3 (1972).

——, 'The Soviet Military and Soviet Policy in the Middle East 1970–1973', *Soviet Studies,* Vol. 26, No. 4 (1974), pp. 502–21.

Dinerstein, Herbert S. 'Soviet Doctrine on Developing Countries: Some Divergent Views', Rand Corporation, P. 2725 (1963).

——, *War and the Soviet Union* (New York: Praeger, 1959).

Dmitriev, E. 'Soviet-Arab Friendship: A New Stage', *International Affairs,* No. 8, (Moscow, 1971), pp. 66–8.

Documents on the USSR–USA Summit Talks (Moscow: Novosti Press Agency Publishing House, 1973).

Draper Theodore *Israel and World Politics* (New York: The Viking Press, 1968).

Dvorzak, L. *Mirovaya sistema sotsializma i razvivayushchikhsiye strany* (Moscow, 1965).

Easton, David *A Framework for Political Analysis* (Englewood Cliffs, NJ: Prentice-Hall Inc., 1965).

——, 'An Approach to the Analysis of Political Systems', *World Politics,* Vol. 9 (April 1957), pp. 383–400.

Ebel, Robert E. *The Petroleum Industry in the Soviet Union* (New York: American Petroleum Institute, 1966).

Eisenhower, Dwight D. *The White House Years, Vol. I, Mandate for Change* (New York: Doubleday, 1963).

——, *The White House Years, Vol. II, Waging Peace* (New York: Doubleday, 1965).

Enayat, H. 'Islam and Socialism in Egypt', *Middle Eastern Studies*, Vol. 4, No. 2 (1968), pp. 141–72.

Eran, Oded and Jerome Singer, 'Exodus From Egypt and the Threat to Kremlin Leadership', *New Middle East*, No. 50 (1972), pp. 21–6.

——, 'Soviet Policy towards the Arab World, 1955–71', *Survey*, Vol. 17, No. 4 (1971), pp. 10–30.

Ericson, John. 'The Dislocation of an Alliance: Sino-Soviet Relations, 1960–61', in D. C. Watt, ed., *Survey of International Affairs, 1961* (London: Oxford University Press, 1965).

Evron, Yair *The Middle East: Nations, Super-Powers, and Wars* (London: Paul Elek Ltd., 1973).

Fainsod, Merle *How Russia is Ruled* (Cambridge, Mass.: Harvard University Press, 1963).

Fairhall, David *Russia Looks to the Sea* (London: André Deutsch, 1971).

Fedchenko, A. F. *Araby v bor'be za nezavisimost'* (Moscow, 1957).

Feinberg, Oded. *Soviet Thought on the Role of the Communist Party in The Third World*, unpublished Ph. D. thesis (Indiana University, 1970).

Fleming, D. F. *The Cold War and Its Origins, 1917–1960* (Garden City, N. Y.: Doubleday, 1961).

Fokin, D. F. ed., *Vneshnyaya torgovlya, SSSR (1946–1963 gg)* (Moscow, 1964).

Frankel, Joseph *The Making of Foreign Policy* (London: Oxford University Press, 1963).

Frankland, N. and V. Kine, eds., *Documents on International Affairs, 1956* (London: Oxford University Press, 1959).

Fraser, Lindsey *Propaganda* (London: Oxford University Press, 1957).

Freedman, Robert O. *Soviet Policy Towards the Middle East Since 1970* (New York: Praeger, 1975).

Friedrich, Carl and Z. Brzezinski, *Totalitarian Dictatorship and Autocracy* (New York: Praeger, 1965).

Gafurov, B. G. *Lenin i natsional'no-osvoboditel'noye dvizheniye v stranakh vostoke* (Moscow, 1970).

——, 'Sovetskaya Rossiya i natsional'no-osvoboditel'naya bor'ba narodov srednevo i blizhnevo vostoka', *Voprosy istorii*, No. 10 (1967), pp. 37–54.

Gallagher, Matthew P. and Karl F. Spielman Jr., *Soviet Decision-Making for Defense* (New York: Praeger, 1972).

Garthoff, Raymond *Soviet Military Policy* (London: Faber and Faber, 1966).

Gataullin, M. F. and M. V. Malyukovskiy, 'Yegipetskaya respublika na puti k ekonomicheskoy nezavisimosti', *Sovetskoye vostokovedeniye*, No. 3 (1956), pp. 119–29.

Glassman, Jon D. *Arms for the Arabs* (Baltimore, Md.: Johns Hopkins University Press, 1975).

Golan, Galia 'Soviet Aims and the Middle East War', *Survival*, Vol. 16, No. 3 (1974), pp. 106–15.

——, *Yom Kipper and After, The Soviet Union and the Middle East Crisis* (Cambridge: Cambridge University Press, 1977).

Golan, Matti *The Secret Conversations of Henry Kissinger* (New York: Bantam Books, 1976).

Goldman, Marshall I. 'Red Black Gold', *Foreign Policy*, No. 8 (1972), pp. 138–49.

——, *Soviet Foreign Aid* (New York: Praeger, 1967).

Goncharev, L. V. ed., *Ekonomika Afriki* (Moscow, 1965).

Gorbatov, O. M. and L. Ya. Cherkassikiy, *Sotrudnichestvo SSSR so stranami Arabskovo Vostoka i Afriki* (Moscow, 1973).

Gordan, L. A. and L. A. Fridman, 'Osobennosti sostava i struktury rabochevo klassa v ekonomicheski slaborazvitykh stranakh Azii i Afriki: na primere Indii i OAR', *Narody Azii i Afriki*, No. 2 (1963), pp. 3–22.

L. Gordonov, *Yegipet* (Moscow, 1953).

Gromyko, A. A. *Mirnoye Sosushchestvovaniye – Leninskiy kurs vneshney politiki Sovetskovo Soyuza* (Moscow, 1962).

Guber, A. A. 'Distinctive Features of the National Liberation Movement', *International Affairs*, Moscow, No. 3 (1959), pp. 71–5.

Gumpel, Werner 'Soviet Oil and Soviet Middle East Policy', *Aussen Politik*, Eng. ed., Vol. 23, No. 1 (1972), pp. 104–16.

Guseinov, K. A. *Internatsional'nyye svyazi profsoyuzov SSSR s profsoyuzami stran Azii i Afriki* (Moscow, 1965).

Halperin, Morton H. *Bureaucratic Politics and Foreign Policy* (Washington, DC: The Brookings Institution, 1974).

Harasymiw, Bohdan '*Nomenklatura*: The Soviet Communist Party's Leadership Recruitment System', *Canadian Journal of Political Science*, Vol. 2, No. 4 (1969), pp. 493–512.

Heikal, Mohamed *Nasser: The Cairo Documents* (London: New English Library, 1972).

——, *The Road to Ramadan* (London: Fontana, 1976).

Hoffman, Erik P. and Frederic J. Fleron Jr., eds., *The Conduct of Soviet Foreign Policy* (London: Butterworths, 1971).

Holsti, K. J. *International Politics, A Framework for Analysis*, (Englewood Cliffs, NJ: Prentice-Hall Inc., 1972).

Holt, Robert T. and Robert W. Van de Velde, *Strategic Psychological Operations and American Foreign Policy* (Chicago: Chicago University Press, 1960).

Honta, T. 'Some Problems in the Development of the Oil and Gas Industry in the Ukraine', *Kommunist Ukrainy* (Kiev, January 1967), pp. 9–11; trans. in *Digest of Soviet Ukrainian Press*, PROLOG (April 1967), pp. 10–11.

Horowitz, David *Imperialism and Revolution* (London: Penguin, 1969).

Howard, David H. 'A Note on Hidden Inflation in the Soviet Union' *Soviet Studies*, Vol. 28, No. 4 (1976), pp. 599–609.

Hsun Fu, 'The National Liberation Movement and the Defence of Peace', *International Affairs*, Moscow, No. 3 (1959), pp. 83–4.

Huntington, S. P. and C. H. Moore, eds., *Authoritarian Politics in Modern Society* (New York: Basic Books, 1970).

Hurewitz, J. C. ed., *Soviet–American Rivalry in the Middle East* (New York: Praeger, 1969).

Ikle, Fred C. *How Nations Negotiate* (New York: Harper and Row, 1964).

Institute for the Study of the USSR, *Prominent Personalities in the USSR* (Metuchen, NJ: Scarecrow Press, 1968).

——, *The Soviet Diplomatic Corps, 1917–1967* (Metuchen, NJ: Scarecrow Press, 1970).

Iskendarov, A. A. *et al.*, *Rabocheye dvizheniye v stranakh Azii i Severnoy Afriki na sovremennom etape* (Moscow, 1969).

Iskendarov, A. A. *K voprosu o pomoshchi slaborazvitym stranam*, (Moscow, 1960).

Ismael, Tareq Y. *et al.*, *The Middle East in World Politics* (Syracuse, NY: Syracuse University Press, 1974).

Issawi, Charles *Egypt in Revolution* (London: Oxford University Press, 1963).

Itogi vsesoyuznoy perepisi naseleniya 1970 goda (Moscow: Statistika, 1973).

Ivanov, K. 'A New Arab State', *International Affairs*, Moscow, No. 3 (1958) pp. 53–8. 'National Liberation Movement and Non-Capitalist Path of Development', *International Affairs*, Moscow, No. 5 (1965), pp. 56–67; and No. 2 (1966), pp. 12–22.

'Iz Materialov plenuma Ts. K. Kommunisticheskoy Partii Iraka', *Kommunist*, No. 12 (1959), pp. 104–9.

Jacobsen, C. J. *Soviet Strategy–Soviet Foreign Policy* (Glasgow: R. Maclehose and Co. Ltd., 1972).

Johnson, Lyndon B. *The Vantage Point: Perspectives on the Presidency* (New York: Holt, Rinehart and Winston, 1971).

'Joint Soviet–US Communiqué', *New Times*, No. 28 (1974), pp. 21–25.

Joshua, Wynfred and Stephen P. Gilbert, *Arms for the Third World* (Baltimore: Johns Hopkins Press, 1969).

Kalb, Marvin and Bernard Kalb, *Kissinger* (Boston Mass.: Little, Brown and Co., 1974).

Kanet, Roger E. ed., *The Behavioural Revolution and Communist Studies* (New York: Free Press, 1971).

Kapranov, I. 'Economic and Technical Cooperation Between the Soviet Union and Foreign Countries', *Foreign Trade*, Moscow, No. 6 (1977), pp. 9–17.

——, 'The USSR and Industrial Development in the Newly Free States', *International Affairs*, Moscow, No. 6 (1966), pp. 33–39.

Katz, Zev ed., *Handbook of Major Soviet Nationalities* (New York: Free Press, 1975).

Kennan, George F. *Russia and the West under Lenin and Stalin* (Boston, Mass.: Little, Brown and Co., 1961).

——, 'The Sources of Soviet Conduct', *Foreign Affairs*, Vol. 25, No. 4 (1947), pp. 566–82.

Kerr, Malcolm H. *The Arab Cold War: Gamal Abd al-Nasser and His Rivals, 1958–1970*, 3rd ed. (London: Oxford University Press, 1971).

——, 'Coming to terms with Nasser', *International Affairs*, Vol. 43, No. 1 (1967), pp. 65–84.

——, 'The Emergence of Socialist Ideology in Egypt', *Middle East Journal*, Vol. 16, No. 2 (1962), pp. 127–44.

——, 'Notes on the Background of Arab Socialist Thought', *Journal of Contemporary History*, Vol. 3, No. 3 (1968), pp. 145–59.

Khadduri, Majid *Arab Contemporaries: The Role of Personalities in Politics* (London: Johns Hopkins University Press, 1973).

——, *Political Trends in the Arab World: The Role of Ideas and Ideals in Politics* (Baltimore: Johns Hopkins University Press, 1970).

——, *Republican Iraq* (London: Oxford University Press, 1969).

Khan, R. 'Israel and the Soviet Union: A Review of Postwar Relations', *Orbis*, Vol. 9, No. 4 (1966), pp. 999–1012.

Khrushchev, Nikita 'Za novuyu pobedu mirovovo Kommunis- ticheskovo dvizheniya', *Kommunist*, No. 1 (1961), pp. 3–37.

Kim, G. 'O Gosudarstve Natsional'noi Demokratii', *Aziya i Afrika sevodnya*, No. 10 (1962), pp. 2–6.

Kimche, John *The Second Arab Awakening* (London: Thames and Hudson, 1970).

Kisilev, V. 'Rabochiy klass i natsional'no-osvoboditel'nyye re- volyutsii', *MEIMO*, No. 10 (1963), pp. 93–8.

Klimovitch, L. I. *Islam, yevo proiskhozhdeniye i sotsial'naya sushchnost'* (Moscow, 1956).

Klinghoffer, Arthur Jay *The Soviet Union and International Oil Politics* (New York: Columbia University Press, 1977).

Kohler, F. Goure, L. and Harvey, M. L. *The Soviet Union and the October 1973 Middle East War: The Implications for Détente* (Miami: Center for Advanced International Studies, 1974).

Kolkowicz, Roman *Institutions in Conflict, The Soviet Military and the Communist Party* (Princeton, NJ: Princeton University Press, 1967).

Kollantai, V. M. *Puti preodoleniya ekonomicheskoi otstalosti* (Moscow, 1967).

Kondrashov, V. 'Dva dnya v Asyute', *Sovremennyy vostok*, No. 6 (1960), pp. 29–31.

Konstantinov, Yu. 'Investitsionyy bank sotsialisticheskikh stran', *Vneshnyaya torgovlya*, No. 8 (1971), pp. 12–17.

Korneev, S. G. *Nauchnyye svyazi Akademii nauk SSSR so stranami Azii i Afriki* (Moscow, 1969).

Kovner, M. 'Soviet Aid Strategy in Developing Countries', *Orbis*, Vol. 8, No. 3 (1964), pp. 624–40.

Kozlov, Lt. Gen. S. *et al.*, *O Sovetskoy voennoy nauke* (Moscow, 1962).

Kudryavtsev, V. 'Indestructible Friendship', *New Times*, No. 23 (1971), pp. 8–10.

Kulski, Wladyslaw, W. *Peaceful Co-existence, An Analysis of Soviet Foreign Policy* (Chicago: Henry Regnery Co., 1959).

Kumykin, P. N. *et al.*, eds., *Pyat' decyat let Sovetskoy vneshney torgovli* (Moscow, 1967).

Kutafin, O. E. 'Vzaumootnosheniya postoyannykh komissiy palat Verkhovnovo Soveta SSSR s Presidiumom Verkhovnovo Soveta SSSR i s Sovetom Ministrov SSSR', *Sovetskoe gosudarstvo i pravo* (1966), No. 4, pp. 37–8.

Kuznetsova, N. A. and Kulagina, L. M. *Iz istorii Sovetskovo vostokovedeniya* (Moscow, 1970).

Lall, Arthur *The U.N. and the Middle East Crisis, 1967* (New York: Columbia University Press, 1968).

Landis, Lincoln 'Soviet Interest in Middle East Oil', *The New Middle East*, No. 3 (1968), pp. 16–21.

——, *Politics and Oil. Moscow in the Middle East* (London: Martin Robertson and Co., 1973).

Lane, David *Politics and Society in the USSR* (London: Weidenfeld and Nicolson, 1970).

Laqueur, Walter '*Détente*: Western and Soviet Interpretations', *Survey*, Vol. 19, No. 3 (1973), pp. 74–88.

——, *The Road to War 1967* (London: Weidenfeld and Nicolson, 1968).

——, *The Soviet Union and the Middle East* (London: Routledge and Kegan Paul, 1959).

——, *The Struggle for the Middle East: The Soviet Union and the Middle East, 1958–68* (London: Routledge and Kegan Paul, 1969).

Lee, W. T. *Soviet Defence Expenditure for 1955–1975*, Tempo GE 75, TMP–42 (Washington DC: 31 July 1975).

Legum, Colin ed., *Africa Contemporary Record, Annual Survey and Documents*, Vols. 1–7. 1968/69–1974/75 (London: Africa Research Ltd., 1969; Rex Collings 1970–75).

Lemin, I. M. '"Doktrina Eizenkhyara"—programma kolonial'novo zakabaleniya Blizhnevo Vostoka', *Sovetskoye vostokovedeniye*, No. 1 (1957), pp. 3–21.

Lenczowski, George *The Middle East in World Affairs*, 3rd ed. (New York: Cornell University Press, 1962).

——, *Soviet Advances in the Middle East* (Washington DC: American Enterprise Institute for Public Policy Research, 1972).

Lenin, V. I. *The National Liberation Movement in the East* (Moscow, 1957).

——, *The National-Liberation Movement in the East* (Moscow: Foreign Languages Publishing House, 1951).

Leonhard, Wolfgang 'The Domestic Politics of the New Soviet Foreign Policy', *Foreign Affairs*, Vol. 52, No. 1 (1973), pp. 59–75.

Lezin, V. V. 'K voprosu o gegemonii rabochevo klassa v natsional'no-osvoboditel'noy revolyutsii' in Akademiya Obshchestvennykh Nauk pri Ts K KPSS, *Voprosy mezhdunarodnovo rabochevo i natsional'no-osvoboditel'novo dvizheniya na sovremennom etape* (Moscow: Sbornik Statei, 1963).

Linden, Carl A. *Khrushchev and the Soviet Leadership 1957–1964* (Baltimore, Md.: Johns Hopkins Press, 1966).

Liska, George 'The Politics of "Cultural Diplomacy"', *World Politics*, Vol. 14, No. 3 (1962), pp. 532–42.

Little, D. Richard 'Soviet Parliamentary Committees After Khrushchev, Obstacles and Opportunities', *Soviet Studies*,Vol. 24, No. 1 (1972), pp. 41–61.

Little, Tom *Modern Egypt* (London: Ernest Benn Ltd., 1967).

Lodge, Milton C. *Soviet Elite Attitudes Since Stalin* (Columbus Ohio: Charles E. Merrill Publishing Co., 1969).

Lutskiy, V. B. 'Natsional'no-osvoboditel'naya bor'ba v Arabskikh stran', *Voprosy ekonomiki*, No. 5 (1952), pp. 69–85.

——, 'Oktyaberskaya revolyutsiya i Arabskiye strany' *Sovetskoye vostokovedeniya*; No. 5 (1957), pp. 87–99.

Mackintosh, J. M. *Strategy and Tactics of Soviet Foreign Policy* (London: Oxford University Press, 1962).

Mackintosh, Malcolm 'The Soviet Military: Influence on Foreign Policy', *Problems of Communism*, Vol. 22, No. 5 (1973), pp. 1–12.

Mangold, Peter *Superpower Intervention in the Middle East* (London: Croom Helm, 1978).

Mansfield, Peter ed., *The Middle East, A Political and Economic Survey* (London: Oxford University Press, 1973).

——, *Nasser's Egypt* (London: Penguin, 1969).

Marx K. and Engels, F. *On Colonialism* (Moscow, 1960).

Materialy XXIII s"ezda KPSS (Moscow, 1966).

Maximov, E. 'The Arabs and the West: A Soviet Warning', *New Times*, No. 42 (1959), pp. 15–17.

McAuley, Alistair and Dubravko Matko, 'Soviet Foreign Aid', *Bulletin of Oxford University Institute of Economics and Statistics*, Vol. 28, No. 4 (1966), pp. 261–71.

McBride, Barrie St. Clare *Farouk of Egypt* (London: Robert Hale, 1967).

MccGwire, Michael, *Soviet Naval Developments*, New York: Praeger, 1973.

MccGwire, Michael *et al.*, eds, *Soviet Naval Policy* (New York: Praeger, 1965).

McLane, Charles B. *Soviet-Middle East Relations* (London: Central Asian Research Centre, 1973).

McLaurin, R. D. *The Middle East in Soviet Policy* (Lexington Mass.: Lexington Books, 1975).

Midani, Wasfi 'Savage Repressions against the Syrian People', *World Marxist Review*, Vol. 2, No. 6 (1959), p. 93.

Mikhailov, A. 'Kto oslozhnyaet Sovetsko–egipetskiye otnosheniya',

Agitator, Journal of the Central Committee of the CPSU, No. 9 (1976), pp. 23–7.

Mirskiy, G. *Bagdadskiy Pakt: orudiye kolonializma* (Moscow, 1956).

——, 'Gamal Abd al-Nasser', *MEIMO*, No. 7 (1964), pp. 112–15.

——, 'The Middle East – New Factors', *New Times*, No. 48 (1973), pp. 18–20.

——, 'Tvorcheskiy Marksizm i problemy natsional'no-osvoboditel'nykh revolyutsii', *MEIMO*, No. 2 (1963), pp. 63–8.

——, 'The UAR Reforms', *New Times*, No. 4 (1962), pp. 12–15.

Moheiddin, Khalid 'No More Colonialism for the Arab Lands', *World Marxist Review*, Vol. 1, No. 2 (1958), pp. 74–79.

Moskoff, William and William Benz, G. 'The USSR and Developing Countries, Politics and Export Prices, 1955–1969', *Soviet Studies*, Vol. 24, No. 3 (1973), pp. 348–64.

Mozhaev, G. A. *Mezhdunarodnyye kul'turnyye svyazi SSSR* (Moscow, 1959).

Najar, F. M. 'Islam and Socialism in the UAR', *Journal of Contemporary History*, Vol. 3, No. 3 (1968), pp. 183–99.

Nashashibi, Karim A. 'Foreign Trade and Economic Development in the United Arab Republic: A Case Study', in Lee E. Preston, *Trade Patterns in the Middle East* (Washington, DC: American Enterprise Institute for Public Policy Research, 1970), pp. 73–95.

Nassar, Fuad 'Lenin i osvoboditel'naya bor'ba arabskikh narodov', *Kommunist*, No. 5 (1970), pp. 113–20.

al-Nasser, Gamal Abd *The Philosophy of the Revolution* (Buffalo, NY.: Economica Books, 1959).

Nicolson, Sir Harold George *Diplomacy*, 2nd ed. (London: Oxford University Press, 1952).

——, 'Diplomacy Then and Now', *Foreign Affairs*, Vol. 40, No. 1 (1961), pp. 39–49.

Nutting, Anthony *Nasser* (London: Constable, 1972).

——, *No End of a Lesson* (London: Constable and Co., Ltd., 1967).

Odom, William E. 'A Dissenting View on the Group Approach to Soviet Politics', *World Politics*, Vol. 28, No. 4 (1976), pp. 542–67.

——, 'The Soviet Military: The Party Connection', *Problems of Communism*, Vol. 22, No. 5 (1973), pp. 12–26.

Ofer, Gur 'The Economic Burden of Soviet Involvement in the Middle East', *Soviet Studies*, Vol. 24, No. 3 (1973), pp. 329–48.

Oliver, James H. 'Turnover and 'Family Circles' in Soviet Administration', *Slavic Review*, Vol. 32, No. 3 (1973), pp. 527–46.

Om Kalthum fi al-Ittihad al-Soveti (Cairo, 1970).

Opyt istorii i sotsial'nyy progress v Afrike (Moscow, 1972).

Osborn, Robert J. *The Evolution of Soviet Politics* (Homewood, Ill.: The Dorsey Press, 1974).

Ovsyany, I. D. *et al.*, *A Study of Soviet Foreign Policy* (Moscow: Progress Publishers, 1975).

Page, Stanley W. *Lenin and World Revolution* (New York: McGraw-Hill Book Company, 1972).

Page, Stephen *The USSR and Arabia* (London: Central Asian Research Centre, 1971).

Pajak, Roger F. 'Soviet Arms and Egypt', *Survival*, Vol. 17, No. 4 (1975), pp. 165–73.

Pennar, Jaan 'Moscow and Socialism in Egypt', *Problems of Communism*, Vol. 15, No. 5 (1966), pp. 41–7.

Pennar, Jaan *The USSR and the Arabs, The Ideological Dimension* (London: C. Hurst and Co., 1973).

Petrov, R. 'The Soviet Union and the Arab Countries', *International Affairs*, (Moscow), No. 11 (1972), pp. 22–30.

Petrov, Vladimir 'Formation of Soviet Foreign Policy', *Orbis*, Vol. 17, No. 3 (1973), pp. 819–51.

Phelps-Fetherston, Iain *Soviet International Front Organizations* (New York: Praeger, 1965).

Polmar, Norman *Soviet Naval Power: Challenge for the 1970s*, (New York: National Strategy Information Center, 1972).

Polyakov, N. N. 'Arabskiye strany na puti k ekonomicheskoy nezavisimosti'. *Vneshnyaya torgovlya*, No. 9 (1956), pp. 4–7.

Ponomaryov, Boris 'O gosudarstve natsional'noy demokratii', *Kommunist*, No. 8 (1961), pp. 33–48.

——, 'Under the Banner of Marxism–Leninism and Proletarian Internationalism: The 24th Congress of the CPSU', *World Marxist Review*, Vol. 14, No. 6 (1971), pp. 1–6.

Potekhin, I. I. *Afrika smotrit v budushcheye* (Moscow, 1960).

Primakov, Ye. '"Sbalansirovanyy kurs" na Blizhnem Vostoke ili staraya politika inymi stredstvami?', *MEIMO*, No. 12 (1976), pp. 38–52; and No. 1 (1977), pp. 51–60.

Problems of War and Peace (Moscow: Progress Publishers, 1972).

'Program of Action of the Communist Party of Egypt', *Middle East Journal*, Vol. 10, No. 4 (1956), pp. 427–37.

Qualter, Terence *Propaganda and Psychological Warfare* (New York: Random House, 1965).

Quandt, William B. 'Soviet Policy in the October Middle East

War—I; *International Affairs*, Vol. 53, No. 3 (July 1977), pp. 377–89.

——, 'Soviet Policy in the October Middle East War—II *International Affairs*, Vol. 53, No. 4 (October 1977), pp. 587–604.

Ra'anan, Uri *The USSR Arms the Third World* (Cambridge Mass.: MIT Press, 1969).

Republic of Egypt, Statistical Department, *Annual Statement of Foreign Trade*, (annual).

Reynolds, P. A. *An Introduction to International Relations*, (London: Longman Group Ltd., 1971).

Rimalov, V. *Economic Cooperation Between the USSR and Under-Developed Countries* (Moscow, n.d).

Rivera, Joseph H. de *The Psychological Dimension of Foreign Policy*, (Columbus, Ohio: Charles E. Merrill Publishing Co., 1968).

Rodinson, Maxime *Israel and the Arabs* (London: Penguin Books, 1968).

Ro'i, Yaacov *From Encroachment to Involvement: A Documentary Study of Soviet Policy in the Middle East, 1945–1973* (New York: John Wiley and Sons, 1974).

Rosenau, James N. ed. *International Politics and Foreign Policy*, (New York: Free Press, 1969).

Rozaliyev, Y. 'State Capitalism in Asia and Africa', *International Affairs*, No. 2 (Moscow, 1963), pp. 33–9.

Rubinstein, Alvin Z. *Red Star on the Nile* (Princeton NJ: Princeton University Press, 1977).

Rumyantsev, A. M. ed., *Sovremennoye osvoboditel'noye dvizheniye i natsional'naya burzhuaziya* (Moscow, 1960).

Rush, Myron ed., *The International Situation and Soviet Foreign Policy* (Columbus Ohio: Charles E. Merrill Publishing Co., 1970).

Rusk, Dean 'Parliamentary Diplomacy: Debate versus Negotiation', *World Affairs Interpreter*, Vol. 26 (1955), pp. 121–38.

Samilovskiy, I. V. *Nauchnyye i kul'turnyye svyazi SSSR so stranami Azii i Afriki* (Moscow, 1963).

'Save Our Lives', *World Marxist Review*, Vol. 6, No. 6 (1963), pp. 93–6.

Sawyer, Carole A. *Communist Trade with Developing Countries, 1955–1965* (New York: Praeger, 1967).

Schwartz, Joel and William Keech, 'Group Influence on the Policy Process in the Soviet Union', *American Political Science Review*, Vol. 62, No. 3 (1968), pp. 840–85.

Schwartz, Morton *The Foreign Policy of the USSR: Domestic Factors* (Encino Cal.: Dickenson Publishing Co., 1975).

'Scientific Relations Between the Soviet Union and the Arab Republic of Egypt', *Novosti Press Release* (Cairo, 1973).

Seale, Patrick *The Struggle for Syria. A Study of Post-War Arab Politics, 1945–1958* (London: Oxford University Press, 1965).

Sergeev, C. 'K voprosy kategorii vsemirnyi rynok', *Vneshnyaya torgovlya*, No. 4 (1963), pp. 17–24.

Sharabi, H. B. *Governments and Politics of the Middle East in the Twentieth Century* (Princeton NJ: D. Van Nostrand Co. Inc., 1962).

Shepilov, Dmitri T. *Suetskiy vopros* (Moscow, 1956).

Shmelyov, N. 'Stoimostnyye kriterii i ikh rol' v ekonomike razvivayushchikhsya stran', *MEIMO*, No. 6 (1968), pp. 40–52.

Shulman, Marshall *Beyond the Cold War* (New Haven Conn.: Yale University Press, 1966).

——, *Stalin's Foreign Policy Reappraised* (Cambridge Mass.: Harvard University Press, 1963).

Skilling, H. Gordon and Franklyn Griffiths, eds., *Interest Groups in Soviet Politics* (Princeton NJ: Princeton University Press, 1971).

Slussor, Robert M. *The Berlin Crisis of 1961: Soviet–American Relations and the Struggle for Power in the Kremlin, June–November 1961* (Baltimore Md., Johns Hopkins University Press, 1973).

Smirnov, V. and I. Matyukhin, 'USSR and the Arab East: Economic Contacts', *International Affairs*, No. 9 (Moscow, 1972). pp. 83–8.

Smith, Glen Alden *Soviet Foreign Trade: Organisation, Operations and Policy, 1918–1971* (New York: Praeger, 1973).

Smolansky, O. M. 'Moscow–Cairo Crisis, 1959', *Slavic Review*, Vol. 22, No. 4 (1963), pp. 713–26.

——, 'Soviet Policy in the Middle East', *Current History*, Vol. 74, No. 433 (1978), pp. 5–10.

Snyder, Richard C. Bruck H. W. and Burton Sapin, *Foreign Policy Decision-making: An Approach to the Study of International Politics*, (New York: Free Press, 1962).

Sovetsko–arabskiye druzhestvennye otnosheniya (Moscow, 1961).

'The Soviet Attitude to the Palestine Problem: From the Records of the Syrian Communist Party, 1971–72', *Journal of Palestine Studies*, Vol. 2, No. 1 (1972), pp. 187–213.

'Soviet Muslims in Mecca', *News*, No. 22 (1954), p. 28.

'The Soviet–UAR and Soviet–Indian Treaties: A Comparison', *Survival*, Vol. 13, No. 10 (1971), pp. 349–54.

'The Soviet Union and the Arab World', *New Times*, No. 31 (1972), p. 1.

'The Soviet Union's Liquid Gold', Interview with Valentin Shashin, Soviet Minister of Oil Industry, *New Times*, No. 4 (1971), pp. 13–16.

Spandaryan, V. 'Nasha torgovlya so stranami Yugovostochnoy Azii i Blizhnevo Vostoka', *Vneshnyaya torgovlya*, No. 11 (1957), pp. 61–9.

Spector, Ivar *The Soviet Union and the Muslim World, 1917–1958* (Seattle: University of Washington Press, 1959).

Spravochnik Partiinovo rabotnika, Vol. 7 (Moscow: Izdatel'stvo politicheskoy literatury, 1967).

Sprout, Harold and Margaret Sprout, *The Foundations of International Politics* (London: Van Nostrand Co. Inc., 1962).

——, 'Geography and International Politics in an Era of Revolutionary Change', *Journal of Conflict Resolution*, Vol. 1, No. 1 (1960), pp. 145–61.

'SSSR i Arabskiy Vostok' *Sovremennyy vostok*, No. 3 (1957), pp. 1–3.

SSSR i strany Afriki, 1946–1962 gg. Dokumenty i materialy, Vol. 2 (Moscow, 1963).

SSSR i strany vostoka; ekonomicheskoye i kul'turnoye sotrudnichestvo (Moscow, 1961).

SSSR, Ministerstvo Inostranykh Del', *SSSR i Arabskiye strany 1917–1960; dokumenty i materialy* (Moscow, 1961).

SSSR, Ministerstvo Vneshney Torgovli SSSR, *Vneshnyaya torgovlya SSSR za—god*, Moscow (annual).

Staar, Richard F. ed., *Yearbook of International Communist Affairs, 1976* (Stanford Cal.: Hoover Institution Press, 1976).

Starko, G. 'How to Solve the Oil Problem', *New Times*, No. 35 (1958), pp. 13–15.

Starushenko, G. 'Mirnoye sosushchestvovaniye i revolyutsiya', *Kommunist*, Vol. 39, No. 2 (1962), pp. 78–89.

'Statement of the Meeting of Representatives of Communist and Workers' Parties, Moscow, November 1960', *World Marxist Review*, Vol. III, No. 12 (1960), pp. 3–29.

Stepanov, L. 'Soviet Aid and its Critics', *International Affairs*, No. 6 (Moscow, 1960), pp. 20–7.

Stephens, Robert 'The Egyptian–Soviet Quarrel in 1972: Russia, the Arabs and Africa' in Colin Legum, ed., *Africa Contemporary*

Record: Annual Survey and Documents 1972–1973, Vol. 5 (London: Rex Collings, 1973), pp. A20–A35.

——, *Nasser* (London: Allen Lane, The Penguin Press, 1971).

Stern, Geoffrey 'The Foreign Policy of the Soviet Union' in F. S. Northedge, ed., *The Foreign Policy of the Powers* (London: Faber and Faber, 1968), pp. 69–111.

Stockholm International Peace Research Institute, *The Arms Trade with the Third World* (London: Paul Elek Ltd., 1971).

——, *World Armaments and Disarmament SIPRI Yearbook 1974* (Cambridge Mass.: MIT Press, 1974).

Suez, the Soviet View (London: Soviet News, Booklet No. 21, 1956).

'XX S''yezd Kommunisticheskoy Partii Sovetskovo Soyuza i zadachi izucheniya sovremennovo Vostoka', *Sovetskoye vostokovediye*, No. 1 (1956), pp. 3–12.

Tansky, Leo *US and USSR Aid to Developing Countries: A Comparative Study of India, Turkey and the UAR* (New York: Praeger, 1967).

Tanter, Raymond and Richard H. Ullman, eds., *Theory and Policy in International Relations* (Princeton, NJ: Princeton University Press, 1972).

Thomas, John R. 'Soviet Foreign Policy and the Military', *Survey*, Vol. 17, No. 3 (1971), pp. 129–57.

Thornton, Thomas P. *The Third World in Soviet Perspective*, (Princeton, NJ: Princeton University Press, 1964).

Tomashevsky, D. 'Some Questions of International Relations Research in the Light of Lenin's Teachings', *International Affairs*, No. 6 (Moscow, 1970), pp. 72–80.

Tomashpol'skiy, L. 'Mirovoi energeticheskiy balans: problemy poslednei treti veka', *MEIMO*, No. 2 (1967), pp. 15–29.

Trevelyan, Humphrey *The Middle East in Revolution* (London: Macmillan, 1970).

Triska, Jan F. and David Finley, *Soviet Foreign Policy* (New York: Macmillan, 1968).

'Trudyashchiyesya Vostoka v bor'be za prava, nezavisimost', i mir', *Sovremennyy vostok*, No. 5 (1959), pp. 35–42.

Tuzmuhamedov, R. *How the National Question was Solved in Soviet Central Asia* (Moscow: Progress Publishers, 1973).

Ulam, Adam B. *Expansion and Coexistence, Soviet Foreign Policy, 1917–1973*, 2nd ed. (New York, Praeger, 1974).

Ul'yanovskiy, R. A. 'Agrarnoye preobrazovaniye v stranakh Blizhnevo i Srednevo Vostoka, Indii i Yugovostochnevo Azii', *Narody Azii i Afriki*, No. 2 (1961), pp. 14–30.

——, 'Agrarnoye preobrazovaniye v stranakh Blizhnevo i Srednevo Vostoka, Indii i Yugovostochnevo Azii' *Problemy vostokovedeniya*, No. 1 (1961), pp. 13–34.

——, 'Ekonomicheskaya nezavisimost-blizhayshaya zadacha osvoboditel'novo dvizheniya v Azii', *Kommunist*, No. 1 (1962), pp. 96–108.

——, 'Imperialisticheskaya politika 'pomoshchi' S. Sh. slaborazvitym stranam Azii', *Narody Azii i Afriki*, No. 2 (1962), pp. 39–57.

——, 'Nauchnyy sotsializm i osvobodivshiyesya strany', *Kommunist*, No. 4 (1968), pp. 92–107.

——, 'Sovremennyy etap natsional'no-osvoboditel'novo dvizheniya i krest'yanstvo'. *MEIMO*, No. 5 (1971), pp. 91–104.

The USSR and the Middle East: Problems of Peace and Security, 1947–1971. Documents and Other Materials (Moscow, 1972).

USSR Central Statistical Board, *Narodnoye Khozyaistvo SSSR v . . .* (Moscow: Statistika Publishers—annual).

——, *Narodnoye Khozyaistvo SSSR, 1922–1972* (Moscow: Statistika Publishers, 1973).

——, *Narodnoye Khozyaistvo SSSR za 60 let* (Moscow: Statistika Publishers, 1977).

——, *The USSR in Figures for 1976* (Moscow: Statistika Publishers, 1977).

UAR Central Agency for Public Mobilisation and Statistics, *Foreign Trade of the UAR* (Cairo—annual).

——, *Monthly Bulletin for Foreign Trade* (Cairo).

——, *Statistical Handbook, 1952–1964* (Cairo, 1966).

UAR Department of Information, *The Charter* (Cairo, 1962).

——, *Al-Jumhuriya al-Arabia al-Muttahida Fi Ithna Ashar Aman* (Cairo, 1964).

——, *President Gamal Abd al-Nasser's Speeches and Press Interviews* (Cairo, n.d.)

——, *UAR Yearbook* (Cairo—annual).

UAR Department of Statistics and Census, *Annual Statement of Foreign Trade* (Cairo—annual).

UAR Federation of Industries, *Yearbook* (Cairo—annual).

UAR *Majmu'at Khutab wa Tasrihat wa Bayanat al-Rais Gamal Abd al-Nasser* (Cairo: Maslahat al-Isti'lamat, n.d.).

UAR Ministry of Education, Department of Statistics, *Comparative Statistics of Education, 1953/1954–1961/1962* (Cairo, 1962).

UN Department of Economic and Social Affairs, *Demographic Yearbook* (annual).

——, *Economic Developments in the Middle East, 1957/1958, 1959/1961.*

——, *Yearbook of International Trade Statistics* (annual).

UN Food and Agriculture Organization, *Production Yearbook.*

——, Food and Agriculture Organization, *Trade Yearbook.*

——, *World Economic Survey, 1958* (New York, 1959).

UNESCO *Basic Facts and Figures, 1961* (Paris, 1963).

——, *Statistical Yearbook* (annual).

——, *Statistics of Students Abroad, 1962–1968* (1971).

——, *World Communications,* 5th ed. (Paris: 1975).

——, *World Survey of Education, Vol. IV: Higher Education* (Paris, 1966).

US Arms Control and Disarmament Agency, *World Military Expenditures and Arms Transfers, 1966–1975* (Washington, 1976).

US Central Intelligence Agency, *Communist Aid to the Less Developed Countries of the Free World 1976,* ER 77–10296 (Washington DC: August 1977).

——, *Prospects for Soviet Oil Production,* ER 77–10270 (Washington DC: April 1977).

——, *Soviet Economic Plans for 1976–80: A First Look,* ER 77–10471 (Washington DC: August 1976).

US Congress, Joint Economic Committee, *Dimensions of Soviet Economic Power* (Washington DC: US Government Printing Office, 1962).

——, *Economic Performance and the Military Burden in the Soviet Union,* (Washington DC: US Government Printing Office, 1970).

——, *New Directions in the Soviet Economy* (Washington DC: US Government Printing Office, 1966).

——, *Soviet Economic Prospects for the Seventies* (Washington DC: US Government Printing Office, 1973).

US Department of State, Bureau of Intelligence and Research, Research Memorandum, *Educational and Cultural Exchanges Between Communist and Non-Communist Countries* (various years since 1963).

US Department of State, *The World Strength of the Communist Party Organizations, 1957,* No. 4489R9; *1958,* 4489R10.

Ushakova, N. A. *Arabskaya Respublika Egipet: sotrudnichestvo so stranami sotsializma i ekonomicheskoye razvitiye (1952–1972gg)* (Moscow, 1974).

Valkenier, Elizabeth Kridl 'New Trends in Soviet Economic Relations with the Third World', *World Politics,* Vol. 22, No. 3 (1970), pp. 415–33.

——, 'Recent Trends in Soviet Research on the Developing Countries', *World Politics*, Vol. 20, No. 4 (1968), pp. 644–60.

Vasilyev, Y. 'Oil Politics Takes a New Turn', *New Times*, No. 39 (1957), pp. 9–11.

Vatikiotis, P. J. *The Egyptian Army in Politics* (Bloomington Indiana: Indiana University Press, 1961).

Vatolina, L. 'Bor'ba Yegipetskovo naroda za mir i nezavisimost', *Voprosy ekonomiki*, No. 2 (1952), pp. 61–73.

——, 'Rost natsional'novo samosoznaniya narodov Arabskikh stran, 1945–1955', *Sovetskoye vostokovedeniye*, No. 5 (1955), pp. 58–68.

Vatolina, L. 'Yegipet i krizis Britanskoy kolonial'noy politiki' in *Imperialisticheskaya bor'ba za Afriku i osvoboditel'noye dvizheniye narodov* (Moscow, 1953), pp. 97–127.

Vatolina, L. N. and Ye. A. Belyaev *Araby v bor'be za nezavisimost'* (Moscow, 1957).

Vermishev, K. 'Ob urobne ekonomicheskovo razvitiya soyuznoy respubliki', *Voprosy ekonomiki*, No. 4 (1970), pp. 127–32.

Viktorov, G. 'Otkrytyye dveri. Kuda?', *Novoye vremya*, No. 40 (1976), pp. 25–8.

Vol'skiy, D. and A. Usvatov, 'Kair-Moskva, fakty i tol'ko fakty', *Novoye vremya*, No. 14 (1976), pp. 18–21.

Walters, R. S. *American and Soviet Aid: A Comparative Analysis* (Pittsburgh, PA.: University of Pittsburgh Press, 1970).

Weinland, Robert G. 'Land Support for Naval Forces: Egypt and the Soviet Escadra 1962–1976', *Survival*, Vol. 20, No. 2 (1978), pp. 73–80.

Wheeler, Geoffrey 'National and Religious Consciousness in Soviet Islam', *Survey*, No. 66 (1968), pp. 67–77.

Wilkenfeld, Jonathan ed., *Conflict Behaviour and Linkage Politics* (New York: David McKay Co., 1973).

Wilkinson, David O. *Comparative Foreign Relations: Framework and Method*, (Belmont Cal.: Dickenson Publishing Co. Inc., 1969).

Wolfe, Thomas W. *Soviet Power and Europe, 1945–1970* (Baltimore Md.: Johns Hopkins University Press, 1970).

Wolfe, Thomas W. *Soviet Strategy at the Crossroads* (Cambridge Mass.: Harvard University Press, 1964).

Zagoria, Donald S. *The Sino-Soviet Conflict 1956–1961* (Princeton: Princeton University Press, 1962).

Zakhmatov, M. 'S. Sh. A. i "obshchiy rynok"', *Vneshnyaya torgovlya*, No. 4 (1962), pp. 25–32.

Zhukov, G. A. 'Two Approaches Toward Cultural Contacts', *International Affairs*, No. 11 (Moscow, 1959), pp. 19–28.

Zhukov, Ye. 'The Impact of the Chinese Revolution on the National Liberation Struggle', *World Marxist Review*, Vol. 1, No. 3 (1958), pp. 14–19.

——, 'Obostrennyy krizis kolonial'noy sistemy', *Bol'shevik*, No. 23 (1947), pp. 51–64.

——, 'Raspad kolonial'noy sistemy imperialisma', *Partiynaya zhizn*', No. 16 (1956), pp. 41–8.

——, *Sovremennyye teorii sotsialisma 'natsional'novo tipa'* (Moscow, 1967).

——, 'Voprosy natsional'no-kolonial'noy bor'by posle vtoroy mirovoy voyny', *Voprosy ekonomiki*, No. 9 (1949), pp. 54–61.

Zimmerman, William *Soviet Perspectives on International Relations, 1956–67* (Princeton NJ: Princeton University Press, 1969).

Zorin, Valerian A. *Osnova diplomaticheskoi sluzhby* (Moscow, 1964).

Zumwalt, E. *On Watch, A Memoir* (New York: Quadrangle, 1976).

Zyzniewski, Stanley J. 'The Soviet Bloc and the Underdeveloped Countries', *World Politics*, Vol. 2, No. 3 (1959), pp. 378–99.

NEWSPAPERS AND JOURNALS

African Digest (London)
Al-Ahram (Cairo)
Al-Akhbar (Cairo)
Al-Anbaa (Kuwait)
Al-Anwar (Beirut)
Al-Jumhuriya (Cairo)
Al-Safir (Beirut)
Arab Report and Record (London)
Arab World Weekly (Beirut)
Congressional Quarterly Weekly Report (Washington)
Egyptian Gazette (Cairo)
The Guardian (London)
The International Herald Tribune (Paris)
Izvestiya (Moscow)
Keesing's Contemporary Archives (London)
Krasnaya zvezda (Moscow)
Le Monde (Paris)
L'Orient Le Jour (Beirut)

Literaturnaya Gazeta (Moscow)
The Middle East (London)
The Middle East Economic Digest (London)
The Military Balance (London: IISS)
The Mizan Newsletter (London: CARC)
New China News Agency Report (Peking)
New York Times
Newsweek (New York)
The Observer (London)
Observer Foreign News Service (London)
October (Cairo)
Pravda (Moscow)
The Scotsman (Glasgow)
Soviet News (London)
Strategic Survey (London: IISS)
The Sunday Times (London)
The Times (London)
USSR and the Third World (London: CARC)

Index